Lesbian Erotics

THE CUTTING EDGE:
Lesbian Life and Literature

THE CUTTING EDGE:
Lesbian Life and Literature

Series Editor: Karla Jay

Lover
by Bertha Harris

Elizabeth Bowen: A Reputation in Writing
by renée c. hoogland

Lesbian Erotics
edited by Karla Jay

Changing Our Minds: Lesbian Feminism and Psychology
by Celia Kitzinger and Rachel Perkins

(Sem)Erotics: Theorizing Lesbian : Writing
by Elizabeth A. Meese

*The Challenge of Bisexuality to Lesbian Politics: Sex,
Loyalty, and Revolution*
by Paula C. Rust

The Search for a Woman-Centered Spirituality
by Annette J. Van Dyke

*I Know My Own Heart: The Diaries of Anne Lister,
1791–1840*
edited by Helena Whitbread

No Priest But Love: The Journals of Anne Lister, 1824–26
edited by Helena Whitbread

THE CUTTING EDGE:
Lesbian Life and Literature

Series Editor: Karla Jay
Professor of English and Women's Studies
PACE UNIVERSITY

EDITORIAL BOARD

Lesbian
Erotics

Edited by Karla Jay

NEW YORK UNIVERSITY PRESS
New York and London

NEW YORK UNIVERSITY PRESS
New York and London

© 1995 by Karla Jay

Library of Congress Cataloging-in-Publication Data
Lesbian erotics / edited by Karla Jay.
p.   cm. — (The cutting edge—lesbian life and literature)
Includes bibliographical references and index.
ISBN 0-8147-4221-1 (alk. paper : cloth). — ISBN 0-8147-4225-4
(alk. paper : pbk.)
1. Lesbianism.   2. Lesbians.   3. Erotica.   4. Feminism.   I. Jay,
Karla.   II. Series: Cutting edge (New York, N.Y.)
HQ75.5.L439   1995
306.76′63—dc20   94-44002
CIP

New York University Press books are printed on acid-free paper,
and their binding materials are chosen for strength and durability.

Manufactured in the United States of America

10 9 8 7 6 5 4 3 2 1

Contents

Foreword

Despite the efforts of lesbian and feminist publishing houses and a few university presses, the bulk of the most important lesbian works has traditionally been available only from rare-book dealers, in a few university libraries, or in gay and lesbian archives. This series intends, in the first place, to make representative examples of this neglected and insufficiently known literature available to a broader audience by reissuing selected classics and by putting into print for the first time lesbian novels, diaries, letters, and memoirs that are of special interest and significance, but which have mouldered in libraries and private collections for decades or even for centuries, known only to the few scholars who had the courage and financial wherewithal to track them down.

Their names have been known for a long time—Sappho, the Amazons of North Africa, the Beguines, Aphra Behn, Queen Christina, Emily Dickinson, the Ladies of Llangollen, Radclyffe Hall, Natalie Clifford Barney, H.D., and so many others from every nation, race, and era. But government and religious officials burned their writings, historians and literary scholars denied they were lesbians, powerful men kept their books out of print, and influential archivists locked up their ideas far from sympathetic eyes. Yet some dedicated scholars and readers still knew who they were, made pilgrimages to the cities and villages where they had lived and to the graveyards where they rested. They passed around tattered volumes of letters, diaries, and biographies, in which they had underlined what seemed to be telltale hints of a secret or different kind of life. Where no hard facts existed, legends were invented. The few precious and often available pre-Stonewall lesbian classics, such as *The Well of Loneliness* by Radclyffe Hall, *The Price of Salt* by Claire Morgan [Patricia Highsmith], and *Desert of the Heart* by Jane Rule, were cherished. Lesbian pulp was devoured. One of the primary goals of this series is to give the more neglected works, which constitute the vast majority of lesbian writing, the attention they deserve.

A second but no less important aim of this series is to present the "cutting edge" of contemporary lesbian scholarship and theory across a wide range of disciplines. Practitioners of lesbian studies have not adopted a uniform approach to literary theory, history, sociology, or any other discipline, nor should they. This series intends to present an array of voices that truly reflect the diversity of the lesbian community. To help me in this task, I am lucky enough to be assisted by a distinguished editorial board that reflects various professional, class, racial, ethnic, and religious backgrounds as well as a spectrum of interests and sexual preferences.

At present the field of lesbian studies occupies a small, precarious, and somewhat contested pied-à-terre between gay studies and women's studies. The former is still in its infancy, especially if one compares it to other disciplines that have been part of the core curriculum of every child and adolescent for several decades or even centuries. However, although it is one of the newest disciplines, gay studies may also be the fastest-growing one—at least in North America. Lesbian, gay, and bisexual studies conferences are doubling and tripling their attendance. Although only a handful of degree-granting programs currently exist, that number is also apt to multiply quickly during the next decade.

In comparison, women's studies is a well-established and burgeoning discipline with hundreds of minors, majors, and graduate programs throughout the United States. Lesbian Studies occupies a peripheral place in the discourse in such programs, characteristically restricted to one lesbian-centered course, usually literary or historical in nature. In the many women's studies series that are now offered by university presses, generally only one or two books on a lesbian subject or issue are included, and lesbian voices are restricted to writing on those topics considered of special interest to gay people. We are not called upon to offer opinions on motherhood, war, education, or on the lives of women not publicly identified as lesbians. As a result, lesbian experience is too often marginalized and restricted.

In contrast, this series will prioritize, centralize, and celebrate lesbian visions of literature, art, philosophy, love, religion, ethics, history, and a myriad of other topics. In "The Cutting Edge," readers can find authoritative versions of important lesbian texts that have been carefully prepared and introduced by scholars. Readers can also find the work of academics and independent scholars who write about other aspects of life from a distinctly lesbian viewpoint. These visions are not only various but intentionally contradictory, for lesbians speak from differing class, racial, ethnic, and religious perspectives. Each author also speaks from and about a certain moment of time, and few would argue that being a lesbian today is the same as it was for Sappho or Anne Lister. Thus no attempt has been made to homogenize that diversity, and no agenda exists to attempt to carve out a "politically correct" lesbian studies perspective at this juncture in history or to pinpoint the "real" lesbians in history. It seems more important for all the voices to be heard before those with the blessings of aftersight lay the mantle of authenticity on any one vision of the world, or on any particular set of women.

What each work in this series does share, however, is a common realization that gay women are the "Other" and that one's perception of culture and literature is filtered by sexual behaviors and preferences. Those perceptions are not the same as those of gay men or of nongay women, whether the writers speak of gay or feminist issues or whether the writers choose to look at nongay figures from a lesbian perspective. The role of this series is to create space and give a voice to those interested in lesbian studies. This series speaks to any person who is interested in gender studies, literary criticism, biography, or important literary works, whether she or he is a student, professor, or serious reader, for the series is neither for lesbians only nor even by lesbians only. Instead, "The Cutting Edge" attempts to share some of the best of lesbian literature and lesbian studies with anyone willing to look at the world through lesbians' eyes. The series is proactive in that it will help to formulate and foreground the very discipline on which it focuses. Finally, this series has answered the call to make lesbian theory, lesbian experience, lesbian lives, lesbian literature, and lesbian visions the heart and nucleus, the weighty planet around which for once other viewpoints will swirl as moons to our earth. We invite readers of all persuasions to join us by venturing into this and other books in the series.

In undertaking this series of books, I did not contemplate editing one of the volumes in it. However, when I chaired a panel on lesbian erotics at the Modern Language Association Convention in 1993, I received fifty abstracts for it, and five hundred scholars filled up a ballroom to hear the resulting panel. I realized that I had fortuitously hit on a lacuna in lesbian scholarship, that is, the critical examination of the cultural production of lesbian erotic material. Like *Lesbian Texts and Contexts: Radical Revisions,* which in some ways served as a springboard for this series, *Lesbian Erotics* attempts to examine as broadly as possible an intriguing topic (and in this case a volatile one as well) that cannot be ignored by a group of people who have been historically defined by what we do in bed.

Acknowledgments

There are many people who contributed to the completion of this collection. First, Michael Moon came up with the title "Lesbian Erotics" for a Gay Studies Division panel for the 1993 Modern Language Association Convention. It was out of a call for papers for that panel that the idea for this collection germinated. I'd also like to thank the Feminist Research Group at Pace University, and especially Mark Hussey, for their feedback on my introduction. Elizabeth Meese and Marny Hall have also acted as invaluable mentors. My collaboration with New York University Press has been made a constant delight and adventure thanks to the warm support and advice of Niko Pfund, Despina Gimbel, and Colin Jones. Finally, I would like to dedicate this volume to Karen Kerner, who has nurtured my intellectual endeavors and fulfilled my erotic dreams.

On Slippery Ground: An Introduction

KARLA JAY

Lesbian Erotics is the first collection of critical essays to investigate the cultural production of sexually charged lesbian images in law, literature, film, and popular culture. Undertaking such a project is no simple matter. The history of lesbian sexuality and eroticism has been an area of intense debate within academia as well as within lesbian and feminist communities. If there were sexually active lesbians before 1900, they were certainly what comedian Kate Clinton would call "stealth lesbians":[1] They may have been there, but almost no one could see them. Lillian Faderman and other social constructionists have posited that relationships between women before 1900 were affectional, romantic, and emotional, rather than genitally sexual, though the fascinating diaries of English gentrywoman Anne Lister reveal she was sexually active as early as the 1820s.[2]

As we come to the end of the twentieth century, the question of whether or not lesbians have sex is still a hotly contested issue. A 1993 anthology entitled *Boston Marriages,* edited by Esther Rothblum and Kathleen Brehony, focused on contemporary nonsexual lesbian relationships. Marny Hall's essay in this volume illustrates how difficult it may be to maintain erotic tension in lesbian relationships. Equally problematic is defining what does or does not constitute lesbian sex or lesbian sexual identification. Consider just two examples: (1) A spread in the March/April 1994 issue of *On Our Backs* implied that mothers and daughters were engaged in consensual lesbian sex; (2) Pat Califia felt it necessary to add a twenty-two page glossary of sexual terminology in *Sensuous Magic.*[3]

1

It may be that the erotic, which includes both sexual and affectional components, eludes definition. Many writers have certainly tried to demarcate its borders. Most widely cited is Audre Lorde's statement that the erotic represents inner power: "The erotic is a resource within each of us that lies in a deeply female and spiritual plane, firmly rooted in the power of our unexpressed or unrecognized feeling."[4] Despite the popularity of Lorde's essay, her assessment is by no means universal. For example, JoAnn Loulan devotes an entire chapter of *The Lesbian Erotic Dance* to an elaborate and detailed description of the erotic. In part, she tells us,

> It can be a rhythm, a simple movement, or swaying in a certain direction. It's her smell or her shape, her eyes, her hair, her stance—an almost chemical attraction. It's a glance, a sideways look, or a full-on, face-to-face stare. It's a hip thing, a swinging foot, a hand lightly touching your knee. . . . It's knowing she is willing: curious, terrified, or eager.[5]

Like Lorde, Loulan appears to prize the abstract or spiritual dimension of love, but there's a strong physical element, too: The erotic may entail an exchange of power that involves a psychical interaction.

The contributors to this collection have come up with an equally broad range of definitions. Donna Allegra locates erotic feeling in "a strong woman being tender to another; a femme yearning for a butch; one woman looking out for and protecting another; a smart and competent woman who is independent, solo, on her own" (p. 76). Anna Livia focuses on a nongenital, sensual experience, that is, taking mutual delight in certain foods. Elizabeth Meese grapples with increasingly complex, evolving sexual identities in cyberspace. "Now it is difficult even to say what is 'lesbian' in lesbian erotics and what might constitute a lesbian erotics, particularly in an arena expanded to include online identities and cybersex" (p. 53). In the end, we may all agree with Anna Livia when she asks, "What is erotic? What is erotic to me? And are these two different questions?" (p. 40).

How can we discuss a concept that seems to have no consensus at all? Perhaps eroticism is ultimately a postmodern notion, an abstraction so slippery and amorphous that we cannot chart its ever-changing surface. Such charting itself might be dangerous in that not everyone would wish to see it mapped or categorized. We can, however, attempt to visualize the elusive, and even to verbalize it, to weave stories around what may turn out to be very limited or very personalized visions. By pluralizing the word "erotic" into "erotics" in the title of this collection, I've attempted to recognize the multiplicity of meanings inherently possible in the word without obscuring the fact that a lesbocentric definition of desire may not be feasible or even desirable at this moment of history. As Marny Hall reminds us, "Perhaps, someday, our sexual maps will become equally cumbersome and we will discard them" (p. 26).

At least, at the end of the twentieth century, lesbians are reading, writing, discussing, and re(de)fining their desire. But this possibility did not always exist: For most of history, lesbian eroticism was erased or, as Terry Castle puts it, ghosted by male writers who made sure that lesbian relationships were never consummated in novels like Daniel Defoe's *The Apparition of Mrs Veal* (1706) and Henry James's *The Bostonians.* Castle refers to this as "the kiss that doesn't happen, the kiss that *can't* happen, because one of the women involved has become a ghost (or else is direly haunted by ghosts)."[6] At the end of the nineteenth century, when those lips did meet in a passionate embrace, writers like Algernon Swinburne, Charles Baudelaire, and Emile Zola, and painters like Henri de Toulouse-Lautrec debased lesbians into "femmes damnées" or members of the demi-monde. These women were created by men for their own sexual gratification and for that of a presumed male audience. Even in the twentieth century, an androcentric vision of lesbians has persisted in everything from Marcel Proust's *Remembrance of Things Past,* to Tom Robbins's *Even Cowgirls Get the Blues,* to lesbian sex scenes in male-oriented and -produced pornography. Pornography produced by and for lesbians may often seem no different, at least to a male heterosexual viewer!

The tension between erasure and titillation has played a prominent role in movies, as well. In this volume Bonnie Burns investigates one telling example, the film *Dracula's Daughter.* The lesbian vampire is emblematic because she is both there (a turn on) and not there (dead and invisible in mirrors). As I pointed out in *Lavender Culture,*

> Most of the films about lesbians are made by men. They often erase lesbianism as in *Fried Green Tomatoes,* where Ruth and Idgie can be read by most viewers as "good friends," despite the semiotic clues of Idgie's Annie Hall-like attire of men's vests and ties. The erotic possibilities are downplayed by a lack of any overt physical affection and by the conflation

of the novel's married Ninny with the rebel Idgie into one character at the end of the film. Conversely, lesbian eroticism in Hollywood films like *Personal Best* and *Lianna* can still be portrayed on the screen more openly than gay male sexuality because the former is still considered titillating for straight men. (Would the respected leftist John Sayles do a gay male movie as steamy as his lesbian *Lianna*? It seems unlikely.)[7]

Because of male hegemony over art generally and over the language of sexuality entirely, lesbians have struggled for centuries to find authentic erotic voices of our own. The struggle is best exemplified in the two published diaries of Anne Lister: *I Know My Own Heart: The Diaries of Anne Lister, 1791–1840* and *No Priest But Love: The Journals of Anne Lister, 1824–1826*. In both of these works, Lister struggles to find words that express not only what she does with various women lovers but also what she feels. Lacking adequate language, she uses the word "kiss" for orgasm throughout, and talks of her desire to have a penis in order to be able to take a lover as would a man.

Lister's diaries were written in cipher, and it is a trope of lesbian literature in general that homoerotic discourse was encoded until well into the twentieth century. For example, in (re)examining the poetry of Emily Dickinson, we can see that a reading that privileges lesbian sensuality, like the astute analysis of Paula Bennett, can uncover clitoral imagery in the peas, berries, and nuts that abound in Dickinson's poetry.[8] Alternatively, lesbian eroticism must often be read in the silent spaces in an otherwise heterosexual text. Often, it is the ellipses or breaks in the text that mark the feelings between women that cannot be spoken, a technique often used by Virginia Woolf and Renée Vivien.[9] Or the perceptive reader can find lesbian erotic tension in the alienated characters, whether male or female, of Carson McCullers or Willa Cather. Or it may be contained in the slyly sexual language employed by Gertrude Stein in many of her texts, including *Lifting Belly* and *Tender Buttons*.

Since the task of decoding lesbian eroticism rests primarily with the reader who is generally a lesbian (or those willing to read as lesbians), in the end we wind up with more questions than answers. When does the implicit become explicit? What is explicit eroticism and how do we recognize it? What lines get crossed so that something becomes labeled "lesbian"?[10]

As painful as it may be to consider, there is no overtly lesboerotic moment in our literature until the pulps of the late 1940s. Even in

Radclyffe Hall's *The Well of Loneliness* (1928), which is so frequently held up as the foremother of lesbian literature, there is nothing that can be read as overtly sexual or even suggestively sexual: Stephen Gordon and Mary Llewellyn never kiss or even hold hands. Stephen Gordon's agonizing recognition of herself as an "invert" is what marks her friendship as lesbian. And with Hall so reticent, who else would dare lay out for us what lesbians desire, what lesbians do? Only Djuna Barnes could facetiously, in the satirical and unsigned *Ladies Almanack,* point out the pleasures of Natalie Clifford Barney's tongue.

Like their counterparts in most of the books of the period, the vast majority of lesbians led encoded lives.[11] We found each other semiotically, spotting a telltale pinky ring, hair a bit shorter than the fashion, or a book "real ladies" wouldn't read in public:

> Lesbian life in America from at least the thirties through the sixties was organized around a highly developed sense of sexual ceremony and dialogue. Indeed, because of the surrounding oppression, ritual and code were often all we had to make public erotic connections. Dress, stance, gestures, even jewelry and hairstyles had to carry the weight of sexual communications.[12]

The erotic life of lesbians and nonlesbians alike was affected by the liberalized attitudes toward sexuality in the 1960s, when the birth control pill freed women for the first time in history from defining sexuality in relation to procreation. Though the majority of lesbians prior to the 1970s considered children to be a product of a heterosexual past (or a bisexual present), still attitudes toward sexual pleasure were influenced by public discussion of the female orgasm. At the same time, the postwar decades of the 1950s and 1960s brought increased persecution for many lesbians in the form of bar raids and government harassment of groups like the Daughters of Bilitis, so that public arenas where lesbians could find one another were often fraught with danger.

In the late 1960s, the second wave of the Women's Liberation Movement advocated equality and social change for women, but the civil rights struggle turned out to be problematic for lesbians. While many, myself included, welcomed and eagerly joined a movement that seemed likely to take up what we then called "homophile issues," support for lesbians within the Women's Liberation Movement turned out to be lukewarm at best and the hostility was often overt. In *The Feminine Mystique,* Betty Friedan set a negative tone when she described lesbians as "spreading like a murky fog over the American scene."[13] In the radical feminist group Redstockings, lesbians soon discovered that the slogan "the personal is political" applied only to heterosexuals: Our problems were considered to have no universal ramifications!

Feminism also dictated a new code of sexual ethics. The creation of sexual proscriptions (for instance, a condemnation of s/m activities) tried to ensure equality during sex as well as in all other aspects of life. Some denounced butch/femme identities as "role playing" and as imitative of male/female relationships. Martha Shelley remarked, "True, some gays play the same role-games among themselves that straights do. Isn't every minority group fucked over by the values of the majority culture?"[14] Some feminists also decried sadomasochistic behavior as evincing a fascistic mentality. In the 1970s, public dissent was minimal, perhaps because some of those who later championed butch/femme identifications or s/m were at that time publicly toeing the party line while privately indulging their fantasies. Also, just as the patriarchal aspects of butch/femme identifications were exaggerated by their opponents, so too was the erotic life of "politically correct" lesbians blandly portrayed as limited to side-by-side sex with simultaneous orgasms.

This atmosphere encouraged lesbians to downplay erotic energy and to define ourselves as political creatures. Prior to May 1970, for an action to take place during the Second Congress to Unite Women, Radicalesbians penned the now-classic "Woman-Identified Woman," a manifesto which proclaimed, "A lesbian is the rage of all women condensed to the point of explosion. . . . Lesbianism, like male homosexuality, is a category of behavior possible only in a sexist society." Presumably, after the revolution, "the categories of homosexuality and heterosexuality would disappear."[15] Perhaps sex itself would disappear.

In retrospect, our error (and as a member of Radicalesbians, I shoulder some of the blame here for the shape of the final piece) was in glossing over the fact that most of us had tons of sexual energy as well as rage. Furthermore, as Amber Hollibaugh and Cherríe Moraga have pointed out, "By analyzing the institution of heterosexuality, feminists learned what's oppressive about it and why people cooperate with it or don't but we didn't learn what is *sexual*."[16]

There was little discussion of what lesbians were actually doing in bed. Lesbian consciousness-raising groups endlessly dissected political and social relationships with gay men, with heterosexual women, with other lesbians and with the world in general, but we were generally skittish at addressing intimate topics or the politics of eroticism. As Marilyn Frye noted, "Lesbian 'sex' as I have known it most of the time I have known it is utterly inarticulate. Most of my lifetime, most of my experience in the realms commonly designated as 'sexual' has been prelinguistic, noncognitive." [17] Frye seems to imply that the sex she had could be neither verbalized nor consciously recognized as lesbian, perhaps even by herself. We knew who was sleeping with whom, but we rarely knew who was doing what with whom. But as Anna Livia points out in this volume, some lesbians clearly enjoyed discussing the merits (or lack thereof) of their previous lovers. And a few pioneers like Betty Dodson publicly and loudly proclaimed the wonders of masturbation and other sexual practices. [18]

The 1970s was a time of relative peace compared to the sex wars of the 1980s. The 1982 Barnard conference on sexuality, during which the antipornography activists were not invited to speak, changed the course of history. At first, an angry debate ensued between those who sought an end to pornography, prostitution, s/m, and "role playing," and pro-sex women, who evolved into several groups, including F.A.C.T. (Feminist Anti-Censorship Taskforce). With Andrea Dworkin, Diana Russell, Kathleen Barry, Pauline Bart, and Jan Raymond in one corner and Carol Vance, Ann Snitow, Joan Nestle, Amber Hollibaugh, and Dorothy Allison in the other, the lesbian/feminist movement seemed about to rip itself apart. Those who didn't take sides (Charlotte Bunch, for example) were often condemned by both factions. The invective has not completely died down, though the issue takes up less space in feminist and lesbian media. In the early 1990s, the passage of an antipornography statute in Canada, which most people believe is based on the work of Andrea Dworkin and Catharine MacKinnon, led to the exclusion of some gay and lesbian material and even to the banning of a work by Andrea Dworkin. For antipornography activists like Dworkin, "erotica is simply high-class pornography: better produced, better conceived, better executed, better packaged, designed for a better class of consumer." [19] Dworkin, MacKinnon, and many others perceive pornography as a textbook for violence against women. But Audre Lorde, for example, would not have called her essay "The Uses of the Pornographic"; she viewed the erotic as a source of energy, not of destruction. For many gay women, male-made pornography is not the same as lesbian-created erotica. Of particular pain to some is the way in which consensual lesbian sexual practices, such as s/m relationships, have been lumped together with heteropatriarchal pornography and concern about violence against women. Much like lovers who quarrel, we have inflicted as much or perhaps more damage on one another than nonlesbians have on us, and our disagreements over the erotic, among other, issues have prevented us from having any sort of unified lesbian agenda. And some younger lesbians now view other feminists, not the patriarchy, as the authoritative power they wish to defy. Meanwhile, violence against women—rape, battery, child abuse, genital mutilation, murder—continues and may even be increasing.

Although antipornography feminists felt that lesbians were their greatest potential allies, ironically some lesbians became great consumers and connoisseurs of the erotic. Beginning in the late 1980s, a wide range of erotic materials by and for lesbians began to proliferate: glossy magazines such as *On Our Backs* and *Bad Attitude;* soft-core erotic novels like *Curious Wine* by Katherine Forrest; hard-core s/m material like *Macho Sluts* by Pat Califia; lesbian sex videos like *Safe Is Desire;* and mainstream movies like *Claire of the Moon.* Erotica (along with mysteries and romances) is now one of the best-selling genres in the lesbian community.

Interestingly, there is little scholarship that examines lesbian eroticism. A few volumes on sexuality, such as the highly successful *Powers of Desire: The Politics of Sexuality,* edited by Ann Snitow, Christine Stansell, and Sharon Thompson, include lesbian perspectives in a generally nonlesbian work. We could claim that this paucity of material is just one of many ways that the scholarly community tends to be out of touch with the world at large, but the issue is really more complex. Poststructuralist theory has shifted our understanding of sex and gender, making sexual identities highly problematic concepts. Perhaps wary of the battles surrounding sexuality, leading lesbian scholars have focused instead on gender (Judith Butler, for example) or on the performative implications of role identification (Sue-Ellen Case).

As a result, there is at this moment rather a lacuna in lesbian scholarship that this volume hopes to address. Some of the essays in *Lesbian Erotics* reflect this gap by calling upon the previous scholarship of lesbians when gender is the issue, and upon the work of male theorists such as Michel Foucault and Leo Bersani when sexuality is the topic. Several of the essays use techniques and issues raised by poststructuralism to look at lesbian sexual practices or literary or cinematic texts and contexts. Judith Butler, Teresa de Lauretis, Eve Kosofsky Sedgwick, and other scholars have examined a continuum of sexual possibilities and gender identifications that make lesbian erotics a rich territory to explore. Postmodernism allows sexuality to be viewed not only as acts but also as a series of fluid and dynamic performances, positions, and surfaces. Essays by Ann Cvetkovich, Colleen Lamos, S. Elaine Craghead, Bonnie Burns, and Karin Quimby, as well as the essay/story by Elizabeth Meese and Sandy Huss, point in this direction.

Other essays, such as those by Jane Garrity, Johanna Blakley, and Sharon P. Holland use elements of current theory to explore the erotic in one novel or the work of one author. The intent here is not to be encyclopedic; rather, a few readings are meant to indicate how we can all explore or reevaluate erotic elements in some of our favorite books.

Because the lesbian erotic past is so murky, the volume also contains two essays by Jennifer Travis and Anna Marie Smith about legal cases. Despite the fact that one is a historical libel suit involving actress Maud Allan's portrayal of Salome and the other is a contemporary British legal case about a teenager named Jennifer Saunders, both outline the difficulties of patriarchal efforts to define lesbianism and lesboerotic sexual practices. They also underscore the dangers of allowing the law to define our sexuality. These essays help ground us in the hegemony of patriarchal law so that the implicit dangers of cultural productions of lesbian erotic material in film and fiction are apparent. In doing so, some of these essays venture boldly into new territory. Like Anne Lister, we are still thirsty for a language of our own.

Finally, as in *Lesbian Texts and Contexts: Radical Revisions,* which I edited with Joanne Glasgow, this collection recognizes the relationship of the author and reader to the text. I have begun here with some of the writers, teachers, and practitioners who are on the front lines. Marny Hall counsels couples whose lack of an erotic life has brought them to her office. Ruthann Robson teaches jurisprudence to a class that would rather discuss the acts themselves. Anna Livia locates the erotic in her own kitchen. Donna Allegra has been nourished by influential images in lesbian erotica but doesn't include explicit sexual scenes in her own writing, much to the chagrin of some editors. Kitty Tsui not only has written erotic poems and stories but also has developed her own body into an art form to combat stereotypes of passive and invisible Asian women. Sandy Huss creates saucy, postmodern scissors. Had this volume room for a hundred additional contributors, each one would bestow her own distinct imprint on it, for our erotic visions and concerns are as varied as we are.

Where *Lesbian Texts and Contexts* challenged the reader to (re)vision literature with radically new eyes, this work hopes to invite readers to consider the implications, variations, and complexities of lesbian erotics. In the end, it is our sexual lives that mark us as outlaws. Therefore, we need to investigate and engage representations of our sexuality to define for ourselves, if we so choose, the scope, shape, and permutations of lesbian erotics.

NOTES

1. Kate Clinton, *Babes in Joyland*. Provincetown, MA: Whyscrack Records, n.d.

2. See Lillian Faderman, *Surpassing the Love of Men* and *Odd Girls and Twilight Lovers*; Martha Vicinus, " 'They Wonder to Which Sex I Belong': The Historical Roots of the Modern Lesbian Identity," in *The Lesbian and Gay Studies Reader*, ed. Henry Abelove, Michèle Aina Barale, and David Halperin (New York: Routledge, 1993), 432–52; Anne Lister, *I Know My Own Heart: The Diaries of Anne Lister, 1791–1840*, ed. Helena Whitbread (New York: New York University Press, 1992) and *No Priest But Love: The Journals of Anne Lister, 1824–1826*, ed. Helena Whitbread (New York: New York University Press, 1993). Terry Castle disputes Faderman's position and, citing the Lister diaries, embraces an essentialist position regarding lesbianism in *The Apparitional Lesbian* (New York: Columbia University Press, 1993).

3. See Esther D. Rothblum and Kathleen A. Brehony, eds. *Boston Marriages* (Amherst: University of Massachusetts Press, 1993); "Liz and Justine," *On Our Backs* 10:4 (March/April 1994): 32–35; Pat Califia, *Sensuous Magic* (New York: Kasak Books, 1993), 131–53.

4. Audre Lorde, "The Uses of the Erotic: The Erotic as Power," in *The Lesbian and Gay Studies Reader*, 339.

5. JoAnn Loulan, *The Lesbian Erotic Dance: Butch, Femme, Androgyny, and Other Rhythms* (San Francisco: Spinsters Book Company, 1990), 3.

6. Castle, 30.

7. Karla Jay, introduction to *Lavender Culture*, ed. Karla Jay and Allen Young (New York: New York University Press, 1994), xxx–xxxi.

8. Paula Bennett, "The Pea That Duty Locks: Lesbian and Feminist Heterosexual Readings of Emily Dickinson's Poetry," in *Lesbian Texts and Contexts: Radical Revisions*, ed. Karla Jay and Joanne Glasgow (New York: New York University Press, 1990), 104–25.

9. See Jane Marcus, "Sapphistory: The Woolf and the Well," in *Lesbian Texts and Contexts,* 164–79.

10. See Karla Jay and Joanne Glasgow, introduction to *Lesbian Texts and Contexts,* 1–9. I am also thankful to Elizabeth Meese for her insights in this area.

11. Some extremely wealthy women like Natalie Clifford Barney and the Marquise de Belbœuf could live as they chose, but they were clearly the exception rather than the rule.

12. Joan Nestle, "Flamboyance and Fortitude: An Introduction," in *The Persistent Desire: A Femme-Butch Reader,* ed. Joan Nestle (Boston: Alyson, 1992), 15.

13. Quoted in Ann Snitow, Christine Stansell, and Sharon Thompson, eds., introduction to *Powers of Desire: The Politics of Sexuality* (New York: Monthly Review Press, 1983), 26.

14. Martha Shelley, "Gay Is Good," in *Out of the Closets: Voices of Gay Liberation,* ed. Karla Jay and Allen Young (1972; rpt. New York: New York University Press, 1992), 33.

15. Radicalesbians, "The Woman-Identified Woman," in *Out of the Closets,* 172–73.

16. Amber Hollibaugh and Cherríe Moraga, "What We're Rollin Around in Bed With: Sexual Silences in Feminism," in *Powers of Desire,* 395.

17. Marilyn Frye, "Lesbian 'Sex,'" in *An Intimate Wilderness: Lesbian Writers on Sexuality,* ed. Judith Barrington (Portland, OR: Eighth Mountain, 1991), 6. What Frye means by "prelinguistic" is unclear.

18. For a more thorough history of this period see *Powers of Desire,* and Alice Echols, *Daring to Be Bad: Radical Feminism in America 1967–1975* (Minneapolis: University of Minnesota Press, 1989).

19. Andrea Dworkin, *Pornography: Men Possessing Women* (London: Women's Press, 1984), 10.

PART I

Reading/Writing/Teaching the Lesbian Body

Not Tonight, Dear, I'm Deconstructing a Headache: Confessions of a Lesbian Sex Therapist

MARNY HALL

1979: Lesbian Bed Death

When I started my career as a lesbian psychotherapist in the mid-1970s, lesbian feminist culture was in high gear. The delights of lesbian love were celebrated in our bookstores and galleries, at our coffee houses and festivals. But despite the siren songs of Meg Christian and Margie Adam and Cris Williamson, not all of us were feeling liberated and lusty. No sooner had I opened my practice than lesbian couples came in complaining of sexual problems. Either one or both partners had lost their desire.

Since my graduate studies program hadn't equipped me for this particular exigency, I signed up for the Masters and Johnson sex therapy training offered by the University of California Medical School. It made no difference that my goal, in contrast to the rest of the sex therapy trainees in my class, was to work exclusively with lesbian couples. We were taught that sex was a natural function—a set of responses so universal that it obliterated differences in sexual orientation, and even gender. Our instructors assured us that if the blocks to eroticism— ignorance, prudery, and performance anxiety—were removed, Mother Nature would reassert herself with vigor, whether our clients were gay or straight, men or women.

The first two libido killers, naiveté and leftover Victorian attitudes, were not my clients' particular nemeses. Unlike the heterosexual clients I was also working with at the time, lesbians seeking treatment for sexual disinterest knew exactly where their clitorises were. Most had long ago given themselves permission to touch their genitals, and many had been stroking themselves with great gusto for years. Such genital conversancy was not necessarily connected with partner sex, however, and partners often worried if there was any variation in their usual sexual frequency. In fact, they seemed to have built in erotic abacuses which were constantly computing the days since they had last "done it." After a sexless month or two had passed, partners often concluded that their stalled passion required jump-starting. At this point some women made trips to the local porn emporium or vibrator store. The romantically inclined scheduled special dates or exotic vacations. The politically correct stalwarts, eschewing such artifice, simply tried to white knuckle their way through disinclination while the astral-minded traced each other's auras with crystals or had their chakras adjusted. When all home remedies failed, they ended up in my office.

By now indoctrinated in the tenets of the training program, I diagnosed these clients' presenting problem as performance anxiety. Misconstruing the normal ebb and flow of sexuality as loss of desire, the partners had become panicky, and their attempted solutions had only exacerbated the problem. According to my mentors in the training program, they had tried to ford the river when they needed to dally on the bank.

The cure for this brand of performance jitters was a goal-free regimen of sensuality. It was up to me to transform these orgasmic overachievers into sensual dawdlers. With that in mind, I gave out massage homework. Clients were told to "explore" each other in certain sequences—find out what sort of touch felt good and talk about it with each other. These exercises were not as effective as my teachers had predicted. Couples in treatment often replaced battles about whether or not to have sex with debates about whether or not to do the sensuality exercises I had prescribed.

In successive rounds of training, my instructors told me that such arguments meant that performance anxiety was not my clients' only problem. The absence of sex might also be the couple's attempt to rebalance an out-of-whack relationship. If partners' boundaries were too permeable, for example, they would feel much too threatened by the additional intimacy of sex. In other words, such couples could stay together only if they *didn't* have sex. If the boundaries of such a couple were strengthened, the need for such symptomatic behavior would wither away and their love life would flourish again.

In the parlance of psychotherapy, many of the lesbian couples I was seeing were "mindreaders." They could describe their partners' feelings in as much detail as their own. Perhaps such attunement was evidence of the permeable boundaries my teachers were warning us about. Maybe such perfect rapprochement made sex redundant, a superfluous form of intimacy. If this were the case, I had to somehow reduce the rapport that for some couples seemed, indeed, to border on the telepathic. If I could fortify each partner's individuality by pointing out the ways she glossed over differences or made unfounded assumptions, perhaps I could curb anti-erotic boundary meltdown. I could also give the couple homework assignments that would continue to emphasize each partner's individuality. Under my guidance, partners would make separate friends, go to separate twelve-step meetings, sleep apart, even jog apart. If they could bear to separate from each other outside the bedroom, perhaps they might be more willing to connect those intimate parts of their anatomy once they slipped between the sheets. Some of my suggestions even seemed to work, at least temporarily.

Meanwhile, like ambitious fledgling professionals of any stripe, we lesbian sexperts were also lecturing and publishing. The first wave of articles on lesbian couples' problems by lesbian professionals tended to mix the cultural and the clinical. Lesbians, went our refrain, hadn't escaped female conditioning. The result—a relentless focus on nurturing—would increase exponentially when two women coupled. This forfeiture of individuality, compounded by our us-against-the-world outlaw stance, created a relational greenhouse effect which suffocated passion. The articles I and my colleagues were writing, for example, "Another Perspective on Merger in Lesbian Relationships,"[1] and "The Problem of Fusion in Lesbian Relationships,"[2] reappeared, often, in popularized form, in the lesbian press. When, shortly after publication of these articles, my clients came in caricaturing themselves as "textbook lesbians" and "merger queens," I laughed ruefully and wondered whether my colleagues and I, in our earnest attempts to write about lesbian bed death, were also authoring a new genre of lesbian self-doubt. In previous eras, lesbians had been sick when they were sexual. Now, compliments of lesbian affirmative therapists, they were sick when they weren't. And therapy didn't seem to be helping. In the long run, my attempts to strengthen my clients' boundaries hadn't worked any better than the massages. Even more disheartening, the ranks of uncured therapy graduates began to include second generation couples: partners I had originally seen together were now bringing in their new partners with the same old problems.

Adding to my skepticism about the effectiveness of sex therapy were the revolutionary ideas of social theorists. All our truths about sex, they maintained, were nothing more than social constructions.

In 1979 a radical historian, Robert A. Padgug, summed up sex both as a set of categories which ordered our experience and a set of relationships which were historically and culturally specific.[3]

And the philosopher Michel Foucault wrote that "modern notions of sex made it possible to group together, in an artificial unit, anatomical elements, biological functions, conducts, sensations and pleasures, and enabled one to make use of this fictional unity as a causal principle, an omnipresent meaning."[4]

If sex was such an endlessly shifting, ultimately unknowable social/historical quark, were lesbian bed death and sex therapy equally chimerical? Were sexual diagnoses nothing more than the codification and dissemination of information which, by creating a feeling of deficiency in particular groups, served other groups? And were we sex therapists actually helping clients or merely benefiting from the proliferation of anxiety-producing social constructions about unhealthy sexual functioning?

1984: Sex and Other Social Science Fictions

My focus was shifting from the bedrock "facts" of sexuality to my position as conveyer (perhaps even self-interested shaper) of these truths. And the change in my perspective was not confined to my office musings. One spring day in the early 1980s, as I sat in the undergraduate psychology library at the University of California at Berkeley catching up on some reading, I took a bathroom break. Sitting in the stall, I began to read the graffiti scrawled around me:

"I would like to make innocent love to another woman. Nice and slow love making. I am a normal person with no crazy desires. Does anyone know of someone?"

Several suggestions followed, each in different script.

"Try Hoyt Hall, the co-op on Ridge Road. There are some nice women living there or ask at the gay/lesbian/bisexual alliance on campus."

"I live at Hoyt Hall. There are only a few lesbians there."

"What's wrong with wanting to lick a woman's cunt?"

"Nothing. It's called homosexual tendencies."

Bemused, I scribbled the restroom commentary down on a scrap of paper, went back to my carrel and picked up Masters and Johnson's *Homosexuality in Perspective* again. "By showing," I read in the foreword, "that there are no physiologic norms clearly distinguishing homosexual and heterosexual function . . . , [Masters and Johnson] invite an abandonment of many of the stereotypes of normal versus abnormal function."[5] I looked at my john door notations again. Apparently, lesbianism had been decreed normal both in the formal sphere of sexology and in the informal, private ruminations of University of California undergraduates. The defiant query, "What's wrong with wanting to lick a woman's cunt?" seemed aimed at the very same disapproving establishment that Masters and Johnson were trying to educate. I wondered if one could always track the latest "truths" across different discourses. Would, for example, the personal musings of nineteenth-century citizens mirror the scientific wisdom of the day as accurately as the bathroom stall had reflected Masters and Johnson? Foraging in the stacks, I found an excerpt from *Sexual Physiology and Hygiene,* a marriage manual written by Dr. R. T. Trail in 1866:

> The frequency with which sexual intercourse can be indulged without serious damage to one or both of the parties depends, of course, on a variety of circumstances—constitutional stamina, temperament, occupation, habits of exercise, etc. Few should exceed the limits of once a week, while many cannot safely indulge oftener than once a month. But as temperance is always the safe rule of conduct, if there must be any deviation from the strictest law of physiology, let the error be on that side.[6]

Rummaging around in Jonathan Katz's *Gay/Lesbian Almanac,* I found an interesting passage from Mary Casal's 1905 diary:

Our lives were on a much higher plane than those of the real inverts. While we did indulge in our sexual intercourse, that was never the thought uppermost in our minds. We had seen over-indulgence on the part of some of those with whom we came in contact, in loss of vitality and weakened health, ending in consumption. [7]

The mirroring was unmistakable. Were lesbians continually refurbishing their identities according to scientific trends? Perhaps the stentorian declamations of experts simply lent authority to popular opinions. Like characters in a cartoon, I imagined us all—scientists and lay people, therapists and clients, students and faculty, even dogs and cats—simultaneously babbling the identical nonsense in different jargon. But something wasn't quite accurate about the cartoon. After all, if the same information was merely reiterated in different registers, how did our truths evolve? When I considered the course of my own career, I realized a system of not-so-subtle rewards existed for those of us positioned to reconfigure information—to tell slightly altered "truths." I remembered, for example, that before I handed them to my clients, I edited the guides to proper massage sequences. I infused them with what I considered to be the necessary esprit de clit by whiting out all references to penises:

Nipple [white space] erections should not get extra attention, although patterns of goosebumps may be given further attention since, if the room isn't cold, this is a sign of successful stroking. [8]

The newly de-dicked sentences earned me special cachet. After all, I had been able to import cutting-edge sexpertise from the mainstream and tailor it in such a way that the marginal status of my lesbian clients was whited out along with the penis references.

But the jelling of certain perspectives into accepted wisdom did not always proceed in such a straightforward way. Imaginative flourishes, misconstruals, and compression of ideas probably accounted for most new truths. For example, when they were first published in journals and anthologies, the articles on fusion in lesbian relationships were complicated hybrids which grafted together notions from mainstream marriage manuals, the sociology of deviance, and gay identity politics. [9] Summaries of the articles appeared in lesbian newsletters and gay studies syllabi, and the community grapevine, in turn, summarized these summaries. Eventually, all the commentary boiled down to one new and quite unintended "fact": Lesbians were "merger queens."

But everyone knows that psychology—a soft science—is always suspect, its findings always fictional. An analysis, however, of the hard science of Masters and Johnson reveals the same process of expedient storytelling.

As couples' therapists and medical scientists, as traditional married partners and nontraditional work colleagues, William Masters and Virginia Johnson were positioned to weave together elements of the warring discourses about sex and gender. Tradition defined women as wives and mothers, and sex as the natural, inexorable conjunction of opposites. In contrast, the sexual and women's liberation movements proclaimed the new woman to be a lusty self-determining female who, by separating procreation from recreation, heralded the triumph of science over nature.

When they set out to write *Human Sexual Response* (1966), the two researchers looked for a bit of neutral ground, an Archimedean Point outside the debate, upon which to build their theories. They found it in the post-Kinsey consensus about orgasms. Whatever their sexual ideology, most Americans knew that almost all men and a substantial proportion of women had experienced orgasms. Consequently, centering their research around orgasms was a safe bet. During laboratory trials—hardly a "normal" setting for sex—Masters and Johnson "discovered" the "normal sexual response cycle." It consisted of orgasms, which they elaborated into a four-phase sequence consisting of excitement, plateau, orgasm, and resolution stages. When women's sexual response data were not parallel to men's, however, Masters and Johnson tried to shoehorn them into a male tumescent/detumescent boilerplate: "Only one response pattern has been diagramed for the human male . . . comparable to three different sexual response patterns . . . diagramed for [the] female. . . . There is a great variation in both the intensity and the duration of the female orgasmic experience." [10]

This finding should have led to a quite opposite conclusion, that is, that women's orgasmic patterns are *not* parallel to men's. Nevertheless Masters and Johnson claimed the four-part human response cycle was universal. And in my training program, this equivalency between men and women was extended to include sexual appetites and genital structures. We were shown color-coded slides depicting penises and vulvas. Matching colors denoted homologous structures. Thus, the scrotum and labia majora were the identical canary yellow, the glans penis and glans clitoris both mauve, and so forth. The message was explicit: the difference between men and women was largely a matter of sex-role stereotyping and quirks, not innate capacity.

But were Masters and Johnson really so intent upon proving analogous male and female sexuality? Was there a hidden agenda? The data about equivalent orgasms and the pictures of homologous genital structures can be read, depending on one's perspectives, in contrary ways. One possible interpretation is that women are the equals of men; another is that men are, themselves, the norm. Women may approximate them, but our orgasms are more diffuse, our dicks (clitorises) diminutive. Thus women can be "liberated" and, simultaneously, reminded of our subordinate position.

1989: Antisex Therapy

The research and conclusions of Masters and Johnson were inseparable from—actually shaped by—mainstream ideology. And my prescriptions for a healthy sex life, despite the lesbian-friendly window dressing I had given it, were laced with the phallocentric values and suppositions that I had imbibed as a trainee. Now that lesbian bed death seemed a particularly oppressive fiction, a "condition" to be deconstructed rather than treated, I could no longer, in good conscience, be a lesbian sex therapist. Instead, I decided I'd become an anti-sex therapist.[11] Instead of trying to goose slumbering libidos, I would simply discuss the politics of sex. Together, clients and I would explore the origins of consensus about sexuality, the ways in which such universal beliefs affected different groups, and the benefits that accrued to the "discoverers" of these truths. In short, I would tell them what I knew. Equally important, by assigning exercises that illuminated the fuzzy provisionality of sex, I would show them that no one, including me, knew anything for sure. Other exercises would, I hoped, isolate, scramble, and desanctify phallic patterns of tumescence and detumescence which had been enshrined as normal sex. And finally, I hoped we would collaboratively design a series of activities which, by defying categorization as sexual or nonsexual, would open a new realm of intimacy for partners.

Among the first couples to experience my antisex approach were two white working-class women I'll call Melanie and Gina. After they had moved in together a few months before, they became increasingly polarized over sex. Gina described herself as "completely shut down" while Melanie complained that her sexuality, an essential part of herself, had no outlet.

Both partners had been raised in families whose ability to nurture them had been compromised by alcoholism, divorce, and economic distress. It was hard to separate such early deprivation from their current sexual problems. From a psychodynamic point of view, their sexual impasse could be interpreted as a struggle to get the special attention that had been in short supply all their lives. I couldn't bypass Melanie's and Gina's feelings of deprivation and abandonment. Entwined with an exploration of these issues was an ongoing discussion of the precepts of antisex.

I described the rather torturous path I had followed to antisex, including my Masters and Johnson training and my own previous hit-and-miss record of treating lesbian bed death. Before they came back the next time, I asked Melanie and Gina to begin a series of experiments which I hoped would blur the line between sex and nonsex. As a beginning assignment, I proposed a massage that would scramble standard erotic/nonerotic zones. They could avoid the standard sequences of working up to the erotic zones by interspersing random touches of noses, nipples, toes, vaginas, and knees or by designating a new sacred zone. If they used the elbow, for example, they could gradually work up to it through a subordination of all the other, now less important, zones. We collaborated on the design of other, similar experiments. On a day before they planned to go to the park and play catch, they decided that along with the ball which they could toss underhanded from the vicinity of their crotches, they could also hurl dirty words at each other. On another occasion, before bedtime, they tied scarves around themselves in such a way that they brushed against their genitals as they were going to sleep. At one point, when she was recounting her early sexual experiences, Gina reported some pleasant erotic encounters with boys in the back seats of cars. Since emotional abandonment continued to be a theme, I suggested that we try to combine both Gina's early memories of sexual experimentation with the forlornness they both felt in the present. Modifying Gina's teen scenario, they disrobed under a blanket in the back of their car and were simply "waifs together," simultaneously naked and woebegone.

At the end of two months of these exercises, Gina and Melanie threw in the towel. They had had enough. When I ran into them six months later, they were succinct about the ineffectiveness of antisex therapy.

"We wanted," Melanie said, "to have a sex life of abandon and you wanted us to abandon our sex life."

Gina added, "I just wanted to be fixed. I didn't want a revolution."

They had, they told me, found a new therapist, who in addition to helping them with their sex problems, had recently officiated at their wedding. When I ran into Gina a year later, she told me they had thrown in the towel on their relationship as well. Her final analysis: "I fell in love. And I found out that I'm really a bottom. I've found someone who can really top me."

Antisex therapy was a bust. Upon reflection, I understood why my approach hadn't worked with Gina and Melanie. Sex may have been a phallocentric social construction. It was also the only way we certified our existences. When we made love, we were "performing" our essences, enacting a pivotal aspect of an embattled identity. Perhaps lesbian bed death was a way of affirming our essences as well. Even if we weren't doing it, we could at least worry about it, talk it over, or confer with an expert. Rather than give up the whole category, and our identities along with it, we would find new techniques, new roles, new therapists, new lovers, or merely new ways to lament the absence of sex in our lives.

1993: Lesbian Bed Death Revisited

The passage of time from 1979 to 1993 has been marked not by a decline in lesbian bed death, but rather by my clients' reluctance to admit they still suffer from it. After years of workshops, how-to books, and butch/femme liberation, something really must be wrong if they're not having sex. Home remedies have also gone through some transformations: handcuffs have replaced crystals, strap-on dildos now sub for plug-in vibrators.

My own brand of sex therapy has changed again. I know too much to do sex therapy. I don't know enough to do antisex therapy. I haven't got any formulas to offer lesbian clients as sex substitutes, and even if I could imagine such alternatives, I don't have the cultural authority to legitimize them.

Now when clients complain of lesbian bed death, I simply try to coax into consciousness the ways their experiences, cultures, and temperaments have shaped their versions of sex. I can only hope that in this process of detailing histories and reactions, partners will come to appreciate the plurality of sexual meanings and how very distinct their maps are. I hope, too, that they will collaborate on mutually inclusive maps.

One of the couples I am currently seeing stopped having sex two years ago. One grew up in El Salvador in an extended matriarchy, the other in Ohio in a series of foster homes. To the Central American woman, constantly supervised by a cadre of aunts, grandmothers, and older sisters, "private parts" meant exactly that: her body was not to be shared with anyone. And, she was taught that every man she encountered would try to inveigle her into sharing it. Her first erotic encounter occurred "in her sleep" with another equally protected girl. "Sex" for her is something entirely different from what it is to her North American lover who, as a foster child, was molested many times. A dangerous male-dominated universe is apparent in both women's stories. Yet phallocentrism has affected each partner so differently that, as a template, it is almost irrelevant. Because their erotic maps are so different, misunderstandings are the norm; any synchronization of desire is rare, unpredictable, a minor miracle.

We have spent many sessions exploring every contrasting detail. Just when I feel we have finally given each difference its due, I discover another nuance which, filtering in from some unexpected source, mediates sexuality in yet another unanticipated way. During the most recent session, they reported they were feeling particularly intimate. Having moved into the bedroom, they were holding each other when one woman interrupted the embrace long enough to take a piece of lint from her partner's eyelash. The lint remover explained that the speck had broken her concentration. Her partner said the removal had interrupted hers. Both partners felt misunderstood, victimized by the other's insensitivity. They were as estranged as they had been when they first came in months ago. We were back to square one. Was the misunderstanding a collaborative way of avoiding a perilous encounter? Or was it simply a clash of physiologies—one partner relying more on sensation, the other more visually oriented? I can't tell without more exploration, more information about their particular maps. I am reminded of Jorge Luis Borges's fable, "Of Exactitude in Science":

> In that Empire, the craft of Cartography attained such Perfection that the Map of a Single province covered the space of an entire City. . . . In the course of Time these Extensive maps were found somehow wanting and the . . . Cartographers evolved a Map of the Empire that was of the same Scale as the Empire and coincided with it point for point. Eventually the mapmakers finding such maps cumbersome, discard them. . . . Now tattered fragments of the Map are still to be found, Sheltering an occasional Beast or beggar; in the whole Nation, no other relic is left of the Discipline of Geography.[12]

Perhaps, someday, our sexual maps will become equally cumbersome and we will discard them. Perhaps the only relic of the days of lesbian bed death will be a quaint jumble of lab equipment and the abandoned offices of sex therapists. On one of their dusty desks, some wild sibyl will have etched the truths that liberate us, once and for all, from the discipline of sex.

NOTES

1. Beverly Burch, "Another Perspective on Merger in Lesbian Relationships," in *Handbook of Feminist Therapy*, ed. L. B. Rosewater and L. E. A. Walker (New York: Springer, 1985), 100–109.

2. Joann Krestan and C. S. Bepko, "The Problem of Fusion in Lesbian Relationships," *Family Process* 19 (1980): 277–89.

3. Robert A. Padgug, "Sexual Matters: On Conceptualizing Sexuality in History," *Radical History Review* 20 (1979): 16.

4. Michel Foucault, *The History of Sexuality*, vol. 1 (New York: Vintage. 1980), xv.

5. H. Tristram Engelhardt, foreword to *Homosexuality in Perspective* by William Masters and Virginia Johnson (Boston: Little, Brown, 1979), vii.

6. Quoted in Michael Gordon, "Marital Education Literature, 1830–1940," in *Studies in the Sociology of Sex,* ed. James M. Henslin (New York: Appleton-Century-Crofts, 1971), 37.

7. Jonathan Katz, *Gay/Lesbian Almanac* (New York: Harper Colophon, 1983), 305.

8. Bernard Apfelbaum, Martin Williams, and Susan Greene, "Couple Sex Therapy Assignments," in *Expanding the Boundaries of Sex Therapy,* ed. Bernard Apfelbaum (Berkeley: Berkeley Sex Therapy Group, 1979), 86.

9. Burch, 100–109, and Krestan and Bepko, 277–89.

10. William Masters and Virginia Johnson, *Human Sexual Response* (Boston: Little, Brown, 1966), 5.

11. Marny Hall, "Ex-Therapy to Sex Therapy: Notes from the Margins," in *Gays, Lesbians and Their Therapists,* ed. Charles Silverstein (New York: Norton, 1991), 84–97.

12. Jorge Luis Borges, *A Universal History of Infamy* (Middlesex: Penguin, 1975), 131.

Pedagogy, Jurisprudence, and Finger-Fucking: Lesbian Sex in a Law School Classroom

RUTHANN ROBSON

Talking about sex in a direct manner can be difficult; most of us have been enculturated to shame, silences, or at best partial entitlement toward sex-talk, particularly in nonintimate situations. Talking about lesbian sex can be especially difficult, not only because nonheterosexual sex is more imbued with shame than heterosexual sex, but also because the very language in which we speak is rooted in the denial of lesbian desire.[1] Talking about lesbian sex in a classroom is complicated not only by the difficulties of sex-talk and lesbian-sex-talk, but by the power and purposes inherent in the pedagogical pursuit. And talking about lesbian sex in a classroom as part of a curriculum devoted to turning students into attorneys can seem absolutely impossible, given the legal regime's prosecution and obfuscation of lesbian sexual desire and practices.

These difficulties are the subject of this chapter, which arises from my experience of developing and teaching a course entitled "Sexuality and the Law" at the City University of New York (CUNY) School of Law. Like many of my colleagues across the United States and Canada teaching similar courses, I have struggled to define the parameters of pedagogy and jurisprudence in a law school course on "sex." However, unlike many of my colleagues, I have not confined "Sexuality and the Law" to minority sexualities or devoted much attention to discrimination based upon sexual status. Instead, the course interrogates "sex" as a subject of legal regulation. Specifically, the course considers the legal treatment of various sexual practices such as reproduction, rape, pornography, prostitution, bestiality, and incest, as well as lesbianism, male homosexuality, bisexuality, heterosexuality, and transsexuality/transgender, as well as resultant jurisprudential issues including consent, privacy, normalcy, and power. The varied list of sexual practices has an equalizing tendency, which forces students to articulate differences, if any, among various sexual practices. This process often leads to extended questionings of "sex" itself, and discussions about whether a specific practice is "sex" or not. Lesbianism is often the centrifugal force of the classroom conversations, perhaps because in this course lesbianism is imbued with professorial authority.

Pedagogy and Boundary Problems

Whoever the professor and whatever the subject, pedagogical relations are often conceptualized as sexual. A psychoanalytic perspective stresses that "all pedagogy comes under the sign of the sexual" because "the ways in which we ordinarily model the relation of teacher and student— no matter how democratic—are always in the long run framed by familial terms" based upon sexual development models, primarily the Oedipal.[2] One can analyze "modes of educative pleasure" based upon sexual acts, supported by Freud and Lacan, so that pedagogy can be phallic (Platonic pederasty in which a "greater" man penetrates a "lesser" with his penis/knowledge) or digital (Socratizing in which a finger penetrates the anal orifice).[3] Given that neither of these modes is intentionally lesbian, one might strive to conceptualize a model of pedagogy based upon lesbian sexuality. Although a few lesbian professors might welcome such a model, I remain rather suspicious of such a project. However, one need not adopt the psychoanalytic model to accept that pedagogical situations have a sexual component: "That the relation between teacher and student is 'erotic' is perhaps the least surprising statement one might make about it, nearly the oldest news in Western writing."[4]

Further, some pedagogical methodologies are more sexual than others. For example, a seminar which has a relatively small number of students and stresses class participation is more "intimate" than a large, formal lecture class. In my own seminars, I have perhaps heightened this intimacy by having class sessions once a week for three hours at the end of the day and by not scheduling a break that would dissipate group energy. This arrangement has caused some of the student smokers to joke about the best cigarette of the week being on Tuesday evenings after "sex."

Such joking highlights the fact that not only are some pedagogical methodologies more sexual than others, but some subjects are simply more sexual than others. Law school classes in tax, administrative law, civil procedure, or federal jurisdiction rarely suggest sexual analogies. By contrast, law school subjects such as civil rights and feminist jurisprudence are often considered more personal, and thus more sexual. As women's studies professor Jane Gurko notes, the ultimate pedagogical and political goal of such courses can be easily interpreted as sexual.[5] When the course title contains "sex," no translation is required.

The explicitly sexualized character of the course as well as my position as a lesbian law professor focuses my attention on three intersecting boundaries. I am often on patrol, checking the security of boundaries which I will call the professor boundary, the story boundary, and the rigor boundary. Of these three boundaries, which I will discuss in turn, the professor/student one is the most complicated and the most vital.

Almost all professors have multitudes of anecdotes about students arriving during office hours to "confess" their "true feelings" of love. For lesbian professors, these anecdotes are further embroidered with confessions of confused or new-found sexuality on the part of previously heterosexual female students, or once in a while, by stuttered explanations mixed with bravado on the part of male students. For me, the simplest problem posed by these events is their physical outcome: none.[6]

In a course in which the explicit task is to address the sexual, the boundaries between professor and student often both intensify and blur in reaction to the hierarchal structure of the relationship.[7] Despite my framing of the syllabus as a series of questions,[8] my authority to create the syllabus (as well as to give the grade in the course) installs me as an expert on the subject of sex. For some students, this power creates an aura of my general sexual competence and expertise, an aura which I can find difficult to resist adopting. In reality, despite my greater scholarly knowledge of the subject, my experiential knowledge of many sexual practices is questionable at best. For some students, perceptions of my lack of particular experiences creates a space for them to attempt to install themselves as experts on particular aspects of sex.

Such student attempts to claim expertise are often accomplished through first-person narratives, implicating what I call the story-boundary. In any three-hour discussion, numerous digressions occur. But when the subject is sex, there seems to be an irrepressible urge to indulge in narration of experiences. This narration can be a method of violating the professor/student boundary: listening to student's sexual experiences makes it more difficult to maintain authority, and being questioned about my own sexual experiences makes it more difficult to maintain formality.

Yet the story-boundary is also intimately connected to what I call the rigor-boundary. This connection is experienced by many women's studies professors who seek to maintain a classroom atmosphere of academic analysis, notwithstanding an underlying politics of consciousness-raising. While personal stories do have a place, I often find myself restricting students' personal revelations, lest the classroom discussion become a series of stories about students' own lives and their neighbors' lives, as well as the lives of TV talk-show guests. My professorial interference with student narratives has been criticized by students in political terms as repressive, conservative, and unfeminist. Yet I perceive the necessity for rigor in arguably political terms as well. Much of legal doctrine pertaining to sexuality is faulty precisely because it is limited by the sexual experience of those empowered to pronounce the doctrine. I do not want the class discussions merely to recapitulate and reposition these experiential limits: I want the class discussions to investigate limits and their consequences.

Pedagogical rigor is important not only in class discussions, but also in every aspect of the course. Some of my attention to this boundary is admittedly caused by external pressures. While lesbian and gay studies have become somewhat respectable within the academy, their existence is still quite contested and controversial, especially in conservative institutions like law schools, and "sex" as a curriculum subject is hardly secure.[9] Thus, part of the pedagogy is often an indirect attempt to forestall labels like "frivolity" and "perversity." Such accusations can be mitigated by substituting "theorizing" for "talk," "sexualities" for "sex," adding a syllabus with appellate court cases and law review articles, and demanding a paper of publishable quality, preferably a law review casenote, as a course requirement. Nevertheless, many students state that they do not want the word "sex" on their law school transcript. While I refuse to rename the course, I strive for a reputation for rigor. My response to concerns about having "sex" on a law school transcript is to tell students that "sex" will only be negative on the transcript if it is accompanied by a failing grade. And yes, students have failed.

Legal Education, Diversity, and Lesbian Sex

Although I might be on pedagogical boundary-patrols in any academic institution, pedagogy in the legal context possesses some important distinctions. Law school has heightened seriousness, preparing students for a standardized examination and entrance into a "profession" of power. Contemporary pedagogical theories, especially postmodernist and feminist ones, stress empowerment in the interpretation of texts.[10] Despite a school of narrative theory within legal scholarship, most scholars admit that the law is vitally different from literary (or other) texts because it is enforced by the power of the state. Or, to put it most succinctly, we do not read United States Supreme Court opinions because they are artful literature, but because they are written in blood and backed by the United States Army.[11] Thus, even a *liberal* legal education (a rather rare animal) is fundamentally different from a liberal arts education. A liberal arts education strives to empower individual students, while a liberal legal education has as its ultimate goal the production of lawyers who will empower others through advocacy.[12]

When the course content is sex, liberal legal pedagogy requires an interrogation not only of one's own sexual practices, but also of the legal treatment of sexual practices of others. The necessity for such an interrogation is most apparent in the criminal context. Lofty discussions of whether or not some act constitutes sex and whether it should or should not constitute criminal sex are often grounded by elements of criminal statutes, case precedents, and theoretical perspectives on criminal justice, feminism, and liberalism. Lesbian s/m always provokes a good discussion in these instances, usually generated by a lesbian student.

The inclusion of lesbian students in the classroom is vital. A necessary aspect of the education of lawyers who will serve a range of disempowered persons is student and professorial diversity. Most law schools pay lip service to this requirement, but only a few have striven to realize it.

Teaching at the City University of New York, a historically diverse institution, insures that there will be actual variety in the classroom. Even in a self-selected elective such as Sexuality and the Law, there will be students along various race, class, age, culture, dis/ability, gender, and sexuality axes, as well as diversities in theoretical sophistication, academic performance, and life—including sexual—experiences. As a professor, I generally appreciate being in an institution with multiple constituencies, have advocated even more diversity within the institution, and have castigated other institutions for their lack of diversity. Nevertheless, diversity is problematic to me as a lesbian professor teaching about sex in a legal context.

The first problem is inherent in the statement "as a lesbian professor." The conflation between sexuality and identity is much contested, not only in the realm of identity politics ("it does/does not make a difference if one is a lesbian") but also in the realm of identity itself ("it makes no sense to label oneself a lesbian").[13] Within the classroom, identities struggle with reification: students may attempt to resist, but habitually (and repeatedly) start sentences with statements such as "as a lesbian," "as a gay man," "as a straight woman," "as a regular guy," and "as an incest survivor." Interestingly, the next statement from students asserting an identity may intentionally undermine the validity of the asserted identity category. Such undermining can be an attempt to forestall accusations from fellow students, such as "That doesn't mean anything" or "You weren't always, according to what you said last week." Unlike the students in class—and unlike my approach in this article—I never categorize myself as a lesbian professor, although this fact is well known to the students. Within the classroom dynamic, my lesbianism is submerged into the identity of professor. It is perhaps the very diversity in the class that mandates the submergence necessary to facilitate among differing articulated standpoints. The lesbian students often experience this stance as betrayal, while the nonlesbian students seem to wait for me to put my professorial imprint on a specific lesbian perspective, which will both settle the disputes among lesbian students and serve to neutralize the "authority" of my comments.

The second problem is that the classroom identity statements are relatively public acclamations that rest upon partial and privatized disclosures. Students will often confess certain aspects of their sexual lives during office appointments, sometimes as related to their interest in developing a casenote paper topic or in a more general conversation. For example, in any particular classroom I might know that a particular student is a "gay man" who sleeps with women, a previously heterosexual woman debating lesbianism, a former prostitute, a virgin, an s/m lesbian, or a previously lesbian woman now married. Of course, I do not know who else in the class knows what; I am only certain that students in the class know facts about each other's sexual histories that I do not. This situation often gives classroom discussions a subtext that bubbles to the surface as when one student runs crying from the room or when a student lashes out at another student. It can also influence my choice of materials to assign.

The third and last problem is the most vexing one. Diversity becomes uncomfortable when the subject is lesbian sex. I often cannot help but feel that the same conversation among lesbians would be of a much higher quality. I censor my own comments and judgments, not just as a professor, but also as a lesbian; I assume that the other lesbians in the classroom censor their own comments as well. We do not disagree as much in this diverse setting as we would among ourselves. But this reluctance to disagree in "public" is not the major drawback of diversity. I am much more concerned with the political implications of any discussion of lesbian sex among nonlesbians. Even given this self-selected group at a progressive law school, I am nevertheless wary of exploitation and appropriation. Lesbian sexuality belongs to lesbians and should not be commodified for nonlesbians, especially men.[14] I often find myself, however, in the position of facilitating discussions about lesbian sex among nonlesbians, including men of various sexual identities. When such discussions are closely textual, based upon court cases, I am most comfortable. However, when the discussions contrast the court's language with other texts or experiences, I am most guarded. Unfortunately, given the scant case law sources that raise lesbian sexuality, the class discussions are most often centered on theoretical nonlegal texts or student-related experiences.

Jurisprudence as Hypothetical

Not only is legal doctrine, especially in the form of case law, meager in its treatment of lesbian sexuality, but American jurisprudence is likewise sparse. Part of the struggle of theorizing lesbian sexuality within the law has been the predominance of lesbian imperceptibility, which often works to trivialize the perceptions of lesbianism that do occur. The opposite of trivializing also occurs: Because there is so little legal material relating to lesbian sex, this material is typicalized or made representative. Thus, the relative rarity of appellate opinion concerning convictions for "deviate sex" based upon lesbianism can lead a student (or a scholar) to conclusions that lesbian sex is generally tolerated (because it rarely appears in appellate criminal cases) as well as to opinions that the "deviate sex" described—or not described—in the appellate opinions is typical lesbianism.

Jurisprudence, the philosophy or theory of law, or in more positivist terms, the science of law, is thus relatively ignorant of lesbian sexuality. Positivist conceptions of law require a "rule" to be articulated and then applied—in a scientific manner—to situations shaped as hypothetical. Lesbian sexuality is imperceptible within this positivist paradigm because the rules controlling lesbian sex are only partially articulated, at best. Rules prohibiting "oral/anal contact," the "crime against nature," or "sexual contact between persons of the same gender" are imprecise from a legal positivist perspective because they cannot be "scientifically" applied to a hypothetical lesbian couple. For example, one woman stroking another woman's breasts is not oral/anal contact, but a court could interpret it to be a "crime against nature" or "sexual contact" if "sexual" is not confined to genital.

Pedagogically, I have struggled with materials to assign regarding lesbian sexual expression as regulated by the legal regime, changing the syllabus each year. There is scarce explicit theorizing about lesbian sexuality within the legal realm. While other professors have reported success using the piece I wrote applying the so-called sodomy statutes,[15] I have struggled with the idea of discussing my own work in class, especially when the material is sexually explicit. I have sometimes addressed this problem by assigning cases, but this is also problematic because discussions of legal doctrine and theory are often precluded by the poverty of the factual development within the cases.

My favorite example of factually impoverished cases is *People v. Livermore,* in which the crime seemed to consist of noises inside a tent overheard by state troopers standing outside for ten minutes, until the troopers unzipped the door and shined flashlights to reveal two women lying on a cot "partially covered by a blanket."[16] One needs a fair amount of lesbian imagination to provide sexual content, but whatever sexual content one supplies is conjecture. As one lesbian student asked, "So was she going down on her or were they finger-fucking?"

"What differences would that make under the various statutes?" is my professorial query. By assigning this case in conjunction with various criminal statutes, I had hoped to prompt a discussion not only about vagueness but about the vagaries of statutory drafting and judicial interpretation. But the class discussion is not so easily facilitated.

It seems like every pedagogical problem I have previously identified coalesces in the "finger-fucking" class. Boundaries of professorial relations are implicated: should I explain what "finger-fucking" means to a male student who looks quizzical and thus establish myself as an expert? What if I do not mean the same thing that the lesbian student means by it? What if the lesbian student made a sexual advance toward me last year and I interpret this remark as sexually aggressive? Boundaries of storytelling are threatened: a heterosexual student tells a story about being at camp as an adolescent; a former police officer tells a story about finding teenagers "necking" and not arresting them; a female student tells a story about being in the army. Boundaries of rigor start to dissolve: maybe there is too much laughter. Maybe a student will answer another student's casual inquiry about today's class by saying, "We just talked about finger-fucking." Maybe "finger-fucking" is not relevant to any student's paper or the bar examination or any future court case. Furthermore, the diversity of the class contributes to identity-politics posturing: a lesbian, a gay man, a heterosexual woman, and even a former police officer reannounce their identities, as the other students solidify their own identities in opposition. My knowledge of partial disclosures by students forces me to attend to the psychological dimensions of the discussion. For example, the disclosure of an incest survivor prevented me from assigning another lesbian case which is more explicit but which is incestuous,[17] and my knowledge that one person has reported in confidence as having virtually no sexual experience prevents me from simply assuming that every student knows what finger-fucking means, that it does not mean something like one-finger-fucking-another-finger as one student stated in a droll-enough-to-be-serious tone. And finally, the very diversity of the class makes me pause as a male student struggles to articulate his understanding of lesbian sex and announces that women use their fingers like "little penises," and as a heterosexual woman disagrees and asks a lesbian for a real explanation of what lesbians do in their cots in tents while state troopers listen, and as a lesbian student starts to speak and is interrupted by another male student who says he does not want to hear the details and he is interrupted by another male student who says he really wants to hear all this, and laughs, and turns to look at me.

I reconsider my strategy of never allowing the class to recess.

Instead, I pose another hypothetical. Using that favorite law professorial tactic of changing the facts, I attempt to shift from finger-fucking to a consideration of rationales for the law's obfuscation of lesbian sexual practices. "Any ideas?" I ask.

One student volunteers, "It's because the courts don't want women finger-fucking each other. And if everyone knows exactly what it means, they'll all go camping and try it out."

Everyone laughs. And I laugh with my students as if they are my friends. Someone tells a story. More laughter spills into the hall and someone in the next classroom comes over to say his class cannot hear the tax lecture because of our laughter. And by the end of our class, we are no longer limited by our diversity, but somehow enriched by it, even its problematic identities, partial disclosures, and risks of appropriation.

It is the kind of class that makes me feel that, despite the problems, combining pedagogy, jurisprudence, and lesbian sex is worthwhile. This feeling lasts until my next office hours, when several students have made appointments to pose precise questions about finger-fucking.

NOTES

1. Marilyn Frye, "Lesbian 'Sex,'" in *Willful Virgin: Essays in Feminism* (Freedom, CA: Crossing Press, 1992), 109–19.

2. Juliet Flower MacCannell, "Resistance to Sexual Theory," in *Texts for Change: Theory/Pedagogy/Politics,* ed. Donald Morton and Mas'ud Zavarzadeh (Urbana: University of Illinois Press, 1991), 66–67.

3. MacCannell *quoting* Jane Gallop, "The Immoral Teachers," *Yale French Studies* 63 (1982): 117–28.

4. John Guillory, *Cultural Capital* (Chicago: University of Chicago Press, 1993), 182.

5. Jane Gurko, "Sexual Energy in the Classroom," in *Lesbian Studies: Present and Future,* ed. Margaret Cruikshank (New York: The Feminist Press, 1982), 25, 29.

6. Of course, many teachers and students do not agree with this position. For example, at the City University of New York School of Law, there is no bar to consensual sex between a professor and a student. A proposal to institute such a bar was opposed by many student groups, including the gay and lesbian group, as well as by a majority of the faculty. On the national law school level, proposals to bar professor/student sex are similarly stalled.

My support of a per se ban of sexual relations between professors and students is complicated by my own histories within academic institutions as well as by my belief that any enacted ban would be subject to the forces of homophobia and thus applied in a discriminatory manner against lesbian professors and students. My proposal also privileges the uniqueness of the academic enterprise, given my opinion that very different rules should apply outside academic institutions.

7. As expressed by Jane Gurko:

The problem lies in the fact that any noncoercive power imbalance tends to trigger romantic fantasies on both sides of an unequal relationship, regardless of the sexes involved. It's almost automatic in the classroom: the teacher becomes an object of hero worship, and conversely as "hero," indulges in ego-inflating fantasies of power over her "worshipper." (Gurko, 27)

8. Each weekly unit is presented as a question: "Does 'gender' equal 'sex'?" "Is consent limited to adults?" "Should the law regulate sexual representation (pornography)?" "Does the law adequately distinguish between disease and sex?" "Are sexual minorities 'minorities'?" "Should the law regulate sexual commerce (prostitution)?" "How important are the legal distinctions between sexuality and reproduction?"

9. I have discussed lesbian and gay studies within the academy and specifically the legal academy elsewhere. Ruthann Robson, "Embodiments: The Possibilities of Lesbian Legal Theory in Bodies Problematized by Feminisms and Postmodernisms," *Journal of Law and Sexuality* 2 (1992): 37–80.

10. For example, see Jennifer Gore, *The Struggle for Pedagogies: Critical and Feminist Discourses as Regimes of Truth* (New York: Routledge, 1993); Patti Lather, *Getting Smart: Feminist Research and Pedagogy With/In the Postmodern* (New York: Routledge, 1991); *Texts for Change: Theory/Pedagogy/Politics,* ed. Donald Morton and Mas'ud Zavarzadeh (Urbana: University of Illinois Press, 1991); *Gender in the Classroom: Power and Pedagogy,* ed. Susan Gabriel and Isaiah Smithson (Urbana: University of Illinois Press, 1990).

11. This phraseology is attributed to Robert Cover, making remarks at a conference, as cited in Robert Post, "Tradition, the Self, and Substantive Due Process," *California Law Review* 77 (1989): 559–60. Robert Cover's published work is consistent with this view; see Robert Cover, "Violence and the Word," *Yale Law Journal* 95 (1986):1601. However, as I have discussed elsewhere, scholars as different as Jacques Derrida, the maven of deconstruction, and

Richard Posner, the maven of law and economics, agree that law is based upon state coercion. Ruthann Robson, "Incendiary Categories: Lesbians/Violence/ Law," *Texas Journal of Women and the Law* 2 (1993): 1, 28.

12. For an excellent analysis and feminist critique of liberal legal education as well as CUNY School of Law's unique place within liberal legal education, see Joyce McConnell, "A Feminist's Perspective on Liberal Reform of Legal Education," *Harvard Women's Law Journal* 14 (1991): 77. Much of my discussion concerning liberal legal education in general, and CUNY in particular, is based upon understandings elaborated in Joyce McConnell's work.

13. For a further discussion of such contestations and their relevance for lesbian legal theory, see Ruthann Robson, "The Specter of a Lesbian Supreme Court Justice: Problems of Identity in Lesbian Legal Theorizing," *St. Thomas Law Review* 5 (1993): 433–58.

14. This problem is not unique to pedagogical situations. For example, the poet Chrystos addresses the problem of publishing lesbian erotic poetry in her newest volume. Chrystos, *In Her I Am* (Vancouver: Press Gang Publishers, 1993).

15. Ruthann Robson, "Crimes of Lesbian Sex," in *Lesbian (Out)Law: Survival Under the Rule of Law* (Ithaca, NY: Firebrand Books, 1992). The chapter also appears in the anthology, *Lesbians, Gay Men, and the Law,* ed. William Rubenstein (New York: The Free Press, 1993).

16. *People v. Livermore,* 9 Mich. App. 47, 155 N.W. 2d 711 (1968).

17. While the class does contain a segment on incest, my concern in this segment was not incest. I therefore thought that interjecting incest through the facts of a case and then stating that the incest was irrelevant to the class segment was problematic. The case, however, raises the interesting issue of whether or not penetration is required in convictions for lesbian sex. *Salyers v. State,* 755 P.2d 97 (Cr. Ct. App. Okl. 1988).

THREE

Tongues or Fingers

ANNA LIVIA

What is erotic? And what is erotic to me? And are these two different questions? Where Freudian individualism might reply, "Why yes, of course. Because of her unique psychological makeup, every woman has her own individual erotic responses," historical materialism might say, "Given a particular set of circumstances—economic, cultural, ideological—any group of people will respond in a similar way." Is my sense of the erotic defined by my place as second child, my happy childhood, and the fact that I love my mother, or by my participation in feminist ideology, my class position, and my height? Either way it is lost in the void of the always already constructed, a matter of circumstance, psychological or material. Or do my desires, sexual responses, and fantasies lie outside any socially defined pattern, in a realm of primordial truth? And when we sift through the bright or misty images memory sends us, where do we put the not erotic? In the heart-shaped chocolate box with the romantic? In the cardboard box in the closet with the pornographic? In the hands of the hairdresser with the buzz razor and the sensual?

Being the kind of linguist who is more interested in how most native speakers would understand the word than in what it used to mean a long time ago and in another country, I spent some pleasant afternoons asking friends what they found erotic.

"Butch women. Power. Difference," said one.

"And what do you find sexy?"

"Butch women. Power. Difference," she grinned.

"So the erotic and the sexy are the same? Would you say your lovers were erotic? That making love was erotic?"

"Some of my lovers have been very erotic. Especially the ones who were most different."

"Most different from you or most different from most women?"

"Most different from my experience. I had one lover who was fat, she was very erotic to me. And another had had a cleft palate. I loved to feel the cleft scars inside her mouth with my tongue. It was different. And it was forbidden and it was very erotic."

But another friend said, "Making love isn't erotic. It's more sensual, emotional. The erotic takes distance. I don't look at my girlfriend and think how erotic she is. Though I might if I saw a photograph of her."

"Different," "distant," "forbidden." Interesting words. Next afternoon I reach for a dictionary (*Webster's Unabridged Dictionary of the English Language,* to be precise). After "amatory," "arousing," and "marked by strong sexual desire," Webster's fourth definition of "erotic" is "an erotic poem." The erotic poem defines its own content. A definition in itself.

Another day my friend Lydie leaves her review copy of *Black Erotica* in my university mailbox. I flip through to the editors' introduction: "I met Toi Derricotte almost a year after receiving no response to my letters requesting a submission, but when I gave her copies of the table of contents, an erotic prose poem, and a *Good Vibrations* catalog, . . . she wrote . . . her first piece of erotica."[1] Like Webster's fourth definition, the editors of the anthology had given up on explaining and started exemplifying.

I turn over the pages of the anthology to Audre Lorde's "Uses of the Erotic: The Erotic as Power." "The erotic is a resource within each of us that lies in a deeply female and spiritual plane, firmly rooted in our unexpressed and unrecognized feeling." "Unexpressed," "unrecognized": primordial truthsville. "The erotic is a measure between the beginning of our sense of self and the chaos of our strongest feelings."[2] Between the inchoate and the chaotic: swirling anarchic mists.

It would appear, then, that the erotic is difference and distance, genesis and chaos, defined by example and lost in the void of the always already. Yet a million people use that word weekly if not daily, and they must think they know what they mean by it. When things get this complicated, I know I am going about them the wrong way. Clearly there is something of the sexy, and something of the sensual, something of the passionate and something of the empowering in erotica. Since drawing lines around a definition has not worked, any more than it did for the editors of Webster's dictionary or the *Black Erotica* anthology, let's try inclusion. What various and variegated things have turned me on, made me wet, hardened my nipples . . . ah, but here I fear the return of the primordial: the body as proof, as the one anchored term in the whole signifying net, the truths of the body which in their physical reality defy the upper echelons of abstract thought. The body is no more truthful, no more innocent of society's dictates than the psyche. Each is molded, pummeled and constructed by language, by ideology and by the daily grind of the workaday world. For "yes, there is a real world," as my friend Patricia Duncker says, "the one we die in—this is a much disputed fact in some university departments of English."

To speak the truths of my body would, anyway, require a more sustained consciousness than I can honestly claim. I have not always been aware of the responses of my body, nor of what they were responses to. Born in Ireland, I grew up in Africa. I remember the sensation of my eyes opening to the wide horizon and the vastness of the sky. Until then my sight had been blocked by buildings, people, cars, clouds, fog. And there were bright colors, fierce in the endless sunlight, sharp as European hues were muted. The noises around me were more distinct, away from the incessant background rumble of traffic, radios, sirens, voices. Here there were voices, but they spoke in other languages, languages with clicks in the throat, new places to make words.

And the food. The things you put in your mouth and make part of your own body. In Ireland I would go for walks with my mother and she would bend down and reach into the grasses by a stream and break off something green and fresh and strong-smelling and put it in my mouth. I would crunch and suck and roll the stalks or the leaves or the petals across my tongue and my whole mouth would fill up with the taste, the smell, the texture. In the new country, whose name was "Africa" in my child's ears, and which was so big you could not get to the sea without driving driving driving for days, the car covered with dust, and the windscreen smeared with the legs and wings of tiny insects, in that new country were a hundred new tastes that my tongue did not recognize. Warm milk straight from the cows' udders. Plates of things I had never seen before and all with names: green and prickly, yellow and bumpy, red and purple with a thousand slippery seeds. And the meat of animals: elephant, fat and rich; hippopotamus, like beef; rhinoceros like venison, they said, but what was venison? Little flying things with wings which came in around the mosquito netting, dazed by the light and warmth of the candles which lit the house. You pulled off the wings and crunched the delicate little body which tasted like anchovies, perhaps, but anchovies were so long ago and used to get spread on toast with butter.

And the smells were so strong, as though our noses had only just opened like the wings of a butterfly after it fights its way out of the cocoon. In Ireland there was the smell of the rain and cut grass, but in London nothing smelled, people kept their noses clean and dry, when they weren't covered by an enormous hanky and a million sneezes. Here there were the sweet smells of camellia and orange blossom, the strong musky smell of sweat, the rich stench of shit and the bitter stink of dead things rotting, all mixed together in the same piece of air.

Then there was the feel of things: flowers which squirted liquid like a water pistol, dirt road under bare feet, the sharp prick of christ thorn, petal gardens made of bougainvillea blossoms. The sensation of hands sinking into thick, dark mud, the squish of mulberries trampled underfoot, staining the skin a deep purple-red.

Is this erotic, my sensual history? Or does it sound like background? Are you waiting for an encounter, skin on skin, flesh touching flesh? There were encounters. Mwela, the daughter of one of the farm servants was the same age as I, and we played together often. She would fill a bucket full of water at the tap near the dam and carry it down to the hut next to the enormous antheap. Then she would pull her dress over her head and pour the cold water over her body. One day I went with her and the bucket was heavy against my leg and the hut so dark I couldn't see anything until I had blinked and blinked like she told me so I'd get used to it. My body was so white in the darkness of the hut and hers so black, and we tickled each other with loofahs that grew on a tree on the farm.

Five years later there was Llonka from Mozambique. I was twelve; she was eighteen. We were the only girls at a school of a hundred and sixteen boys. I would lie on her bed and she would play the guitar and sing songs by Joan Baez. Or I would lie on flat rocks sunning my back like a snake and dream of kissing her. She kept promising I could come and visit her in Lourenço Marques during the holidays, but I never did.

Is it erotic yet? I remember the slap of the loofah against Mwela's skinny shoulder, how the water ran in trickles down her back. Her hand on my little flat chest: could anyone really be that white? I would run my fingers along Llonka's bare arms, pretending to admire her watch or her blouse. I would look at her and think how much I wanted to stroke the fine hairs on her legs. And I would think of putting my mouth on hers and dream of touching her with my tongue, and one day I did but that's another story.

Are sex and bodies erotic? Are trees and water lapping lapping not erotic? There were many incidents involving genitals, like the time the boy on the next farm made me pull down my underwear so he could see my vagina, or bathing with my two brothers because it was the dry season and the dam was empty and all our water had to be brought from Luanshya in Jannie's truck. I pulled my brothers' penises because they looked so funny; they seemed so vulnerable with those little pink slugs hanging between their legs, whereas my body was neat and trim with everything properly tucked away.

These were sexual experiences but not sensual, not like the day the ants came. I had a dream one night that there was an ant on my face and I kept flicking it off and it just kept coming back, as though it could fly. I would pick it up and throw it on the floor and then I would feel it on my cheek, on my eyelids, in my nostrils. I woke up, and there was an ant on me and it kept coming back till I lit the candle by my bed and saw that my hand and arm were black and shiny, the bed glistened and it moved softly up and down in a wave. And then I realized that it was covered with ants, that I was covered with ants, that my room had been invaded by a whole army of ants. I ran to wake my brothers and we went to my mother's room which the ants hadn't reached yet. She gathered up her bedclothes and told us we would have to sleep in the duck house. So we ran out of the house in the middle of the night and laid down blankets and pillows on the straw in the duck house. Then we all curled up together, my big brother, my little brother, my mother, and me.

In the morning Washing, one of the indoor servants, began to run around outside calling, "Bwana, Missis. Bwana, Missis." He was scared because the Lenshina riots were happening just across the border in the Congo and the farms were not always safe.

My mother called to him, "We're in here, Washing. In the duck house." And he came and peered around the side of the door, only it was too dark for him to see very much.

"There are ants in the house," my mother told him. "They're everywhere."

"No ants, Madam," said Washing.

"Last night," said my mother, "The house was full of ants."

Washing looked perplexed and went to talk to Simon, the farm overseer. I couldn't understand what they were saying because they were speaking Simon's language and he was from the north. Soon Simon came into the duck house. He looked at us all bundled up in blankets on the straw and burst out laughing. He had an enormous, deep-bellied laugh.

"So the ants came," he said in English.

"Yes," smiled my mother. Everyone liked Simon. He always knew everything.

"Then you will have to sleep in the duck house every year. If the ants' road is through your house, they will not change their road for anybody."

The night of the ants was far more memorable, more full of sensual feelings than rooting around in my little friends' vaginas with a lolly stick.

But now you are getting impatient. This is an anthology of writing about lesbian eroticism and so far in this essay all you have had are childhood memories and abortive definitions.

I was fourteen. We moved to London. I'd come straight from Swaziland, the last hut on the mountain, surrounded by herds of cows and streams and pools and rocks that were good to climb and aloes that cut your legs if you ran too close. London was cold, dark, noisy. It never let you be. Bodies were muffled under heavy clothes; you could not tell what shape anyone was and no one had feet. I closed up. It was grey and ugly and you could never get away from all the other people. And then—here it is, the really erotic part—I started going through the preliminaries to sex with men: sleeping over at parties, getting felt up, touching clothed crotches. At sixteen, sex happened. Full penetrative heterosexual sex. Dull but necessary. Certainly nothing to fantasize over. My fantasies were about softness and kissing. Most of my time I spent with my best friend. As long as I was with her, I was happy. A sense of calm contentedness, of perfect peace would fill me as I walked into her house and sat down to do the crossword in the English *Times* newspaper with her mother while she made coffee. I loved her and her little brother and her mother and her father and her house and her bedroom and her bicycle saddle because they were hers.

My thoughts about my best friend's bicycle saddle would more easily enter into the erotic canon than my feelings as I parted my legs for some bloke to fuck me. "Sex is boring," I wrote on the toilet wall at school. It was the seventies; the sexual revolution was in full swing. Women were liberated, and sex was necessary. It seemed that I had given up the all-over, generalized sensuality of my African childhood for sexual activity focusing almost exclusively on the genitals. I hated London in my first few years there. If you wanted to go somewhere, instead of walking you had to buy transport. If you got hungry, you didn't just pick fruit from the mango tree, you had to pay money. You didn't make toys out of bits of wire and the inner tubes of tires, you went to a shop and bought them. You could not just drift over to a friend's house on Saturday morning, you had to phone first. And instead of a multiple of sensory experiences, of sounds, sights, smells, tastes, and touches, there was the once-removed distraction of television, which was hard to concentrate on. I would look and fidget and get up and wander around—you actually have to learn how to watch television—and there was sex.

At first I gave in completely to the heterosexual imperative and felt glad and relieved that I was attractive to men. As I realized how important sex was to them, I began to understand the power that gave me. I did not come to this understanding all by myself; sex was undergoing an immense process of recodification, first in the mouths of the sex and love generation, then from the feminists who followed them. I became consciously sexually active somewhere in between the two waves. Women were meant to throw off Victorian prudery and take men to bed, but we were also supposed to have orgasms. An avid reader and discusser of *Cosmopolitan* and *Forum,* I learned large doses of vocabulary and many prearticulated opinions with which to discuss sex, positions, erogenous zones, contraception, and postcoital triste. I told the men I was fucking exactly what I wanted them to do and how I wanted them to do it. I bought a vibrator so I could have orgasms any time I wanted. Between my eighteenth and twenty-fourth birthdays I got through a lot of men—some pleasant and attentive, others narcissistic and dull. But I didn't touch myself lovingly, didn't spend hours lying on my bed thinking about sex and imagining new, delicious sensations to give to my, or my lover's body.

You may find this quite irrelevant, but I spent very little time thinking about food, or music, or flowers, or how things looked. I ate bacon sandwiches, absorbed the popular music of the time without paying it any attention: David Bowie; Patti Smith; Crosby, Stills, Nash, and Young; a little later Bob Marley, Johnny Rotten, Sid Vicious. I had a friend who had lost her sense of smell and I remember wondering how she had come to notice, my own sense of smell was so seldom tested. I cared very little what things looked like, could never recall the color of men's eyes or whether a particular program had been in color or black and white. I did not know how to appreciate that new country, and what it seemed to offer meant little to me. I read a lot of books, took a lot of exams, and learned two more languages.

Then I became a feminist, and everything changed. We embarked upon a momentous task: that of reexamining everything. All our most fondly held beliefs were minutely analyzed to see which benefited men, which women, to pinpoint the patriarchal influence in every nook and cranny of our daily lives. Pretty soon the movement got as far as sex. When I became a lesbian at twenty-four, there was a fairly strict set of rules about how to, and more importantly, how not to, have sex. These rules were gently imparted to me by my friends, in workshops on sexuality at conferences, or in articles on how to rid oneself of heteropatriarchal thinking on all fronts.

"Cor, what a dish," I would enthuse. "Don't half fancy her." (A common expression of appreciation for the physical charms of a woman one would like to go to bed with.)

"How can you talk like that, Anna?" my friends would protest. "She's not just a body, you know."

I read articles about penetration and how heterosexual it is. Nice lesbians did not put things in their girlfriends' vaginas, and they did not call the women they had sex with their girlfriends either. "Girl" was for females under fifteen. From fifteen to eighteen they were "young women" and after that they were "women."

Sometime in the early eighties I went to a conference on "Sex and Sexual Practice," which was for lesbians only. There were many different workshops but only one on "what lesbians do in bed." And no, the others were not "what lesbians do in the shower," "what lesbians do on the kitchen counter." They were on the history of the patriarchy, prostitution, pornography, and how to combat them. I walked into the "what lesbians do in bed" workshop and everyone was sitting, or standing, in a circle—the room was packed—looking at each other, shuffling their feet, and waiting for someone to say something. We went round the circle saying our names and explaining why we had come to the workshop.

"To find out how other dykes go about it," said one.

"To pick up some tips," said another.

"Because sex is a great unspoken mystery. We're all lesbians and we all fancy women and we see each other at dances and conferences and benefits, but when they're over, we all get on the bus and go home and close the bedroom door and no one ever talks about what she does there."

This sounded good but the premise was entirely false, since I had either slept with, or one of my ex-lovers had slept with, almost everyone else in the room (with the exception of the two women who had just arrived from Australia) and we all talked about each other constantly and especially about what sex had been like, what we'd done together, and how we'd liked it.

(On a wet weekend in Wales once a lover and I had been eating dried fruit. I looked at the dried apricot halves and said to her,

"What do these remind you of?"

She gazed for a while and then giggled, "Oh, that one's just like Edith's."

"And this one's like Evangeline's."

"And this would have to be Esmee's. Remember I said she had that little fold of skin right here?"

I got a letter from that ex-lover recently telling me she had kept those dried apricots for ten years and had only just thrown them away.)

Well, then my friend Artemisia walked into the room. We had finished introducing ourselves and explaining why we were there and somebody had to say something. So Artemisia grew brave, and she opened her mouth and said,

"Well, there are really only two ways of going about it, aren't there?"

That got our attention. Yes, yes, we mouthed, tell us, Artemisia.

"There's tongues," she said, "Or fingers. Tongues or fingers," she said. And the day was saved.

She was my lover's ex-lover so I knew exactly what she meant.

From merely boring, sex quickly became deeply boring. I could have had more fun with a wet loofah and a bucket of cold water. Though that was not how I thought at the time. Mostly I did not think, or at least not about sex. I thought about the revolution and how I wanted it like a lover, more than a lover actually. Then some revolutionary feminists began to announce that everyone had sadomasochistic fantasies—and if they didn't they were lying—but that we must look at where these images came from and the damage they did to women. This pronouncement baffled me. I had no fantasies of any kind, except about finding someone soft of body and fierce of brain who I could hold in my arms and tell all my secrets. I still didn't masturbate without a vibrator. Couldn't be bothered, took too long and made my wrist hurt and besides the revolution was waiting. Food had shrunk to bowls of raw chick peas with lentils; clothes were uniformly navy blue; I couldn't even listen to wimmin's music, there didn't seem to be anything there. We had given up the patchouli of the seventies for warm water and soap; feminists did not use scent.

I wonder sometimes where I kept myself back then. I was an intellectual. I talked (knowledgeably) about Michel Foucault and Jacques Lacan and Antonio Gramsci and Louis Althusser and film theory and Sally Potter and Chantal Ackerman, though these were soon replaced by Mary Daly and Janice Raymond and Marilyn Frye and Sheila Jeffreys. It was a long exercise in intellectual and analytical rigor accompanied by thoroughgoing sensory deprivation. Though I suspect I got more extreme doses than my lesbian feminist sisters, many of whom continued to wear pink and eat salmon and who assured me there was more to wimmin's music than sweet voices and predictable harmonies.

The one area of sensual delight which was condoned by my community was the novels of the black American (as we British called them) women writers: Alice Walker, Audre Lorde, Gloria Naylor, Toni Morrison, out of reach of political correctness because they were black and could therefore write about whatever they wanted (a new twist on black as Other). I do remember a certain discomfort occasioned by the avocado scene in *Zami: A New Spelling of My Name,* however.

And now the nineties are hurling themselves forward to collide with the twenty-first century, and I live in California, in the Bay Area— Berkeley to be exact. I moved here in 1990, and while I would like to declare that I made the move entirely to improve my sex life—doesn't everyone like to imagine themselves the complete hedonist?—I have to admit there were a few other important motives like getting a Ph.D. in a country that still had enough money to support students. So what do we conclude on the weighty topic of eroticism? That fully half of it is climate while the other half is fashion? I like heat and light, but I have many friends in London whose erotic lives are rich, exuberant, and exhilarating, even in the middle of winter, so we have to rule out climate as anything but an idiosyncratic factor. As for fashion, the erotic fashions of the Bay Area are in extraordinary conflict. It is still America and so in the grip of the peculiar fervor of the fundamentalists and their fetal hysteria. Those people must walk around wearing those ghastly pictures of tiny torn limbs and bloody flesh because they get a kick out of it. Isn't that what personal adornment is all about? At the same time the Bay is home to branding, or, if your skin does not keloid sufficiently, piercing, and public sex clubs. On one and the same day, in the same paper, I can read an article about angry mobs attacking abortion clinics and humiliating doctors, and a letter from some bloke who has heard that by slowly widening the urethra a man can insert his penis into that of another man. I am "gobsmacked." You probably do not know what that word means. Just re-read the long sentence two before this and look at your expression in the mirror. There you are. That's "gobsmacked." What I'm trying to say is, eroticism may very well be a heavily cultural phenomenon, but this is not my culture. When my friend Leslie tells me she is studying the leather community in her Queer Theory course, I imagine a set of uncomfortable furniture from Scandinavian Design.

As for climate, it's warm and sunny here, and my shoulders are almost always bare. There are squirrels and raccoons and doves and hummingbirds, and I lie on my bed listening to "Ardon' gli incensi" from the opera *Lucia di Lammermoor* and tears slip blissfully down my face. I ride my bike down to the Berkeley Marina and gaze out at the huge vista of the hills of Marin County, the Golden Gate, and San Francisco shaking off the last tatters of its daily fog while the boats in the harbor bob about, their sails swaying gently, and they make me happy. I have a girlfriend who eats meat, whose ambition is to taste every animal that is not endangered, and I cook them for her. Almost all my friends have been some kind of vegetarian, so I'm no longer well acquainted with meat, but I go out and buy two chicken breasts and then, in the middle of the Berkeley Bowl, where all the lesbians in the Bay Area buy their organic artichokes, I remember a meal I once ate in an Indian restaurant. I am standing, gripping my shopping trolley, and thinking of the taste in my mouth of chicken, baked in a sauce of . . . was it yogurt? cottage cheese? and the thick creamy texture of that sauce on my tongue, and the smell of the herbs—turmeric? garam masala? cumin? And when I get to her house I bake the chicken breasts in a thick cream I have blended and we eat it together, my girlfriend and I. She raises her eyebrows and gazes at me with a thoughtful expression while we eat. She dips her forefinger in the yogurt, sour cream, and feta sauce.

"What does this remind you of?" she asks, eyebrows now lowered, moving her dripping forefinger toward my mouth, darting it back suddenly into her own. My teeth bite down on emptiness. And I want to run my tongue over every inch of her skin, lick the muscles in her upper arms, hide my nose in her hair and smell the thick long black weight of it around me. I needed to enjoy the weight and wetness of my own tongue in my mouth before I could get interested in someone else's. I needed to enjoy again the touch of my own skin, the smell of my own breath, the surge of my own blood, the weight, heat, and delight of the world.

Her roommate's friend, Pat, comes in. I watch as she lays a journal on the table and begins to read. Presently she gets up, walks over to the fridge, takes a frozen quiche out of the freezer, opens the door to the microwave, places the quiche inside, presses five buttons and returns to her seat to resume reading. In precisely five minutes an electronic buzz sounds three times. She gets up again, takes the quiche out of the oven, returns to her place, cuts the quiche into three pieces, picks up a fork and puts the pieces in her mouth, one after the other, while she is reading the journal. I watch her take a potato from the vegetable rack, cook it in the microwave, put it on a plate with safflower margarine and eat it, while reading the journal. I watch her take a piece of corn from the fridge, cook it in the microwave, put it on a plate with safflower margarine and eat it. Then I watch her pour water into a cup from the tap, heat it up in the microwave, place a herbal tea bag in the water, and drink it. I do not know what her erotic fantasies are: dildos, chains, handcuffs, or soft bodies and vast wet marshes, but I know I could never go to bed with her.

NOTES

1. Miriam DeCosta-Willis, Reginald Martin, and Roseann Bell, introduction to *Erotique noire/Black Erotica* (New York: Doubleday, 1992), xl.

2. Audre Lorde, "The Uses of the Erotic: The Erotic as Power," in *Erotique noire*, 78–79.

FOUR

Staging the Erotic

ELIZABETH MEESE AND SANDY HUSS

In this double endeavor, Sandy Huss and I will present critical fictions that provide contexts for thinking and writing about lesbian erotics. The lesbian erotic was a much simpler subject in the period of what passed for (though never was) an uncontested lesbian identity politic, days of unchallenged agency and the speaking (out) subject. Not that it was ever easy to achieve such a state of identity and autonomy, and this illusion of the singular certainly exacted its price. Now it is difficult even to say what is "lesbian" in lesbian erotics and what might constitute a lesbian erotics, particularly in an arena expanded to include online identities and cybersex. That the "I" is "non-self-identical" turns this definitional task into a genuine conundrum.

In "Imitation and Gender Insubordination," Judith Butler explains the "non-self-identical" subject as follows: "there is no 'I' that precedes the gender that it is said to perform." [1] Further, she asks, "If a sexuality is to be disclosed, what will be taken as the true determinant of its meaning: the phantasy structure, the act, the orifice, the gender, the anatomy?" [2] Possibly all of the above or none.

We might also say that the erotic, as not generalizable from one person to the next, or even necessarily from one time to the next, is also "non-self-identical," hence our difficulty in writing about it, and also our compulsion to write it again and again. The forms or shapes of erotic styles result from complex "psychic identifications," [3] the precise nature of which I could never tell you, about myself, my lover, or any one else. Perhaps the "lesbian erotic," then, is a double-double play.

I'm not the only one who has trouble with this subject. On December

13, I posted a plea for help on the electronic network's Sappho bulletin board. On December 17, the activity report from the bulletin board came: 263 posts in the four-day period following my post. I received four responses to my plea. One suggested I read Audre Lorde on the power of the erotic; another, from a professional acquaintance, directed me to an article she had written on the erotics of Djuna Barnes's *Nightwood*. (I read them both.) The most extensive discussion of the subject came from a woman named mitch.bot who identified herself as "the scary SM dyke that likes to dress as a cub-scout." She wrote:

> "the lesbian erotic" doesn't mean much to me, cuz there isn't just one. some lesbians get off to the stuff that's made by het men for het men. Like Playboy and Penthouse and some of the raunchier stuff like "Lez on Lez" videos where skinny girls with big blonde hair lick each others shaved pink pussies.
>
> That doesn't work for me.
>
> What works for me is POWER. A strong femme dyke that can tear you apart with her wit, strength, and pure sexyness. A smart confident butch dyke that knows you'll do anything to get a taste of what she's got to offer. The dynamics of struggle. Femme on Butch, Butch on Butch, and Fierce Femme on Fierce Femme.[4]

My other correspondent contradicted mitch.bot, saying no to power and yes to conventional beauty, but agreed on the erotic dimension, the necessity for intelligence.

When we move onto the fiber optics, complications multiply. In "The Virtual Orgasm," Susie Bright reports overhearing a phone sex conversation during which the speaker represents herself as a 38C-25-36. She gets the client off in under a minute, upon which Bright exclaims: "That man didn't talk to *you*. . . . He talked to an hourglass figure with a breathy little voice who made him climax so hard he didn't even have a chance to say good-bye." To which her friend responds, "Oh, it's me all right. It's me every time. . . . Welcome to futuresex, Miss Sexpert. You can be any BODY you want to be on a fiber optic network. But there's always a piece of me in every blonde, redhead and stunning brunette I deliver over the phone lines."[5] I imagine that a lot of people might want to know WHICH piece, and probably hope for more than one.

"Femme on Butch, Butch on Butch, Fierce Femme on Fierce Femme," how will I recognize them on the Net? Will I know how to pick my pleasure? Cyberspace confronts us with the ultimate deconstruction of identity categories: you are what you say you are when you say it. As the hacker Anon of Ibid puts it, "Whether my name is 'Anon,' which must 'mean' anonymous, or whether my name is 'Susan,' or 'SpaceCase' or whatever, I 'am' not that name, I 'am' not those things, all I am here is these words before you, you choose whatever mental picture you like to accompany that, but it isn't my job, is it, to facilitate that process any more than makes me happy?"[6]

Perhaps this sounds depressing to be unable to specify a lesbian erotics, but to me it seems perfectly compatible with recent developments in gender theory and, in itself, might actually be a source of pleasure rather than frustration. For example, Butler, regarding identity categories as trouble sites, observes of the "lesbian": "In fact, if the category were to offer no trouble, it would cease to be interesting to me: it is precisely the *pleasure* produced by the instability of those categories which sustains the various erotic practices that make me a candidate for the category to begin with."[7] Certain benefits might even accrue from this instability. Another writer on the Net puts it, "When your net-acquaintance turns up in one game as a white male, another as a black lesbian and the next as a tri-sexual alien, you're going to have to start learning to deal with people as they are rather than what they appear to be. . . . If we can't cope today with people on the Net who change their net.sex, net.race and net.species on a regular basis, how are we going to be able to cope in the future when we can do it in real-life as well?" — an interesting doubling here, where within the space of virtual reality, one encounters people as they really ARE, rather than as they appear to be.

The erotic requires endless renewal in order to live up to its name, that is, to be synonymous with our expectations. Since eroticism is a mental effect, it is particularly risky for me to offer examples, although I attempted that in my book *(Sem)Erotics—Theorizing Lesbian : Writing* and will again. Inspired by my Sappho correspondent and my lover, what I thought I might do is offer a mental movie on the lesbian erotic. I imagine making a film in which my lover strips for me, over and over again. Her performance is long and varied. The music changes. Her clothes change too.

First, Peter Gabriel is singing "Steam." My lover is hot. She's wearing black velvet pants, a poet shirt, and fuck-me pumps. Her eyes are closed, and she's moving to the music as she kicks off her shoes and takes off her pants. She's my dream. She's singing along with the music, asking for steam, like steam heat, sizzlingly hot. She takes off her ruffled shirt and stands in front of where I'm sitting on the sofa. She's ready for it. Now Prince is singing "Wanna Melt with U." All three of us are busy, urging and merging, top to bottom. We're moving. My lover makes an entrance into the bedroom. She is dropping her cream-colored silk pants on the floor. She shimmers, dancing a little to the beat. Slowly, teasingly, with a smile, she unbuttons her blue shirt and throws it over me. We're melting into each other. We're gonna fuse. Yes, I say. And Prince sings about doing it doggy style. Just like that, saying how we love it like that. There are other wonderful scenes in our movie. We let Prince sing some more. I start singing along with him on "Continental." Let me do it to you, girl. You need it. You want it. You like it when I do. We're on the floor now, getting busy. I think the best scene in the movie is the final one. My lover puts Terence Trent D'Arby on the cd player. He's singing "Succumb to Me." I want to do that with her. She undulates to the music like something under water, gracefully. She strips slowly, first pulling off her stockings and twirling them from her finger as though she were a vamp in a movie. She takes her time, like a person who is preparing for something special. She takes off her black leather skirt, and is wearing nothing underneath. The beat starts to throb, to insist: Give it up to me baby, give it to me good. Now she's wearing only her soft pink cashmere sweater, and it rubs against her nipples. I can only hear the beat. I can only hear what I'm saying to her. Oh, and I almost forgot her pearls. I can see her asking for me. We always have such a great time together.

I think our movie is erotic. You might not. Since my lover is doing this for me, I would say that she is acting like a lesbian. You might not. To my mind, she is incredibly sexy and beautiful when she is writing or reading, thinking or talking. That much is undeniable. You can see for yourself.

[Sandy, wearing pearls, pink cashmere sweater, black leather skirt, stockings and black suede pumps, steps to the podium.][8]

You can't help but have questions about ✄: their sex, race, age, class— even though you think you're not supposed to. Is it an accident that the same info satisfies both readers of fiction & demographers? Do you want to sell them something? How much do you need to know? Highest level of formal education? Last major appliance they purchased? Marital status? What they drive? Who they owe?

Let's start with sex (the doctors do)—or, as ✂ have been taught to say, gender. ✂ really can't say. The language that raised them thought of itself as mom & dad/male & female/man & woman 'til death do us part, and it reared ✂ as a girl. ✂ know better. But sometimes they are called upon to identify. When that happens, given the choices usually understood, they choose woman. In some company they say lesbian. In others, dyke. But they'd almost always rather say that they are what they're most certain they aren't. That is, girl. Not because they missed the point of the second wave—quite the contrary—but because political correctness makes ✂ squirm. Discipline isn't, usually, their thing.

That's the girl in them, their indolence. All they really wanna do is take their shoes off, get high, and fuck. Listen to music so loud that it vibrates in their bones. Lie right in front of the speakers, if possible. Fuck there too. Reading is nice, if no one calls on them later, asking their opinion. ✂ don't ever want to write another paper—unless they could use it to seduce someone. Long books are the best, nineteenth-century novels the best of those, but anything that can be counted on to require hours of their absorption will do. They like a good love story—and can read almost anything as if it were one. They sucked down *Pride and Prejudice* a dozen times before they noticed its obsession with class. Of course, ✂ didn't think much about class then. They have many unhealthy addictions: coffee, cigarettes, bubble gum, drugs. For the first three items they'll stir their butt and drive to the store, but their lovers have almost always procured their drugs for them. Whatever gets doled out, ✂ do. Sometimes they ask for more.

Surroundings matter: they like a roof. And comfortable furniture. An armchair big enough for them to get their feet up in, or better still, a couch. Nice stuff to look at. Lots of light in the daytime. Lots of dark at night. ✂ love magazines about decorating houses and dressing up: they could spend hours looking at the pictures. But shopping is almost beyond them: ✂ like to stay home better than anything. They don't know what they'd do without catalogues. If they have to go anywhere, they'd prefer it was the beach—where they can lie around with impunity.

It's the girl part of them that fucks. Most of the time. ✂ are actively passive. The noises that escape them! The ease with which you can tie their hands! If you want them to spread their legs, just tell them how hot they are. 'Course, you gotta keep telling them. It's not that they forget—they just want reassurance that you remember. The payback: you've never felt more powerful. Don't forget to bite: their favorite part of their body is wherever you've left your mark. ✕ love penetration: whatever you've got, feel free to stick it anywhere. Again and again. Oooo. Once more. Think you could fuck them stupid?

Go ahead. Try.

But be careful with ✕: they fall in love like nobody's business. (Of course, it's always business to somebody.) Crush is their favorite mode. Thinking about you gives them pleasure upon pleasure, and the more they think, the more they know how to make you happy. If you're not wary, they'll bond in a way that makes crazy glue seem feeble. Try to let them down easy & they set their phone on redial. Permanently. They'll dog you for life, remember your birthday, your sister's birthday, maybe even fall in love with your sister. It's not that they're fickle: they just love to be in love.

The feminine ✕ hate the news in all its forms: its forms are always the same. War. War. War. Rape Rape Rape. Torture. Poverty. Cities burning. Disease unchecked. Oceans brimming with toxicity. New laws against sex. New laws against drugs. The same old laws against stealing. And the obligatory image of a darling young woman on a swing pumping herself into oblivion. The girl knows—as girls have always known—that no one's in charge (there is no plan), and we've long since run out of money. Science is run by guys like Jonas Salk—who tested the polio vaccine on his family. The girl votes—teeth gritted—not, as is alleged, for the cutest guy, but for the guy with the smartest wife—or the most flamboyant lover. Or—if she gets the chance—for an African American or a woman.

There's more girl parts to ✕. They can get engrossed in a mirror. They like talking to kids, retarded people & crazies. Sometimes. Sometimes it's as tedious as talking to anybody else. They used to get their period, so they know the cost of tampons and ibuprofen, but they had that part of themselves cut out (and don't miss it). They hate to fight. Stalkers give them the willies. They're suckers for romance. Flowers. Surprises. Serendipity. They can make a house look clean without cleaning it. And they can think of a zillion things that need cleaning—if they let themselves think that way. Most girlie of all: they were nuts about their mother—who taught them that a clean house is a sign of a person with too much time on her hands. Their mother's house was filthy filthy filthy. ✂ miss her terribly.

There's not a person on the planet who wasn't raised as a boy, and ✂ are no exception. They can't get enough of t & a, the money shot, wet hot beaver. Girls with long hair make them think of sex. Girls with short hair too. They've got an erection half the time—on a good day more. What they've got between their legs isn't as big as they'd like, but it's plenty big enough for you. They know they could provide the definitive fuck: let them in just once and die happy! Tenderness & petting make them a little bored: fast hot sex is what they like—then, let's eat! It's economical, in fact, to fuck in the kitchen. And of course they talk about you with other guy-type people—if the boys will let them: that's one way guy-types court each other. Nothing turns ✂ on like a shiny new car, unless it's a song about one. "Little Red Corvette," for example. ✂ know who jerked off on the moon, who showed their dicks to Everest. ✂ move in those circles.

They love the company of boys. They'll play any old game in the rainy mud and then take a nice hot shower. Hiking, camping, feats of endurance: ✂ are your man. ✂ look at a house—they don't confuse it with a home—and see a wall that needs moving. ✂ know just who to call: they revere Skilled Labor. And they're never so proud of themselves as when the neighbors want to hire Their Workers. Tools! ✂ have a thing for tools. They want their own—no sharing! Needle-nose pliers. Ratchet sets. Tin snips. Those things you put in screens with. Pots & pans with but one esoteric use—like corn bread molds & fish poachers. Mechanical pencils, air pressure gauges, lemon zesters, staple guns. Scissors for hair, scissors for yard goods, scissors for paper. And the most indispensable tool of all: a big purple silicone dildo.

✂ in their boy-mode even like that list of tools: they still think a line can get them somewhere.

While we're talking about conversation, it's why they can't get enough of the news. All that information! They fill lulls with it. Not that they can pronounce it anymore. They're suspicious, of course, of their sources—and they know that they don't always know who it's popular to trust. But they always have a good enough idea of what's going on that they can rehearse the issues during an election year. Voting's important to the boy side of ✂: he believes in representation. In having a voice. The masculine ✂ don't really count on any big changes in the way things are run—and are pretty sure they'd be the first to be incommoded if there were. It's a little hard to believe how much they already pay in taxes—a lot of it for stuff they don't believe in. He thinks it's normal to be self-centered—of course he has a self!—and that self's not only limited, but—let's be realistic here—powerless. ✂ are not such a prick that they believe they're dirty mortal scum, mere droppings from the filthy cunt of some inevitably fallen woman. After all, they were raised as a girl. Since they don't believe in perfection they don't have to believe in damnation. On Saturday & Sunday they sleep in.

✂ identified with their father and still do. Natch: he was the major competition for their mother's affection. In public Mom would say, "I guess you can tell who fathered this kid." In private she'd try to help ✂ cover up that forehead—the telltale sign. Bangs? Maybe a side part? That was back in the days when dad & ✂ still had some hair in the vicinity of their brow.

Dad died on the block where he was born. He had long since given up on hitting it rich, and his lungs paid a premium for every noxious job he put his brain to. But he hung in there, left no debts, and his kids can take care of themselves. They know how to work. They're resourceful. They don't need to be bossed. ✂, tough guy that they are, hold their head up. When they think about books, they want to write one—why not?—they can suspend disbelief as well as anybody else. Better. Why let other people represent their lives for them? ✂ have their own voice. They could make a killing, get really rich, never again have to work. They might write such a strange book that it would change the language, make the world a better place. And they just know they could edge out Dr. Ruth as the favored white guest on Arsenio.

Not that they're white exactly.

✂ aren't exactly anything. The girl & boy stuff they've just rehearsed feels so arbitrary. And it's not that they're some third thing, either. They're so many they can't get a grip on what to call themselves. Nonetheless, they buy stuff. You sellers out there can rest easy. (For a long while they bought that boy & girl stuff, for example.)

"Are they sexually active?" the gynecologist in you asks. If ✂ answer, "Yes," your next question will be, "What do you do for birth control?" (You haven't noticed yet that ✂ have had that handy operation, since you're pretending that you're interacting with ✂ as human beings and not trying to sneak a look at their New Patient Information. ✖ don't mind, by the way, that your attention is divided. They're pretending they're not even in the room, that this conversation isn't happening.) If ✖ answer, "No," they're afraid you'll fail to look for something important. Like the something that killed their mother. If they say, "Lesbian sex" (a category about which ✖ have infinite doubts), you raise your gloved hand like a crossing guard & say, "Say No More!" What ✖ really want to tell you is that of course they're sexually active: they've got a brain. To answer this question they didn't need to haul ass up onto a table and spread their legs.

✖ answer to Miss, Sir, or Ma'am, to You Guys, to All You All. They get it up for hunks of silicone and chunks of silicon. The last thing they want is climax, the most they hope for, indiscretion. But they can't seem to hang on to fine distinctions. How is sensual different from sensuous — or from sentient? About this ✖ have nothing to say. But they speak anyhow, they just won't cut it out: they say: We lust. We are.

NOTES

1. Judith Butler, "Imitation and Gender Insubordination," in *Inside/Out: Lesbian Theories, Gay Theories,* ed. Diana Fuss (New York: Routledge, 1991), 18.

2. Butler, 17.

3. Butler, 26.

4. mitch.bot, e-mail to author, 13 December 1993.

5. Susie Bright, *Susie Bright's Sexual Reality: A Virtual Sex World Reader* (Pittsburgh: Cleis Press, 1992), 60–61.

6. scotto, "Issue Two: Identity Hacking," *Fringe Ware Review* 2 (1993): 10.

7. Butler, 14.

8. Huss's section of the paper is an excerpt from her novel in progress: *east toledo elegy: a rant.*

FIVE

Give Joan Chen My Phone Number Anytime

KITTY TSUI

I was born in 1952 and raised to be a nice Chinese girl. But nice Chinese girls don't grow up to be dykes or rebels. And I turned out to be both!

I grew up in silence. Though I was part of a large extended family, we ate our meals in silence. There was no conversation or laughter, just the sound of soup spoons and chopsticks against the rice bowls. I was not encouraged to talk, express emotions, show feelings, or ask questions. I grew up with a heritage of silence.

I was a girl born into a traditional Chinese family. I was raised to be seen but not heard, raised to excel in book learning but not to be curious about the world, raised to be a wife but not to be a person of my own.

As a child my most prized possession was my library card. I loved to read so much that I walked to and from school, a distance totaling six miles, with a book in my hand, oblivious to traffic and other pedestrians. As a preadolescent I dreamed of being a writer, of creating myth, mayhem, mystery, melodrama, and magic.

As a Chinese girl I grew up as a second-class citizen. I was the firstborn, but I was not a son. Since the disappearance of prehistoric matriarchies in China, women had been regarded as little more than chattel. Daughters were neglected in favor of sons. In poor families midwives drowned girl children at birth as a routine matter of course. A female owed her allegiance first to her father, then to her brothers, her husband, and her sons. Women were forced into arranged marriages and were not allowed to own property or hold political office. In the wealthy classes, polygamy was widely practiced. Second wives and concubines were subordinated to the principal wife.

Women were inferior, even expendable, but probably the most extreme manifestation of the subordination of women was the widespread practice of foot binding. Originated by court dancers in the Tang Dynasty (618–907 A.D.), the custom gained popularity as a status symbol. Starting at the age of four, the feet of girls were bound, causing the arches to break and the toes to turn under the foot. By the nineteenth century, women of all classes, save for the very poor (for obvious economic reasons), had bound feet.

Women walked on their three-inch "golden lilies" with mincing steps and a hip-swaying gait that was alluring to male eyes. Men were also drawn to the delicateness of the small feet. Connoisseurs alleged it made sex more exciting as the muscles of the vagina were tightened. Whatever feelings it stirred up for men, there can be no doubt that the pain was excruciating during childhood and continued throughout a woman's life.

As a Chinese woman I have a great heritage of rejection to overcome. In addition to having to deal with a culture that idealized the mutilation of women's bodies, I also had to overcome the sociological and psychological rejection of women. Growing up in Hong Kong, I heard all around me mothers shouting at their children: "*Say nui, mow no, mow yung*" (Dead girl, no brain, no use). And, "*Ngai ge sai yun tow!*" (Your dead head).

We were not just naughty children or bad girls. We were dead girls. What a way to begin life! Hearing myself called dead girl so many times I was sure I *was* a dead girl. Meaningless, useless, worthless. In addition, I was always told what I couldn't do, what I couldn't say, what I couldn't be. I could dream, but I could never be.

When I was growing up in England, Hong Kong, and San Francisco, I read everything I could get my hands on. But none of the books I found spoke of experiences similar to my own. In England I was the only Chinese child in the school. In Hong Kong I went to an exclusive school for rich kids and foreigners. In San Francisco I was an immigrant child. I was different everywhere. Everywhere I went, I was an alien in a foreign land. I started writing to fill the silence and to turn the years of isolation and rejection into affirmation.

My first byline appeared in the teenagers' section of the *South China Morning Post*, a major English daily in Hong Kong when I was twelve.

In 1983, *The Words of a Woman Who Breathes Fire* was published. It was the first book written by a Chinese American lesbian. Ten years later my byline had appeared in publications locally and nationally, and I had been included in over twenty-two anthologies worldwide.

I was raised by traditional parents to be a nice Chinese girl. I don't know when they first suspected that they had a rebellious, spunky nonconformist on their hands. But when they decided to curb my independence by forbidding phone calls, enforcing curfews, and even accompanying me the three blocks to the library, I left home for good. I was seventeen years old, adrift in the land that my Asian American ancestors called *Gum San* (Gold Mountain).

I lied about my age and got a job making salads (canned fruit in jello molds on pieces of iceberg lettuce) in a hospital kitchen. Having graduated early from San Francisco's academically elite Lowell High, I enrolled first in Chinese Studies and then in the Creative Writing department at San Francisco State. I lived in a small, sunny apartment in the Haight-Ashbury and typed my stories on my mother's old portable Olivetti. It was while I was in college that I came out as a lesbian.

You're probably wondering what the hell any of this has to do with lesbian erotics. The answer is: plenty! For me, writing is not just a discourse from the heart or a mere catharsis of feeling. What I write is shaped by my history and experiences both as a Chinese woman and as a lesbian.

Writing is a ritual. For me, writing is often a painful process done in isolation. I write to dispel stereotypes, to give my characters voice, breath, life. I write to fill the void, to reclaim my heritage, to affirm my history, to celebrate truth, to define my existence as a woman of color and as a lesbian. I write because my anger and my pain are too explosive to keep inside.

Chinese is my first language. But I was fluent only in the words my parents deemed it necessary for me to know. I was certainly not taught the words for breast, cunt, ass, orifice, or orgasm. There were no words for sex; therefore, sex did not exist. We never talked about the acts between married men and women, never mind lesbian sex!

I came out as a lesbian when I was twenty-one, but I didn't start writing about sex until almost a decade later. Sure, I wrote love poems, but I never wrote about sex. I was, after all, a nice Chinese girl, and we didn't talk about things like that.

Han Suyin wrote: "As a picture encompasses a universe of cognition, so should words, like stones, embody a permanency of meaning, to bear witness to enduring reality."[1]

Writing is an intimate act, as intimate as the act of sex. Writing about sex is a celebration and a public affirmation of private feelings.

This is a poem I wrote in 1973 entitled, "my poem":

> it is five-thirty.
> i could not sleep,
> missing you.
> thoughts accumulate
> in windswept patterns
> in my mind:
> a book i read
> rituals i perform
> the woman i love.
> my hands dream
> the tender places of
> your body.
> my poem—
> being friends,
> that sense of sharing.
> my poem—
> being lovers
> that storm in our eyes.[2]

Fifteen years later I wrote a poem called "gloriously" in which I named fifteen body parts including cunt, clitoris, and ass, words for which I still do not know the Chinese translations.

When I realized I was a lesbian, I came out to the world. It never occurred to me that I should stay in the closet. Loving women was the most natural thing in the world. My sexuality is a personal expression of intimacy and intensity. As a lesbian, my sexuality is also an act of political rebellion against the patriarchal norm. Anytime you choose to act in a way that does not conform, it is an act of rebellion.

I had been writing for years, yet in two decades of work it was not my words that made sparks fly, but images of my body that generated controversy. In 1988, *On Our Backs,* a lesbian sex magazine, featured their first Asian American model on the cover, me.

I was raised as a nice Chinese girl. I was a quiet, shy, demure girl. Bookish even. I was short and skinny, had bow legs and wore spectacles. In my adolescence I was what was known as a "late bloomer." When all my friends were buying bras, I was still wearing undershirts. I hated gym class not because I hated sports but because I had to undress in public. Yikes! I started dating in high school at the late age of seventeen. I may have been flat-chested (how I hated that word!), but boys never failed to admire my legs.

Like most of you I grew up in a world surrounded by images of heterosexuality. I dated boys. I liked making out in the park and fondling cocks that grew and hardened magically in my hands. I remember the first time I felt a jolt of electricity for someone of my own sex. She was my best girlfriend in high school, a shy Chinese girl much like myself. She had come over to spend the night as she often did. I saw her dark nipples through her sheer nightdress. It sent waves of shock and delight through me.

I squelched the feeling very fast and didn't explore my desires for women until many years later. It was a typical San Francisco summer, gray, cold, and foggy. I was living with a boyfriend in a large flat in the Fillmore district. All of a sudden it was as if I had inhaled some mysterious gas, and I was smitten. Suddenly I was in love. But not with any *one* woman. I was in love, unexpectedly and inexplicably, with *all* women! Needless to say, after years of being attracted to the male organ and the male physique, this came as a big shock.

I grew up in my body, but she was a stranger to me. I wanted to be a girl with curly, blond hair and blue eyes, not the skinny Chinese girl with straight bangs who stared back at me out of the mirror. It was only in the stories I made up that I was a girl with blond hair and blue eyes.

I grew up with no images of Chinese women. What little education I received about my own culture was limited to poets, painters, philosophers, and calligraphers who were, without exception, all male.

I was ignorant of women like Empress Wu who was responsible for instituting the competitive system of imperial examinations by which men could attain a government post, or Wu Tsao, a poet and lover of women, or Ch'iu Chin, a revolutionary, a poet, and a lesbian, or even Hua Mulan, the famous woman warrior who impersonated a man to take her father's place in the army. I was not told the true stories of the battalions of women who fought in the Taiping Rebellion or of the silkworkers in Guangdong who resisted marriage and banded together as "sworn sisters." I did not even know my grandmother's name or her place in history. She was just an old lady, my grandmother.

Alice Walker wrote: "If we kill off the sound of our ancestors, the major portion of us . . . is lost."[3]

When I was a teenager I visited San Francisco's Chinatown often. My grandmother lived in a tiny apartment above the Golden Phoenix Restaurant, and whenever I visited, we would indulge in my favorite ritual, eating. Chicken chow mein, Yang Chow fried rice and apple pie at Ping Yuen on Grant Avenue. Or dark cubes of grass jelly swimming in liquid cane sugar at Uncle's Cafe.

On Saturday mornings, after dim sum with *poa poa*, I would walk a block to the Great Star on Jackson. There, in the darkened theater I would spend hours entranced by the sight of brave men—and often women—battling bandits, demons, and wicked warlords with bamboo staves, swords, or using their hands or even fans as lethal weapons. The women warriors featured in these immensely popular low-budget swordplay epics made in Hong Kong were fearless. They possessed superior strength and supernatural powers. They were skilled in swordplay and in martial arts. They could catch an arrow between their teeth as easily as reciting a verse of a poem. Many times they masqueraded as men in order to travel unmolested; sometimes they cross-dressed to escape male eyes and inadvertently attracted attention from female eyes! Fortified with popcorn and Coke, I tumbled headlong into these wildly fantastic escapist fantasies. When the fantasies were played out, I had no choice but to return home to my own body.

When I discovered women, it was as if I had entered Paradise! Everything was new, yet everything seemed comfortably familiar, like an old pair of jeans or a faithful canine companion. The arms that enfolded me were soft yet strong and firm. The lips that caressed me were warm and lingering. The thighs that gripped me were soft as silk and strong as steel. The fingers that opened me were sure and unrelenting. My heart opened, my body sang under the hands of women as it had never sung before.

In 1981 I discovered an old boxing studio in the neighborhood where I lived and started training with weights. I had never liked team sports, so this solitary pursuit was ideal for me. There was no women's changing room (in fact, I don't recall any women at all) but soon I was hooked! Not only did training with weights sculpt my body, but the physical discipline challenged my spirit. I began to like my body for the first time in my life; I also felt strong, sure, positive, and ready for anything!

In 1986 my best friend of thirteen years, Anita Taylor Onang, died of cancer. I had been weight training on and off since 1981 and falling on and off the wagon for as long. When Anita died, I wanted to die, so I picked up the bottle and drank and drank. One morning I woke up with the startling realization that she didn't want me to die. I got my gloves, weight belt, and knee wraps out of the closet and went back to the gym. With the help of an old coach from the boxing studio I trained like a fiend for three months and entered the bodybuilding competition at Gay Games II, my first contest. To my shock, I won the bronze medal in the women's lightweight division in the physique contest.

A group of my friends sat in the front row and cheered. Even they couldn't believe their eyes. This shy, nice Chinese girl had taken off her clothes and taken the stage by storm!

In 1988 English photographer Jill Posener approached me to be part of a book she was editing on women bodybuilders. As an aside she mentioned that she was also the photo editor for *On Our Backs*. Would I consider posing for her camera? I replied bluntly that I did not read the magazine and did not care to pose for pornographic photographs, lesbian or not!

Bodybuilding is often called the ultimate sport. Not only must a dedicated athlete train with weights five or six times a week, often in a double split routine (training different muscle groups twice a day), but she also must follow a strict dieting regimen, practice her posing routine daily, cross-train by engaging in rigorous aerobic activities to burn off body fat, and get as dark a tan as possible (to show off the muscles to their maximum advantage). Bodybuilding is a full-time activity and often a jealous mistress.

For me, bodybuilding is a way of redefining beauty in a patriarchal society that defines beauty in terms of face, tits, and ass. When I bodybuild, I am proclaiming the whole of my body to be beautiful. Lats. Traps. Biceps. Triceps. Abs. Quadriceps. For me as a Chinese American woman, bodybuilding empowers me to reject both the stereotype of the passive Madame Butterfly and the fiery Suzy Wong/Dragon Lady images.

Controversial cover girl Kitty Tsui, from the Summer 1988 issue of On Our Backs. *Photograph by and courtesy of Jill Posener.*

When I appeared on the cover of *On Our Backs* I heard a lot of talk behind my back. But no one said anything to my face. I heard many things: that I should not have posed naked, that I was "showing off," that I was being exploited as an exotic face/body, that as a role model for young Asian Pacific lesbians, exposing my body to the camera was not a politically correct thing to do.

After much deliberation I agreed to be the *On Our Backs* cover girl because I wanted to challenge the stereotype of Asian women as shy, passive, docile, demure. I wanted to show an image of an Asian woman who is strong, assertive, powerful, and beautiful. One who is proud of her body. Proud to be an Asian American woman. And proud to be a lesbian.

I've lived in my body all my life. For many years, I was a "dead girl." I grew up thinking of myself as insignificant and ugly. I've traveled a long road to reclaim my body and believe in my beauty. Who says Asian women aren't beautiful? Oh, and while I'm on that subject, give Joan Chen my phone number anytime!

NOTES

1. Han Suyin, foreword to *Between Worlds* (New York: Pergamon Press, 1990), ix.

2. Kitty Tsui, "my poem," in *The Words of a Woman Who Breathes Fire* (San Francisco: Spinsters, Ink, 1983), 32.

3. Alice Walker, *In Search of Our Mother's Gardens: Womanist Prose* (New York: Harcourt Brace Jovanovich, 1983), 4.

SIX

Between the Sheets: My Sex Life in Literature

DONNA ALLEGRA

I began reading lesbiana when I was around ten years old, an open-minded adolescent who first found *The Well of Loneliness,* by Radclyffe Hall, on a bookshelf at summer camp. I'd read heterosexual romances and was certainly well exposed to that way of life but hadn't taken to it. Radclyffe Hall's book, however, hit the spot. I saw myself reflected on those pages where Stephen Gordon lived. I, a black girl, Brooklyn-born and raised, had something important in common with this upper-class British noblewoman, something beyond a love for fencing and riding horses.

Avid book reader that I was, I began my search for knowledge and understanding at the library. After two years of hunting, I located a copy of Jeannette H. Foster's *Sex-Variant Women in Literature* from the main branch of the Brooklyn Public Library system. I don't think I ever returned it.

Sex-Variant Women in Literature contained a precious reading list of books with information on lesbians, not that there existed many entire texts, but references to even a whiff of a lesbian character would send me searching through the library's card catalogue. I needed those books to see who I might be, as I'd gleaned a glimpse of my face in *The Well of Loneliness.*

I believed strongly in books then and still do. My adolescent imagination was honed on a literary world which was so forbidden it had to be kept under wraps. I'd discovered soft-core pornography in my early teens and there I was finally able to locate a world of precious stories revolving around lesbians.

Those first guilty readings, under my bed covers, lest my parents find what I had purchased from a drugstore "pornography" section, have left an indelible impression on the shape of my erotic imagination. No matter how embarrassed and ashamed I felt when I went to the cash register to buy these books, it was absolutely necessary for me to have them. I needed them the way I needed food and shelter for survival. I haunted second-hand bookstores where I scrutinized bookjacket covers for words like "unnatural," "strange," and "perverted," which I knew would lead me to my treasure.

I'd happened on Joan Ellis's *Summer Camp* at a drugstore near my junior high school. From there, I happily discovered the 1960s "soft-core pornography" and hunted down books by March Hastings, Sloan Brittain, Randy Salem, Dallas Mayo, Ann Aldrich, a.k.a. Vin Packer (boo, hiss — this lesbian condemned lesbians and regarded them as more of an evil perversion than many heterosexual writers), and Sheldon Lorde. How I longed to be able to mail-order those Fawcett, Tower, or Medallion paperbacks. But I dared not: I was in my teens and didn't control the mailbox key. It wouldn't do for my parents to find out that I indulged in what was deemed "pornography."

After reading a few of these paperback novels, I saved myself from disappointment before purchasing a book by reading the last page. If two women were in conversation or an embrace, the book was likely to have a glad finale. If a man and a woman were kissing, I knew a sad ending had come to the lesbian love story.

I read to find just who I was as a "female homosexual." I did find parts of me in those "lesbian" books, often written by men to titillate other men. Those tales, however, didn't deliver the whole truth. They were no more accurate than television depictions of "real life." But from these books, I caught the scent that put me on the trail of my erotic orientation.

Such were the books that gave me ideas on which to shape my erotic desires as well as clues for a future romantic style. Searching through their pages for guidance as to how to live as a lesbian, I first felt drawn to take the butch stance, that is, to believe that my birthright is to have a femme.

Since then, my lesbian literary selections have broadened, and the particulars have deepened with nuances and added cultural variety. But when I was in my teens and masturbating sometimes every day, I needed to read what was marketed as "soft-core pornography."

My sexual imagination then, and into early adulthood, was keenly focused around both hard-core, heterosexual pornography and those lesbian love fantasies that I found among the "soft-core" drugstore literature. The erotic energy I conjured from reading these two sets of literature was used differently according to my purposes for reading. With the former I jerked off, with the latter, I could fabricate my dreams for romance and sexual fulfillment.

I did not have the opportunity to behave like other teenagers because I knew myself to be lesbian. I found no other girls with whom to explore sexual possibility. I knew too much: that what I wanted was taboo and had to be hidden until I lived independently. Hence, it was between the sheets, using my left hand and reading the pages of books, that my erotic life came into being.

Through *The Grapevine* by Jess Stearn, a journalist's dubious socio-logical study of lesbians, I learned of the Daughters of Bilitis, a national lesbian organization, and got a few copies of their publication, *The Ladder*. Here I found true lesbian fiction. In 1969, when I was sixteen, I could identify only Jane Rule and Isabel Miller as lesbian writers of a more literary order. My drugstore paperbacks' lesbian tales rarely went further than clichéd romances of love and loss.

It never occurred to me to question why my erotic desires were considered fit topics for pornography. In the 1960s, I had no concept of lesbian or gay pride. I didn't believe I was "unnatural" or "perverted," as the societal attitude of the time would have it, but I knew it would be a long time coming before that line of thought changed. "Acceptance" was the most I hoped for. At the same time, the prevailing social order considered any sex on the page pornographic: both the heterosexual books that I jerked off to, as well as the lesbian ones I set my love fantasies to.

In the 1970s, I found a flood of feminist press short stories, essays, poems, and novels. I used to be able to brag that I'd read everything in the Oscar Wilde Memorial Bookstore; now, twenty years later, there is such a wealth of literature that I can't keep up. I even have the luxury of not finishing a few lesbian books because they're too poorly written.

I was a reader before I was ever a writer, but somewhere along the line, I became a writer, as well. I now read my favorite authors with an eye on how they work their craft. The writer in me has her eyes open to learn technique. I want my readers to feel as I did about the authors to whom I looked for revelation and guidance. That communication from page to spirit, that process of recognition, of giving and receiving, opens a door to the erotic.

Audre Lorde takes on that elusive kaleidoscope we call the erotic in her essay "Uses of the Erotic: The Erotic as Power." She tells us, "The very word *erotic* comes from the Greek word, *eros,* the personification of love in all its aspects—born of Chaos, and personifying creative power and harmony. When I speak of the erotic, then, I speak of it as an assertion of the lifeforce of women."[1]

I too come to a realization, and am surprised by it, that the erotic is not just a sexual energy nor exclusively shaped by romantic feelings. Given Lorde's perspective on what is erotic, I can say that I find embers of erotic excitement stirred when I read book reviews, essays, poems, any genre in which the writer conveys a truth that resonates within me.

I read fiction about lesbians because my erotic self needs to sup on words that nourish my hopes and dreams, which reach across all realms on the map of my life. I suspect that erotic self is the primary place I read for—to satisfy its longings for identification.

I think sexual love is the predominant, but not the only channel which carries the erotic. Lorde points out that "the erotic has often been misnamed by men and used against women. It has been made into the confused, the trivial, the psychotic, the plasticized sensation."[2]

While I admire Lorde's writing, I just don't like lesbian erotica. I'm probably one of the few lesbians who will admit this. Contemporary erotica, written by dykes, for dykes, daunts and dismays me. I won't deny that the sex writings I've read have expanded my own work. They have, even as I have not always respected this erotic literature and wouldn't bring it home to mother as the girl I'd like to marry.

A law governing the marketplace that publishers know well is that "sex sells." This maxim has changed the requirements for lesbian writers. Our audience demands and responds to more explicit sexual action and as a writer, I've had to take this fact into consideration. Where I once thought of "fuck scenes" as the stuff of hard-core pornography, by the 1990s it has become standard fare. I'd even say it seems de rigueur in the guidelines from publishers likely to be receptive to my work.

With erotic material a contemporary expectation, I feel pressured to address sexual behavior I might not otherwise be inclined to portray with my characters. The trend toward expanded sex writing is liberating for some writers, but disturbing, coercive, and not welcomed by others. Some editors clamor for sex and more sex, and as a reader, I prefer the love story told with sexual details played as one aspect among many that the author lays before me.

In a letter from Circlet Press, Inc., rejecting a piece I submitted to an anthology of erotica, Cecilia Tan said, "The main reason I cannot use the story is that, although it has 'erotic overtones' there isn't any actual sex in it. My definition of erotica is work in which all the story's elements (plot, characterization, conflict development, etc.) are revealed through the sexual interaction. . . . Everything that I publish is focused on these moments of erotic exchange. The language need not be explicit or vulgar, but the exchange must BE there! And it must be the major focus of the story."[3]

But times have changed since I first started reading to fill my erotic needs, and with the changing times, so have the tastes we are permitted to cultivate. More out-front sex action has been part of the evolution in literature since I came out with books as my primary source for role models. Would I be different if my first exposure to lesbian literature had been through books published by Naiad, Firebrand Books, or Crossing Press, or if I had read *On Our Backs,* where lesbians can openly (gasp!) have sex without love or romance? What if I had grown up with Tee Corinne's collections of stories or *Cunt Coloring Book,* or a JoAnn Loulan self-help book?

Even as I am a skeptical reader of lesbian erotica, I feel defensive on its behalf. I don't think erotica is currently being written at the height of its possibility. I venture to speculate that this is because erotica is still a genre as yet young in its development.

Lesbian culture is similarly in a period of tremendous growth and transition. As herstorians unearth major closeted figures, our heritage fills in the gaps on the spectrum linking Sappho to Radclyffe Hall, Natalie Clifford Barney, Renée Vivien to Jane Rule, Sarah Aldridge, Valerie Taylor, and Paula Christian. Over the past thirty years, thanks to feminists working in concert with, or rather, inspired by lesbian visions and consciousness, the outpouring of literature has expanded like beans set to soak in water overnight.

I would defend lesbian erotica's honor and right to life in the face of attack, but at present it has only slight appeal for me. Even from a writer whose work I highly enjoy and admire, such as Pat Califia, I skip over the sex parts. Little of the sex literature I've read touches on the deeper parts of my humanity where erotic energy resides. When I want the charge of erotic energy to fill me, when I seek to be immersed in the haze of love feeling, I read lesbian love stories.

Along with the giant steps we've taken, our heels are dogged by those who would have us slink back into the closet and remain silent. Lesbian political awareness has received a lot of critical contempt for being the leading edge as well as the consistent voice addressing oppressive mechanisms in our society. Homophobia fomented by the media, and that which resides in our selves, would have some believe that lesbian/feminist ideals are the problem. Terms like "lesbian thought police" imply that we would censor anything not "politically correct." Lesbians are in fact the messengers that the culture wants to kill for bringing the bad news of societal ills out in the open for all the world to see.

An important point to bear in mind as we survey our literature is that lesbians don't see many movies in which our lives are played out. Women's music festivals are a relatively recent phenomenon as a resource where festival-goers can find a multifaceted sampling of lesbians. Despite the fact that images of lesbians are somewhat more available in mainstream magazines and on television than when I was in my formative years, our strongest resource for visions of how we appear to ourselves is still between the covers of a book. Lesbians must of necessity lean more heavily on the page to find the same validation of self that film, popular music, the mall, and other vehicles of art, culture, and commercialism give to hets at the drop of a hat. Given that perspective, I can say I'm still mighty hungry for lesbian love stories.

Only lesbian fiction and poetry give me visions of the women who have fueled and inspired me. As a reader, I want to know what these lesbians are made of. This is the information that arouses and excites an energy in me. Just as when I was a child, I still haunt the bookstores and libraries to find how contemporary lesbians live, especially how we fare in our love lives. The need is an erotic one because the desire for love is so all-encompassing.

At this point the reader might wonder what I find erotic. Here are some images: a strong woman being tender to another; a femme yearning for a butch; one woman looking out for and protecting another; a smart and competent woman who is independent, solo, on her own. This eroticism also includes hearing what kinds of strategies other dykes use to fend off men in the street who make the sexual propositions that have become a part of the contemporary landscape. Like air pollution, billboards, and commercials—noxious elements we just have to live with—I look to see how other dykes respond to ever-worsening male behavior.

Despite Audre Lorde's definition of the erotic and my own sense that my erotic energies have to do with more than romantic notions and sexual activities, the general expectation when you speak of "erotica" is that the discussion is going to be about sex. So let's talk about sex-writings for a hot minute.

Earlier I identified images I found erotic. Looking back to my reading as a younger person and as the adult I am now, it was/is the active love between women that would conjure emotions of sexual feeling in me: that sexual feeling is how we commonly understand the erotic. In that state, a wave of sensation comes over me and my feminist critical sensibility is bypassed as the passions of love are stirred. Figurative sighs of yearning escape my critically pursed lips as I read wholesome lesbian love scenes. Despite the frowning face to accompany my right brain disapproval, I respond to outmoded romantic clichés to which I, perhaps you too, react.

As a forty-year-old reader of lesbian literature, I still crave the lesbian love-life story. I need the characters in the romance-to-a-happy-ending, the relationship-not-working, the fixing-relationships novels. Lesbians are long-gone from the days when *The Ladder* was our only literary journal. Today we have *Sinister Wisdom, Common Lives/Lesbian Lives,* and *Deneuve,* to name a few, and I still tear them open with my teeth when they come in the mail.

As a writer, I'd say the erotic is best employed as a part of a whole piece of literature that includes mystery, suspense, humor, and intrigue. And yet, I have long loved Naiad romances and would put up with some awfully purple prose just for the sake of getting to the love story.

Romances arouse me sexually. A book may not be especially well written or flavored to my taste, but if seasoned with enough of a love story, I will struggle through because I want so very much to read of lesbians loving one another. Such books have a wholeness that covers far more parts of life than episodes of sexual encounter such as the stories in *Serious Pleasure: Lesbian Erotic Stories & Poetry,* edited by the Sheba Collective, or a long work whose motif is sexual conquests, such as *Travels with Diana Hunter* by Regine Sands. I don't believe my preferences here are solely because my arousal mechanism was installed when I was a teenager hunting down soft-core porn to find lesbian love stories.

When I seek erotic arousal from lesbian books, I need to know and have affirmed again and again, the possibility of true-to-life endings for lesbian lovers. This doesn't have to mean a walk hand-in-hand into the sunset. But in nothing and nowhere else in the world I live in could I have seen the possibility of a lesbian happily-ever-after, when I was a teen, outside of books.

Sex without some relationship is a dubious luxury that I may well be able to afford, but I don't invest in it in my own writing. Depictions of desire in the context of love are what turn me on. Who has felt as I have for women? That's what I need to see, and want to show, in living color on the page. And it is not that I'd disallow sex divorced from love for other people.

Too much of the erotica/lesbian porn I've read lacks a plane of emotional involvement, so I turn the page, bored. I've always felt that the sexiest part of a woman was her mind, and it is in my psyche that I know desire.

Erotica is popular these days, yet I rarely see it done in a way I can enjoy. I know lesbians want to read sex writings and these generate a lot of enthusiasm and excitement, but is that more smoke than fire? I wonder what actually turns readers on when so much erotic writing seems so poorly done. I also wonder if the rape culture that we view on TV, in magazines, and in advertising has trained us to respond to coarse, brutal images. Have our circuits been wired to become sexually aroused by something that goes against the grain of natural impulse, like the childhood sexual abuse survivor who continues to be turned on by dangerous sexual situations which she would shun in real life?

I think pornographic writing exploits the appeal of, fears around, and overemphasis on sexuality in American culture. The whole notion of using sex appeal to sell goods and services harkens to the ways sex has been so distorted in our society. Pornography is an evidence of that.

Lynn Yamaguchi Fletcher was speaking of discovering the power of her sexuality, at the 1993 East Coast Lesbians' Festival, when she said, "I read a lot of bad erotica and it distresses me, not only for the trees it destroys, but because of what it perpetuates in ourselves. . . . There is so much hatred of our sexuality built into our culture, . . . built into the ways that we all grow up that it's extremely difficult to separate the strands, to find the health in the disease." [4]

But people read erotic literature anyway. A friend said to me that she reads erotic fantasies to masturbate, that erotica gives her a lot of ways to view lesbian sexuality. Erotica does portray a wide spectrum of ways to perceive sexuality and that includes what some would see as "male" behavior. It gives her loads of ways to be a lesbian.

My friend also said that it is hard to find good erotica, that lesbian erotica is very basic and unsophisticated, but then she forgives it because it takes so long to come out. Part of why erotica is immature is because many of us lesbians come so late into our sexuality. We don't talk about sex to each other in the ways men do.

Like conflict, sexuality is enormously interesting. Any kind of sex is difficult to truly see, embarrassing to behold, and enormously fascinating. You want to watch sex, but only from under cover—few people want to be caught staring. Sex is even hard to talk about. It is giggled over. And still, the promise of even an approach to the topic of nasty, dirty sex draws instant attention from all communities across the board. How come?

Sex is perhaps the most prominent manifestation of erotic energy, as Audre Lorde points out in her essay, "Uses of the Erotic: The Erotic as Power." I'd say sex is the subset that is most often confused with and made synonymous with the erotic. Lorde points out that "we have often turned away from the exploration and consideration of the erotic as a source of power and information, confusing it with its opposite, the pornographic." [5]

Divinities ascribed with our erotic nature, like Venus from the ancient Roman tradition, Aphrodite from the Greek, and Oshun from the Yoruba people of Africa, are commonly described as goddesses of love. They have been degraded to fit male fantasies of their own seduction. The same can be said of Middle Eastern dancing, which is commonly called "belly dancing" and the enormously popular and compelling sabar dance of Senegal, Africa. Both these forms of dance, to speak of examples I am familiar with, were originally celebrations of female reproductive power. Yet, in a distortion of the erotic such as is routinely seen in our culture, these divinities are now presented to us as "sex goddesses" and the dances are said to be about seduction.

This is a frustrating limitation because we've all had moments that we recognize as erotic that had to do with religious feeling, spiritual emotion, physical exhilaration. Sex is part of that spectrum, but in our culture, any sexual love is still largely regarded as the stuff of pornography. Or it is called "erotica" if the writing is of a more literary nature. I find it hard to tell the difference and there are no common criteria. Indeed, debates around "pornography" and its discontents are crucial to a contemporary understanding of what constitutes "freedom."

I also have to ask rhetorically, in dismay, how come black people are eroticized, in pornographic/erotic literary myth? Our sexuality is supposed to be more potent than the assumed-to-be-white reader. I think and sputter with rage about Artemis Oakgrove's *The Throne Trilogy* as one of the most wretched examples of erotic writing. Oakgrove isn't even subtle in the ways she depicts black characters. The writing calls on stereotypes, for example, the sadistic black butch in *Nighthawk,* in order to achieve its effect on the reader.

I am not flattered when I, as an African Caribbean American, am attributed to be "hot" just by virtue of being black. I feel nervous and sad when white friends attempt to jest along lines like, "Once you go black, you never go back." I also know that along with attributes meant to be taken as positive, there is a host of negative ones, unspoken and unquestioned.

I'd say lesbians, as a group, have seemed to be more sincere in community efforts toward unlearning racism, but I see its tracks in the best of us. I've found more blondes, as the object of desire, inhabiting books all across the board than have ever populated the earth.

What erotic literature actually lives up to Audre Lorde's description, as a bridge that connects the political and psychological, a bridge that "is formed by the erotic—the sensual—those physical, emotional, and psychic expressions of what is deepest and strongest and richest within each of us, being shared: the passions of love, in its deepest meaning"?[6] Not much that I've read. Lesbian life stories which have erotic aspects woven into the tapestry have touched on that ground. There we leave genre descriptions and start talking about capital L-Literature.

I don't doubt that erotic literature, Lorde's or Tan's or your own definition, can inspire the better parts of ourselves, lay out a further vision to guide the reader, or provide clues for the next turn in the road. As we learn better ways to write of the erotic, it can nourish our imaginations with further possibility. These are necessary for the pilgrims, and I am one such, on that path to the interior. I am still looking to find erotic truth on the page, between the sheets and anywhere else I can find it.

NOTES

1. Audre Lorde, "Uses of the Erotic: The Erotic as Power," in *Sister Outsider: Essays and Speeches* (Freedom, CA: Crossing Press, 1984), 56.
2. Ibid., 43.
3. Cecilia Tan, Letter to Donna Allegra, 4 January 1994.
4. Lynn Yamaguchi Fletcher, Untitled Talk, East Coast Lesbians' Festival, Ponyville, PA, 4 September 1993.
5. Lorde, 54.
6. Ibid., 56.

PART II

Qu(e)eries into People, Theories, and Deeds

SEVEN

Camille Paglia and the Problematics of Sexuality and Subversion

S. ELAINE CRAGHEAD

Camille Paglia, in the introduction to *Sex, Art, and American Culture,* gives the following as one reason for the proliferation of articles about her during the early 1990s:

> I like reporters and enjoy talking to them. With most academics, I feel bored and restless. I have to speak very slowly and hold back my energy level. . . . My manic personality, which frightens and repels academics, seems perfectly normal to media people, who are always in a rush and on a deadline. [1]

I hardly think that, at least on the surface, it is any "normal"-seeming behavior of Paglia's that has intrigued either the reporters who have written about her, or the journals that pay for their articles, or especially the readers who "tune in" to Paglia's latest "shocking" statements. Paglia fails to recognize, at least in the above quote, which is to frame our reading of her most recent publication, just why she is this strange popular icon that has garnered attention from all quarters—the talk-show circuit, TV news magazines, newspapers, "hip" periodicals such as *Zone, SPIN,* and the *Village Voice,* a film (by Monica Treut), established mainstream journals (for example, *Harper's* and *Vanity Fair*), popular magazines like *People* and *Spy,* and academic publications from the *Harvard Crimson* to the *Chronicle of Higher Education.* But most interesting to note is the amount of attention which Paglia has received from publications geared toward gays and lesbians—the *Advocate, NYQ, On Our Backs,* and *Out/Look*—and from writers such as Ruby Rich in the *Village Voice* who focus on questions of sexuality that surround Paglia's persona.

Writers like Rich are attempting, largely for more "mainstream" audiences, to expose the conservatism inherent in Paglia's stance, underneath its shocking veneer. Her sexual stance is what makes for her popularity, in its paradoxical outrageousness and adherence to a neoconservative ethic: she not only fuels the backlash against feminism, but she also rejuvenates otherwise worn-out stereotypes of gays and lesbians, which these very publications and writers have worked to overthrow. Exposing this lack of subversion in her work is crucial, for Paglia provides the perfect new facade for what is merely the reproduction of conservatism: hers is a false front of subversion, a so-called leftist attack on liberalism which *claims* to make issues of sexuality visible and to provide a forum for the serious discussion of these issues.

Yet this visibility comes at a price, for in much the same way that the July 1993 cover of *Vanity Fair* (depicting k.d. lang being shaved by Cindy Crawford) reinscribes "lesbian" with a masculine-encoded, perhaps parodic and certainly non-"sexy" persona, Paglia refuses to disrupt the myths that surround the concept of lesbian sexuality. Paglia even plays lesbians against gays in an article entitled "Homosexuality at the Fin de Siècle," attempting to solidify a historical separation between gay males and lesbians, and to drive a wedge between them at a moment in which some political alliances have formed: "Gay men and straight men have much more in common than do gay men with lesbians or straight men with straight women. Every man must define his identity against his mother. If he does not, he just falls back into her and is swallowed up."[2] Therefore, men in general must form "group alliances" (when have they not?) and reject their connections to women. Though Paglia seems to be attempting to make bridges here between hetero and homo, it is among males only, the "complex" creators, and thus she merely replicates the standard division between the "sexes." Rather than pointing to the material alliances among gay men and lesbians, at least in their relative pathologizations and lack of civil rights, Paglia points to what she sees as their material differences—namely, their relation to sex and lust:

> Gay men may seek sex without emotion; lesbians often end up in emotion without sex. Male homosexuality, pushing outward into risky, alien territory, is progressive and, overall, intellectually stimulating. Lesbianism,

seeking a lost state of blissful union with the mother, is cozy, regressive, and, I'm sorry to say, too often intellectually enervating, tending toward the inert.

Male lust, I have written elsewhere, is the energizing factor in culture. Men are the reality principle. They created the world we live in and the luxuries we enjoy. When women cut themselves off from men, they sink backward into psychological and spiritual stagnancy. [3]

Thus, not only do men have the ability to cut themselves off from women and become "intellectually stimulating," but if women decide to cut themselves off from men (and this seems to be the construction of "lesbian" inherent in this passage), then "stagnancy" ensues as well. Thus Paglia finally undermines *only* lesbianism here, for "male lust" obviously flourishes in a hetero economy; women who choose other women as sexual partners are being denied any real *sex*uality here at the expense of their male counterparts. But in what ways does this construction differ from standard hierarchies based on biological sex differences? And why would the gay media continue to give space to "outrageous" statements such as these, as though they are worthy of careful consideration?

Because they are. Because gay and lesbian publications cannot afford *not* to take up the problematic of Paglia and what she stands for, especially when more "mainstream" audiences continue to feed upon her statements as well as her persona. Because regardless of whether Paglia suddenly finds herself unpopular in the various interviewing forums, her past and current popularity represent an event of importance which has occurred, and the conditions for that occurrence will not disappear so easily as Paglia herself may. For the early 1990s not only witnessed a backlash of conservatism, but also the mass definition/ visualization of "lesbian" through an inundation of information, relatively speaking, on a subject/entity heretofore little known or discussed in popular media. And Paglia's appearances and interviews aid in developing that picture, helping to shape it partially from "within," since she has claimed to be a lesbian, but she is also mainstreaming herself by making it quite clear that she no longer defines herself as such or aligns herself politically with lesbians. Thus how do(es) Paglia and her sexual persona help to shape the definition of lesbian that is being constructed and disseminated? How is Paglia able to fuel simultaneously a conservative ethic and a definition of "lesbian" from "inside"? And how is her definition of "lesbian" being deployed?

In her essay entitled "Imitation and Gender Insubordination," anthologized in *Inside/Out*, Judith Butler investigates the relationship between "I" and "lesbian," arguing that "identity categories tend to be instruments of regulatory regimes, whether as normalizing categories of oppressive structures or as the rallying points for a liberatory contestation of that oppression."[4] Yet she goes on to admit that these identity categories are "necessary trouble."[5] That is, having seen the damage that can be done by them, gays and lesbians might tend to resist these labels, given that they are political categorizations that can lead to facile assessments, to limiting identity politics, and eventually to damaging, persistent stereotypes. But insofar as labeling is a necessary part of how we come to see ourselves and others in relation to the world, and is a means by which political action may be taken, labeling is then both a process and product that cannot be fully erased as a means of critiquing modes of intelligibility and thereby gaining political power through visibility. If we say, "I refuse to call myself a feminist" or "I refuse to call myself a lesbian," though the statements admittedly differ from "I am not a feminist" and "I am not a lesbian," the former set of statements still immediately places us as "reactor" within a particular language game, in a position which is other-than-feminist, other-than-lesbian, though "feminist" and "lesbian" are themselves terms which lack easy definition and coherence. But such statements would probably be read by most feminists and/or lesbians as a denial of the political importance of collectivity and as a move from "outside" to "inside" (the mainstream), from margin toward center. Yet if we say, "I am a feminist" or "I am a lesbian," we are, of course, in danger of being too easily, too superficially read by those who, like Camille Paglia, dump almost all feminists and lesbians (other than herself) into one lump sum of misdirected hostility, constipated desires, political short-sightedness, and/or humorlessness. Yet what is initially interesting about Paglia is that she turns this game of naming to her advantage by appropriating, and attempting to resignify, both positively and negatively, the very terms/groups that she attacks. That is, all other lesbians have not been able to truly satisfy either Paglia's sexual desires/fantasies or her intellectual standards, yet Paglia has, for "most of [her] life," "identified [herself] as a lesbian." And all other feminists, according to Paglia, whine "about the culture, about 'Big, Bad, Daddy Patriarchy,'" but Paglia, who supports elitism, the traditional literary canon, and blames the victims of date rape, is "a *real* feminist."[6] This move on her part is the negative of what various politically, socially, and/or economically disempowered groups have done—to take a pejorative term which has been used as a means of oppression and reappropriate it through a largely internal resignification. Within particular groups, these terms lose their demeaning, humiliating intention, though resignifying outside of the group may be quite gradual or even nonexistent. Paglia, in contrast, has taken the (proud, self-ascribed) labels of still-disempowered groups and, riding on the sword of the conservative thrust against "political correctness," has reappropriated, after a few wild lunges against feminists and lesbians, terms which have spoken and generally continue to speak for often radical, certainly leftist politics, in order to resignify "feminist" and "lesbian" under her neoconservative rubric.

Paglia's "feminism" thus means to make a mere pretense of "breaking the rules," to attempt "subversion," or "transgression," a so-called "undermining" which is not part of a process whose end is to dismantle dominant discursive practices, but is to be "played" out at the expense of discourses—feminism and gay studies—which are already marginalized within academia and, more generally, within the neoconservative hegemony of the United States. The reality that Paglia's work denies is that, despite neoconservative portrayals of academia as "dominated by radicals," the "radical" undermining of oppressive structures, even within academia, is by no means a *fait accompli*. Nothing, finally, is truly being subverted by Paglia, for her work simply reifies patriarchal "logic" and its attendant assumptions about the relationships among biology and gender, gender and sexuality, which, albeit *ostensibly* outmoded within academia (generally speaking), and certainly within academic feminism (at least), continue to surface and to find an audience within the academy. Paglia attacks "feminist theory" in the academy as though it still clings to a monolithic, transhistorical model of "Patriarchy," a move which at once denies recent theorizations which are based upon much more complex models of the relationships among gender, sexuality, and power, and simultaneously exposes Paglia's own lack of scholarly investigation. Too busy attacking Gloria Steinem and Susan Sontag, feminists working in a humanist tradition that has not been the dominant paradigm in American academic feminism for the last ten years, Paglia ignores the work of Teresa de Lauretis, Judith Butler, Linda Hutcheon, Linda Nicholson, and numerous others whose work makes it quite clear that Paglia attacks a target which no longer exists as she describes it. Yet the dangers here are in the misleading of readers, perpetuating the assumption that Patriarchy-As-Ogre feminism is still a predominant mode of academic feminism, and reproducing dominant discourses of gender and sexuality, found everywhere from academia to political rhetoric to advertising: how does Paglia's belief that lesbians are "withdrawn from the instinctual rhythms of nature"[7]—if they were truly instinctive, how could one withdraw from them?—differ from the neoconservative rhetoric on the dangers of the dissolution of the "natural"—if it were natural, how could it dissolve?—unit of the nuclear family, or from television commercials which consistently depict heterosexual coupling as the ideal?

Yes, the game remains the same: the self-avowed anti-poststructuralist has used her knowledge of language games and the power dynamics within academia to position herself as the constructed "male" that she claims to be and to allow her persona the agency to continue to speak. Paglia obviously knows the rules here and pretends to run against them while using them to full advantage, yet never attempts to disrupt the game: she does a bad makeover job, puts a new face on old patriarchy, and becomes a father-figure-in-drag. Once again, the bad little feminists and/or lesbians are unceremoniously shoved to the merely reactive position of "whiners." According to Paglia's game rules, this essay can be no more than an extended "whine." Yet to accept her "you react, you lose" strategy is to lose. The only way to win here is to force others into another-than-passive stance on Paglia, to resignify her work within another game, one in which she, as the cultural icon, does not do the signifying, but is (re)signified: to "win," the game itself must change.

Paglia's popularity has, in spite of the applause which she has received from some quarters of academia, been surprising to many academics, especially feminists: the reasons for this surprise include Paglia's obvious "sour grapes" attitude toward the academy, fueled by her anger over the "past twenty years of 'poverty and neglect'" and by her desire for revenge against "those who have not been sufficiently 'respectful'";[8] the lack of recognition by Paglia of her indebtedness to previous scholarship; and perhaps especially, her lack of references to recent scholarship in *Sexual Personae*. She has thus positioned herself as the "shock jock" of the academy, by refusing to do her "homework," and also by playing on the fears and prejudices of both the disempowered and empowered, respectively. Feminists, and more especially those working in gay studies, "cannot afford" to overlook or tacitly "ignore Paglia, to return her texts unread": [9] the right, and the pseudo-leftist "radicals" who appreciate her radical-for-the-sake-of-being-so "radicalism" have actually applauded her work. Oddly, even Greil Marcus (whose *Lipstick Traces* fuses poststructuralist and new historicist paradigms into a radical reworking of the "secret history" of this century and who has discussed the recent academic insistence upon finding "subversion" nearly everywhere, calling for a reexamination of this admittedly overdetermined term) actually lauds Paglia's *Sexual Personae,* calling the text "close to poetry." Poetry it may be, for it takes only a few minutes to discover that in her "notes" section, Paglia includes no works published within the ten years preceding the publication of *Sexual Personae,* with the exception of a critical edition of an author's collected works. And most of the works listed are "primary"; virtually no critiques of Freudian psychoanalysis, feminism, or poststructuralism appear in her endnotes: Paglia's voice thus booms alone, gaining power through the absence of critical voices which would otherwise have the power to turn her own into a mere whisper, and to expose her "radical" statements as nothing more than hollow echoes.

This lone, wry, often harsh voice which shuns recent scholarship might lead one to admire secretly Paglia's pseudo-maverick position in *Sexual Personae* as a Marcus-like radical maker-of-her-own-truth, as a system-bucker who refuses to make the critical "nods" that are generally required by the publishers of academic texts. But in Paglia's refusal to acknowledge much important critical/theoretical work produced in the 1980s, in her seeming to change, to "free up" the academic publishing game by side-stepping the task of rigorous interrogation of other critical and theoretical texts that might have encouraged or provoked a *dialogue* of sorts, what Paglia has finally produced is merely a pseudo-critical *diatribe,* a blast of sometimes-humorous one-liners. The aim of this approach appears to be at least threefold: to lull ingenuous readers and those already hostile toward the academic "game" into complicity, conformity (often through laughter, the shared joke); to offer some readers the vicarious glee of playing nonconformists by constructing along established neoconservative lines of logic that left theory is *itself* conformist; and to enrage simultaneously those (like the so-called humorless lesbians and feminists) whose politics are antithetical to Paglia's.

If Paglia is tired of being ignored by "the powers that be," what better way of gaining attention than to adopt a stand-up comic persona, to play Joan Rivers and strike out at the academic "big guns"? Her audience chuckling or furious, Paglia remains where she wants to remain—the focus of their attention.

Ironically, along with the humor, both the quickness of the read and the similarity of *Sexual Personae*'s style to Paglia's speech acts (recounted and recorded in interviews with lesbian writers Susie Bright and Ruby Rich, as well as "mainstream" writers and now filmmaker Monica Treut) often actually work to engage or dupe (when not hopelessly frustrating perhaps any reader to the point of giving up). This barrage of bullets often doesn't repel/repulse its audience, for at least two reasons: first of all, Paglia moves easily, sneakily from descriptive statements into causal statements and back into description, glossing the difference, and secondly, Paglia's target remains elsewhere: "those" other feminists, who almost always remain, strategically, unnamed. In the former case, any response (as always, in the defensive position) is difficult as well as tedious, requiring a taking apart of the text in a line-by-line fashion (not a task for the faint of heart, high of blood pressure, weak of stomach, or left of center). In the latter, response of the clear, well-aimed sort is equally difficult (again, where to start?) in that to argue against her views on feminism is to take them on (the views as well as the unnamed feminists) in a piecemeal fashion, and to accede from the outset that there may be some feminists who are "guilty" of the "crimes" of which Paglia accuses them (just as there may be some feminists who actually share Paglia's politics). In either case, she "wins."

Paglia thus positions herself as the one who is honest and forthright in the game. She is the holder of all the cards, the source of parody, and the teller of truth: "First of all, you have to realize that I am playing a game. My remarks about lesbians are my form of guerrilla warfare. It is a criticism that comes from within, because for most of my life I have identified myself as a lesbian, so there is a lot of parody in what I'm saying." [10] *First of all,* the very notion of the game, as well as this game-playing posture, oddly, even paradoxically, reverberating a kind of "ludic postmodernist" [11] paradigm—a position that she of course intends to controvert in *Sexual Personae*—reveals a major problem in Paglia's stance.

In the description of her multilayered, self-defined sexuality, as well as in her own adoption of an overtly "male" position, Paglia allows for herself the "play," both (with)in and (with)out, which she denies to other women, who are "physically and psychologically . . . serenely self-contained. They may choose to achieve, but they do not need it," for neither women nor men may "escape from the biologic chains that bind us"; "the radical disjunction between the sexes . . . begins and ends in the body":[12] "Women know they're women, because they have their period. . . . They don't have to prove they're women. . . . Women are content with things as they are. Women lack the violent aggression to change, to revolutionize. They don't like causing pain. They are happy when the people around them are happy; otherwise, they are emotionally parched."[13] Of course women always remain "they": Paglia separates herself from her own "biologic chains," the "natural" position of "woman" just as she separates herself from "other" feminists and lesbians. And given women's "content" nature, how then would Paglia justify her own need to achieve, her "male" position? An advanced level of testosterone? This contradiction between the humanist epistemology of difference to which Paglia subscribes in *Sexual Personae* and the ludic postmodern articulation of difference to which she adheres in self-descriptions in various interviews of course generates the very controversy for which Paglia aims, and is analogous to her dualistic within-and-outside-of-"lesbian" stance; in my opinion, these splittings account for much of the attention given to her work, especially by those involved in lesbian studies.

The questions of how to signify "lesbian" or what constitutes a lesbian (con)text have, since the publication of Adrienne Rich's landmark essay, continued to be debated within lesbian studies in the work of Bonnie Zimmerman, Marilyn Farwell, Deborah McDowell, Barbara Smith, and others. It is this "playing" of the debate, of the indeterminacy of "lesbian," and thus of what remains the gap between identity politics and poststructuralist critiques of the stability and "naturalness" of any subject position which fuels Paglia's odd popularity. It may be that in some ways, by essentializing nature, reading it as a "pure" space aside from/outside of the discourses which construct our readings of it, and by extension reading sex (as opposed to gender) and thus *sex*uality in similarly essentializing ways, Paglia's work may be attractive to those who, fearing the poststructuralist denaturalizing of "identity," opt for simplistic either/or politics. To latch onto Paglia is, then, on the one hand to deny that "there is no such thing as woman," and on the other hand to wonder how it is that Paglia-the-subject-position is able to construct and reconstruct herself continually at will. The desire to pin her down (metaphorically, of course) and to answer the perhaps unanswerable questions that surround our constructed notions of sexuality in a more popular forum is nearly irresistible to an area of study that is given relatively little visibility even within academia. Paglia is perhaps seen by those who continue to interview her as not only a catalyst for a controversy on the Morton Downey, Jr., type show, but also perhaps as an eventual generator of more meaningful dialogue, given her supposed exposure of hidden, silenced voices and lives.

But why do the popular media continue to give Paglia a platform from which to speak, given the ironically homophobic nature of her remarks? Oprah Winfrey has declined to have members of Neo-Nazi, Skinhead, and Klan groups on her show, aware that, to some members of her audience, their remarks may be persuasive; she may be doing more harm than good by allowing them to air their racist views. But Paglia is *not* seen as perpetuating homophobia for precisely the reason that Neo-Nazis *are* seen as racist: Neo-Nazis do not claim to be Jews; Paglia claims a lesbian alliance. This is what continues to make her remarks popularly acceptable. After all, how could a lesbian be homophobic?

And what may be the effects of teaching the works of Camille Paglia, especially to undergraduates? Her statements have found an appreciative audience which needs no augmentation in the classroom. Printing her statements in this essay may be another question, for it is no longer up to "us" to even "give" her a platform from which to speak, since that platform has been and continues to be provided by the hype-machines of the multimedia outlets; Paglia will have a platform as long as we tune in, as long as she is shocking enough to maintain our attention. The bind here is that to heed Teresa Ebert's advice and refuse to ignore Paglia is necessary; to (necessarily) reproduce her words is, again, to buy into her game, to perhaps reproduce, even through critique, the "politics of the outrageous."[14]

The problem with the kind of "outrageous" exposure which Paglia gives to lesbians, especially as far as her interviews are concerned, is also reminiscent of the *Basic Instinct* controversy. The film was picketed by gay and lesbian rights activists for its depiction of lesbians as pathological killers without conscience. On a 1992 *Maury Povich Show* entitled "Lipstick Lesbians," three lesbian guests disagreed about the film's potential danger for and damage to the gay community: two of the women claimed that this was simply the "first step" made by Hollywood to include lesbian characters in starring roles and that they believed that more positive roles should and would follow; the third woman criticized the film's lesbian characters based upon the material conditions of gays and lesbians in this country and within its film industry. How many full-fledged lesbian characters do we see in popular films grossing well over $100 million, as *Basic Instinct* has, as opposed to the X-rated, late-night cable variety (that inevitably depicts lesbianism as a mere stepping-stone to a full-fledged heterosexual relationship anyway)? And how are the few gay or lesbian characters that we do see simply reproducing the rampant homophobia with which gays and lesbians are faced every day? How exactly can we call *Basic Instinct* or Paglia's remarks "subversive" in terms of the ways in which they depict female homoeroticism? What dominant discourses about female-to-female sexuality are being disrupted? Are we not witnessing the further pathologizing of the already (overly) pathologized?

By employing Freud unproblematically to examine sexual personae, Paglia reaffirms this pathologization of other-than-"standard"-heterosexuality: lesbians are seen by her as somehow stunted, having failed to reach the space/place of bisexual desire (which appears to be nothing more than the convenient appropriation of heterosexual structures, made desirable). Her position thus includes an inherent homophobic element. As Freud "reads" dreams in order to expose the repressed desires of his patients, Paglia "reads" literature in *Sexual Personae* to expose the "truth"—that Dickinson "is the female Sade," for instance, since "her poems are the prison dreams of a self-incarcerated, sadomasochistic imaginist" (624), or that "Christabel is Coleridge dreaming aloud" (341). A little biographical information goes a long way with Paglia-the-Freudian psychoanalyst: her readings of Dickinson, Coleridge, and others confuse narrative voice with the subject position we call "author"; she sees "self-projection" in the poetic voice (643) in much the same way as Freud constructs Dora's narrative(s) for her, filling in gaps to produce his own "truth." The core of Dora's "trouble," according to Freud, is her repressed desire for Frau K.; homosexuality is the basis of her neurosis, what has made her "ill." And what is attractive to Paglia about Dickinson and Coleridge (who, like Dora, have become their texts, as the texts become them) is the sexual violence of the images in their poetry: we are to enjoy, as voyeurs into the newly exposed "deviant" mind of the poet, the textual "play" of this projection outside of the self, finally given a glimpse of the "real" Dickinson or Coleridge, believing that we can reach into their minds in a way that biography and/or history will not allow. For Paglia's insights, as Freud's, position themselves as transhistorical, never the products of particular historical moments, but "true" now and forever, and thus *Sexual Personae,* which posits itself as historically based from the outset—"Art and Decadence from Nefertiti to Emily Dickinson"—is, in spite of the inclusion of "data," "facts," a text which simultaneously *denies* historically based constructions.

Homosexuality is rooted in the (biologically linked) psyche, according to both Paglia's Freud and Paglia herself. (Of course, Paglia fails to note that Freud's texts have been deployed, by the very poststructuralists she claims to oppose, to counter the kind of essentialist use which Paglia makes of those texts.) Paglia claims, for instance, that male homosexuality is based upon one of two scenarios: either the male identifies "with the mother, perceived as a goddess," or turns away "from the mother" which leads to a "disdain" for "femaleness and esteems perfected masculinity." And, as noted above, lesbianism is based upon a desire for a "blissful union with the mother" which is "regressive."[15] All of this is, of course, based upon an outmoded conception/construction of "mother" and employs the equally outdated foundation of (nuclear) "family" to establish a theoretical framework. All we can hope, I suppose, is that Paglia's work may function in some arenas to show the inadequacy of such uses of the Freudian models of desire and to point out the flaws in these unproblematized models by the very pushing of those theories to such an absurd extent.

Paglia further pathologizes lesbians by directing "guerrilla warfare" against a largely closeted, certainly marginalized group, a move which reverberates a kind of oppression in its intent, even coming from "within" as she claims. For Paglia constantly plays on the "lines," the boundaries between positions which she adopts and discards at will, verbally, a strategy which makes the material finally meaningless. Thus, Paglia taunts us all—she is a nonacademic academic, a nonfeminist feminist, a female who claims to be a "male," and now a once-lesbian-nonlesbian lesbian, who adopts a position of bisexuality, yet also professes an attraction almost exclusively to straight women and gay men, and thus claims for herself a kind of nonsexual position of sexuality, whining that she hasn't had sex in ages because lesbians are "sexually inert,"[16] that she desires the "virility" of and from men, but refuses to do the "nursing and caretaking and all the stroking you have to do to keep men going from day to day."[17] Paglia sums up her own (non-) position: "I consider myself neither gay nor straight, neither male nor female, and neither human nor animal."[18] Again, her "play," in adopting multiple positions at once from which she claims to speak, is simultaneously nearly inspiring in its range of desires, its seeming inclusion, in one subject, of an incredible "polymorphous perversity," and is at the same time a kind of safe, paradoxically nonsexual position, speaking all and no sexual possibilities and potentialities. Sexuality is made abstract, into mere metaphor. It is no wonder, then, that in Madonna, Paglia sees a "kindred spirit,"[19] another "real" feminist.

Though the release date of the film *Truth or Dare* followed that of the publication of *Sexual Personae,* both texts emerged during the early 1990s amid much discussion of their shock factors, largely because of their discussions/"exposures" of sexualities. Moreover, the former text mirrors the contradiction between Paglia-the-self-constructed subject and the theoretical framework (if we can call it that) for *Sexual Personae.* Both Madonna and Paglia frame their texts/subjectivities around the telling of "truths" about others' sexualities, themselves remaining somewhat nebulous or contradictory, sexually indeterminate. In *Truth or Dare,* Madonna performs an act of autoeroticism on stage to "Like a Virgin," gigglingly "outs" her then-friend, sometime-lesbian Sandra Bernhard, cavorts in bed with her gay male dancers while commenting on their anatomy, insists that she had a sexual relationship with her childhood friend, Maureen McFarland, spars with her then-lover Warren Beatty, performs oral sex on a mineral water bottle, claims that Sean Penn is the "love of her life," playfully bares her breasts for the camera, and lusts for actor Antonio Banderas. Madonna emerges at once as polymorphously perverse, sexually subversive, and yet comfortably heterosexual: Bernhard, McFarland, and the male dancers are those "outed," while Madonna's only overt claim to a homosexual experience is in the safe, distant past and about which she (with help from the camera and director Keshishian) controls the telling. During McFarland's denial of their sexual relationship, the camera cuts more than once to Madonna, who makes statements such as "what a liar!" after having seen the filmed interview, in order to undermine McFarland's statements, to solidify her own truth, or rather her own position in this pseudo-"daring" game of truth that she plays.

It should be noted that Madonna's "game" differs from Paglia's in that the former makes little or no claim herself to be the arbiter among whatever media or knowledges may take her as an object of examination/critique, whereas Paglia has clearly limited criteria about how the "knowledge" which she produces is read. And *Truth or Dare* foregrounds Madonna's own duplicity and anxiety over self-representation, whereas Paglia's comments always gloss her own duplicity. Still, both Madonna and Paglia produce constructions of sexuality-as-mere-metaphor-for-materiality: like Madonna, Paglia, even in overtly claiming a position of bisexuality, remains sexually indeterminate through her gender-bending and multiple attractions: she refuses to be confined to a label as she confines others—sadomasochist, demon, vampire, feminist. The label of "bisexual" thus becomes inadequate, standing for a kind of (nonsexual) polysexuality. Desire and its effects are hardly material, but made into mere "play," a kind of abstract *textual* eroticism happening elsewhere, once-removed from the physical. As Paglia notes in *Sexual Personae,* the academic "dare" that she constructs as "truth" has become a stand-in for herself, seducing (unwitting) others for her. Thus she actually does to herself here what she does to the literary figures that she discusses (at last no gap, no contradiction): text and author are coequal. Too bad that in her own case the assumptions of neither text nor subject position are ever interrogated or critiqued.

Like Madonna, Paglia lures her reader into her text with the expectation that, between its covers, all will be exposed, overthrown: the history of visual arts and literature (that is, "high art") will be overthrown, exposing their inherent decadence, their sexual subversions. Yet "high" art remains so, and the most decadent thing about Paglia's *Sexual Personae* and the text that is Paglia is the lack of an analytical and/or self-critical basis (under the guise of such a foundation); like Madonna and

Freud, Paglia posits herself as *teller* of truth, closeting her position as *framer*, maker of truth for all others except herself.

And the "truth" that Paglia tells is merely a negative deployment of "lesbian": she has certainly helped to "out" the image to the public, but in doing so she has, like Clinton (in backing down on his proposal to allow gays and lesbians in the military to be open about their sexualities without fear of reprisal), done much more damage than any possible good. These seemingly open-minded discourses did not and will not subvert, nor were they *subverted by*, on the surface, dominant ideologies. The undermining of their own "subversive" strategies comes from the speakers, from Paglia and then Clinton, and now others who are complicit in perpetuating these discourses, who pretend a sympathy or alliance; the undermining from "within" means that the images and definitions that are popularly disseminated are doubly damaging. And the cost of such visibility in this historical moment may be too high a price to pay for those actually living on the margins and those attempting to effect political change and to dismantle dominant discourses about sexuality.

NOTES

1. Camille Paglia, *Sex, Art, and American Culture* (New York: Vintage Books, 1992), xii.

2. Paglia, *American Culture*, 23.

3. Ibid., 24.

4. Judith Butler, "Imitation and Gender Insubordination," in *Inside/Out* (London: Routledge, 1991), 13–14.

5. Butler, 14.

6. Susie Bright, "Girl Talk: Susie Bright Undresses Camille Paglia," *NYQ* (10 November 1991): 26–28.

7. Ruby Rich, "Top Girl," *Village Voice* (8 October 1991): 31.

8. Francesca Stanfill, "Woman Warrior: Sexual Philosopher Camille Paglia Jousts with the Politically Correct," *New York* (4 March 1991): 28.

9. Teresa Ebert, "The Politics of the Outrageous," *Women's Review of Books* (October 1991): 12.

10. Bright, "Girl Talk," 26.

11. See Teresa Ebert, "The Difference of Postmodern Feminism," *College English* 53 (1991): 886–904.

12. Camille Paglia, *Sexual Personae: Art and Decadence from Nefertiti to Emily Dickinson* (New Haven: Yale University Press, 1990), 19–21.

13. Stanfill, 28.
14. Ebert, "Outrageous," 12.
15. Paglia, *American Culture*, 23–24.
16. Susie Bright, "Undressing Camille," *Out/Look* (Spring 1992): 9.
17. Bright, "Girl Talk," 27.
18. Stanfill, 27.
19. Ibid., 23.

EIGHT

Taking on the Phallus

COLLEEN LAMOS

The dildo has long been a source of titillation and embarrassment. The stuff of off-color jokes often told by men at the expense of intellectual or "masculine" women, the dildo has circulated within popular culture, satiric tales, and subliterary, pornographic genres in the West since at least the seventeenth century.[1] The use of dildos has been proscribed in various ecclesiastical codes, while commercial possession of dildos is illegal in some states.[2] Despite its bad reputation, especially its association with misogynistic and homophobic representations of women, the dildo raises important, although disconcerting, questions about lesbian sexuality and its relation to heterosexuality in general and to the phallus in particular.

My aim in this essay is twofold. First, I will survey the role of the dildo in contemporary lesbian discourse. Historically the scandal of lesbian sexuality, dildos have lately become a popular topic in lesbian sex advice manuals and in discussions of lesbian sexual practices. The depiction of dildos in lesbian pornography is increasingly common, and the sale of dildos in shops and mail-order catalogues that serve lesbians has grown enormously.[3] The result has been an explosive controversy over the meaning of the dildo and the nature of lesbianism; Sheila Jeffreys, for instance, recently complained of the "onslaught of dildos in lesbian sex magazines" and the attendant commodification of lesbian sex.[4] This debate has far-reaching implications for lesbian and gay theory in general.

My second aim is thus to examine the dildo in terms of Judith Butler's groundbreaking work in *Gender Trouble* and *Bodies That Matter*. The

dildo exemplifies her concept of lesbian sexuality as a "subversive repetition" of heterosexual norms, for the dildo both imitates and undercuts
the phallicism of the penis, discrediting phallic power while simultaneously, and paradoxically, assuming such power for itself. Applying
Butler's theoretical model, and drawing on post-Lacanian feminist psychoanalysis, I argue that the dildo undermines the authority of the penis,
demystifying the latter's phallicism through its simulation of the penis.
However, the dildo also points to an apparent problem with Butler's
enterprise, which relies upon the pragmatic assumption of an identifiable
lesbian sexuality in contrast to heterosexuality, while calling into question that assumption on a theoretical level. I will try to show that
"lesbian" sexual identity is ironized precisely within contexts and discourses that are designated as "lesbian." Although lesbian sex advice
manuals at times deny the dildo's phallicism or try to naturalize it as
somehow feminine, I claim instead that the dildo opens up the possibility
of sexual practices beyond the limits of conventional gender (male/
female) and sexual (hetero/homosexual) identities.

The long-standing association of lesbian sexuality with the dildo
has typically reinforced the belief that female same-sex relations ape
heterosexual roles, albeit in a pathetic, degraded, or even sexually provocative fashion. Yet, as Butler has argued, the notion of lesbianism as a
"bad copy" of heterosexuality may be critically reworked in order to
overturn the idea that heterosexuality is the natural origin from which
homosexuality is perversely derived. According to Butler, "the parodic
replication and resignification of heterosexual constructs within nonheterosexual frames brings into relief the utterly constructed status of
the so-called original." [5] Such a resignification mimes or re-cites sexual
norms and thus exposes the ways in which heterosexuality is continually
performed. Because these norms derive their authority from repeated,
regulated enactments, their staged repetition in homosexual contexts
effectively deauthorizes them.

How can the dildo—the butt of homophobic humor and fodder for
heterosexual pornography—be recast from a fake penis to a parody of
the penis's phallic pretensions? To answer this question, I will examine
contemporary lesbian sex advice manuals, which include reports of actual lesbian sexual practices, as well as contemporary pornography produced by and for lesbians, although not exclusively consumed by them.
These popular discourses shed light on the empirical contingencies of

Butler's theory. Her claims for the subversive effects of parodic imitations of heterosexual norms depend upon those imitations being received as such by particular audiences. In short, specific contexts of interpretation are crucial for Butler's argument to work. We need to ask: When, where, why, how, and for whom is the repetition of a sexual norm subversive instead of self-validating? The effects of a performative repetition cannot be determined in advance, and any particular performance has multivalent effects.

Partly in response to questions such as these, Butler has shifted the emphasis in her recent work. Instead of distinguishing between straight norms and their queer parodies, she stresses the fact that heterosexuality is performatively constructed through constant, albeit failed, imitations of its own gender and sexual ideals. Homosexual (per)versions of those ideals merely make explicit their performative enactment.[6] Nevertheless, the displaced citation of heterosexual practices in nonheterosexual contexts again raises the problem of the determinacy of straight and gay contexts, and of heterosexuality and homosexuality in general. Is it possible to demarcate such contexts and to draw conclusions regarding the functions of a practice within them, such as the use of dildos, when the force of Butler's logic is that such demarcations are also undermined by the same performances that constitute them? In other words, can a clear distinction be drawn pragmatically between heterosexual and homosexual contexts, while arguing that these two domains are in theory mutually constitutive of each other? This question confronts the inevitable dilemma of a lesbian and gay theory that critiques the foundational division between heterosexuality and homosexuality. The dildo poses this dilemma in an especially useful way because the dildo blurs the boundary between heterosexuality and homosexuality, while its interpretation is highly variable and context-specific. By examining the significance of the dildo within indicatively lesbian contexts, I hope to sharpen the question not only of what lesbians do in bed, but of who lesbians supposedly are.

The meaning of the dildo in popular lesbian discourse centers on three related issues: (1) as an artificial commodity or prosthesis, the dildo implicitly denies the notion of a "natural" lesbian sexuality or of sexual desire springing "naturally" from gendered bodies; (2) as a fetish object, the dildo is aligned with other fetishistic practices, such as sadomasochism; (3) as an assertion of male identification, the dildo participates in butch/femme sexual styles. The dildo appropriates the symbolic power with which the penis has traditionally been endowed and transfers it onto a nonanatomical, commercially manufactured part. Moreover, the overt artificiality of the dildo reflexively denaturalizes the penis-as-phallus, revealing the penis as only one among many possible phallic symbols. Butler argues, "the more various . . . the anatomical (and non-anatomical) occasions for its symbolization, the more unstable [the phallus] becomes" (*Bodies* 90). As a fetish in the psychoanalytic sense, the dildo takes the place of or cites the phallus, thereby demonstrating its psychic transitivity. Because the dildo is morphologically similar to the penis, it both reiterates the identification of the penis with the phallus and also displaces the penis-as-phallus in a double gesture that ambivalently endorses and discredits phallocentrism. This equivocal movement of the dildo accounts for its controversial status in current lesbian discourse. Yet, by alienating the phallus from the penis, and by claiming phallic power for itself, the dildo puts the phallus into circulation as a continually displaced signifier. Finally, because it is an imaginary penis, the dildo foregrounds the imaginary construction of body parts, natural or prosthetic, including the penis.[7] The masculine identification implied by the dildo is therefore not a betrayal of a woman's essential femininity; instead, the dildo and related butch/femme sexual practices open up multiple identificatory possibilities foreclosed by our culture's gender norms.

The dildo appears to confirm the popular belief that lesbians imitate and want to be men, a view stated famously and influentially by Havelock Ellis, the turn-of-the-century sexologist who asserted with confidence that, "in [female] homosexuality, the use of an artificial penis is by no means uncommon and [is] very widespread."[8] It is thus unsurprising that the dildo was decried by many lesbian feminists in the 1970s and 1980s as a straight male fantasy, a myth contrived by jealous men who could not imagine two women sexually satisfying each other, or else disavowed as a retrograde, male-identified practice stemming from false consciousness or penis envy. Like the butch lesbian, it was relegated to the benighted, prefeminist past, the product of outdated notions of sexual inversion. Echoing the orthodox feminist view, Mariana Valverde believes that "dildoes . . . are virtually unknown among lesbians," despite their presence in male pornography where "lesbians are depicted with penis-substitutes, presumably so that the male reader can imagine himself replacing the dildo by the 'real' thing."[9] Likewise, Sheila Jeffreys claims that "the use of dildos" among lesbians is "rare" although it "has always been a common motif of men's sexual fantasies about" them.[10] But do lesbians really use dildos, and if they do, are they really lesbians? The 1979 *Gay Report* by Karla Jay and Allen Young, which surveyed 1,000 lesbians, concluded that "regular use of the strap-on dildo was almost nonexistent."[11] In their 1978 study of lesbian and gay sexual practices, sponsored by the Kinsey Institute, Bell and Weinberg make no mention of dildos at all.

More recent lesbian sex advice manuals exhibit a tolerant if ambivalent attitude toward dildos. An informal survey conducted by JoAnn Loulan in the mid-1980s reported that 10 percent of lesbians use dildos,[12] yet in her best-selling advice manual Loulan seems uncomfortable with them, or at least with the term: "Dildo. Yuck. Can't we find another word? How about Agnes of Goddess? Fortunately, we now have at our disposal dildoes that no longer look like penises. . . . We now have made things that fit into all kinds of orifices . . . and come in all sorts of colors and shapes" (98). Like Sophie Schmuckler who "tried to make this desire [for a dildo] ok by thinking that if [her lover] really did have a penis it would be quite natural just hanging there with her clit and cunt," and that "it would be very friendly and for both of our pleasure,"[13] Loulan tries to feel good about vaginal penetration by naturalizing it as a lesbian act. "Some lesbians think penetration is a heterosexual activity. . . . Personally, I enjoy having people explore my vagina. There's nothing heterosexual about that" (98). Loulan's uneasiness mounts as the difference between heterosex and lesbian sex becomes less and less clear. Turning to the topic of strap-on dildos, not just vibrators, Loulan offers a more ample defense of sexual pleasure:

> Some people say, "Now that's really male-identified." I say, why not? Why should men be the only ones who get to put something in a woman's vagina and still keep two hands free? I think it's wonderful because it gives you more opportunities to feel her up. What else is wonderful about you and your partner both having vaginas is that you can take turns wearing the harness. (99)

Loulan is quick to seize on the logistical possibilities afforded by the dildo, although the two-hands-free argument may seem like an endorsement of the missionary position for lesbians. Moreover, by claiming an equality of sexual relations achieved by exchanging not just the dildo but the harness, so that both partners can "take turns" being "male-identified," Loulan assimilates the dildo to the egalitarian ideals of lesbian feminism.

Since Loulan published her equivocal affirmation of the dildo in 1987, lesbian popular culture in the United States has undergone a veritable sexual revolution, motivated in part by growing alliances between lesbians and gay men within a resurgent gay rights movement. Rapidly changing lesbian sexual practices include what Jeffreys calls an "avalanche of dildos" (29). The rise of the dildo in contemporary lesbian sexual representation and practice is evident in the pages of *On Our Backs,* a popular lesbian pornographic magazine, and in the substantial increase in the sale of dildos by shops that serve a lesbian clientele. This phenomenon, like the return of butch/femme sexual styles, seems at first blush atavistic, a regression to precisely those gender roles that feminism has tried to overcome. Nevertheless, the writers of lesbian pornography, sex guides, and mail-order catalogues stress in various ways that the dildo really isn't what it looks like and, in some cases, no longer looks like what it is.

Dell Williams, the owner ("gardenkeeper") of Eve's Garden, a sex toy store that caters to women, explains to the readers of her mail-order catalogue that "we don't think of dildos as imitation penises. . . . They're sexual accessories. Not substitutes." [14] Williams calls them "vaginal massagers" instead, which are marketed in a variety of shapes dubbed "The Dolphin," "The Whale," and "Lilith," and which, she explains, are also useful for exercising vaginal muscles. The more daring among the lesbian avant-garde are willing to admit, like Celeste West, that, while "held for years to be politically incorrect by feminists as the embodiment of intrinsic maleness, dildoes have slipped from the taboo charts, approaching Lesbian mainstream." [15] But for West, the author of *A Lesbian Love Advisor,* the question remains, "is the dildo a penis substitute, or is it the other way around? As a rule of thumb, . . . many Lesbians do not use dildoes or even an organic version like carrots" (47). West's sly sexual reference to the thumb, fitting hand-in-glove with the carrot as the image of an "organic" dildo, inadvertently and anxiously implies that dildos are at bottom unnatural.

Pat Califia, the queen of lesbian s/m, is cautious on the subject of dildos, "probably the most taboo sex toys a lesbian could consider using. Relatively few lesbians have ever seen a dildo." [16] The account of dildos in her sex advice manual is rife with contradictions that center on the crucial issue of the dildo's resemblance to the penis. Introducing the matter by distinguishing the use of dildos by lesbians from their representation in male sex fantasies, she claims, remarkably, that, because "the dildoes available in sex shops are usually phallic in appearance, . . . *many lesbians prefer to carve or cast their own*" (50–51, emphasis mine). Like West, Califia's uneasiness with the dildo's phallicism and blatant artificiality leads her to the highly questionable assertion that a uniquely female, noncommercial, "organic version" exists—the supposedly homemade, nonphallic dildo. She continues:

> A real lesbian who wants to play with a dildo has motives that would be incomprehensible to the makers of commercial erotica or to clinical psychologists. . . . She knows that women don't need men to be sexual. . . . It is, after all, just a piece of plastic. Whatever symbolic meaning it has is assigned by our culture. (51)

To rescue the dildo from the hands of (male) capitalists and psychologists, Califia naturalizes the "real lesbian" as one who, even if she uses a plastic dildo, remains sexually autonomous, uncorrupted by its phallic symbolism. Having dismissed those pesky, irrelevant cultural meanings, she states, like Loulan, that strap-on dildos are advantageous because "they leave the hands free to wander" (51). Again, the free, groping hands suggest the sexual—one might say phallic—significance of the hand within the lesbian erotic imaginary.

Subsequent to *Sapphistry,* Califia has published highly successful commercial erotica that depends for its sizzle on the dildo's cultural symbolism, including a collection of short fiction, *Macho Sluts.* The latter contains her famous story, "The Calyx of Isis," which features a butch dyke named Michael, dressed as a Marine Corps officer, who packs a dildo which she compels the masochistic heroine to suck. Yet in *Sapphistry,* as elsewhere, Califia's defensive, "bad girl" stance and the incoherence of her account seem motivated by the suspicion that lesbians who use dildos are, at bottom, aping heterosexuality. "Women who like vaginal penetration may feel ambivalent about it and wonder if it isn't 'sort of heterosexual.' Any technique that two women use to arouse and please one another is a *lesbian* technique" (51). If Califia distinguishes between lesbian sexuality and heterosexuality on the basis of the gender of the partners involved, she is only able to do so by disingenuously denying the dildo's phallicism.

Susie Bright, by contrast, is refreshingly candid on the subject in *Susie Sexpert's Lesbian Sex World,* a collection of essays from her "Toys For Us" column appearing in *On Our Backs* during the late 1980s. Bright neither assimilates dildos to orthodox feminist norms nor denies their cultural significance; in fact, she brazenly jokes that, since "dildos are among the few pieces of sexual turf historically associated with dykes," they may as well use them.[17] Unconcerned with defining what real lesbians (or real heterosexuals) do, Bright discusses sexual acts and pleasures detached from their gender assignments; "fucking knows no gender" any more than kissing does (19). Her description of dildos is in keeping with her expansive vision of sexuality as a realm of opportunities ranging beyond the clitoris and the vagina, including the felicitous introduction of artificial devices, and aiming ultimately at individual rather than coupled pleasure.

> A dildo can be a succulent squash or a tender mold of silicon. Technically, it is any device you use for the pleasure of vaginal or anal penetration. . . . [P]enises can only be compared to dildos in the sense that they take up space. . . . [T]he most glaring contrast is that the dildo is at your service; it knows no desire other than your own or your partner's. (18–19)

Bright emphasizes that "a dildo is a sexual plaything; it is not attached to a human body who has to live with it till death" (30). In her account, the dildo is pleasurable precisely because it is a toy.

Bright's stress on the unnaturalness of the dildo goes hand-in-hand with the implication throughout her work that female sexuality is not natural either. In her recent book, *Susie Bright's Sexual Reality,* she celebrates the multiplicity of practices and fantasies opened up by the very commerce that Califia decries. Alluding to Burger King's advertising slogan and so underscoring the dildo as a commodity (she includes a "Pocket Dildo Guide" and a guide to "Specialty Dildos" for the consumer), Bright writes, "Fucking feels good—that is the basic premise of dildo popularity—and when it comes to penetration, why NOT have it your way? Using a dildo allows lovers to get it on in any shape, size, texture, or color" (29).

Bright's work signals a new, postmodern practice of "lesbian" sexuality that does not attempt to distinguish between lesbian and nonlesbian sexuality, much less between normative and taboo lesbian sex behaviors.[18] Instead, she explores the possibilities of practices beyond the anchors of secure sexual (heterosexual/homosexual) and gender (male/female) identities. In this sense, she offers a hands-on, fully contextual application of Butler's theories. The dildo is a key term in Bright's practical deconstruction of sexual norms.

As we have seen in the sex advice manuals by Loulan, Califia, and Bright, the dildo is threatening and fascinating because it transgresses the boundary between woman-identified lesbianism and male-identified or cross-gendered practices. Indeed, many commentators draw the line separating relatively "normal" lesbian sexuality and pseudo-heterosexual, "perverse" lesbian behavior on the distinction between the vibrator and the dildo.[19] The vibrator is widely recommended to help women, straight and gay alike, to achieve orgasm through clitoral stimulation and comes with the endorsement of sex therapists who encourage the lonely to satisfy themselves. The close association of the vibrator with solitary pleasures and its reputation as a sexual aid imply that, while it does not necessarily involve another partner (and hence perverse sexual techniques), it is not supposed to supplant a human lover, at least ideologically.

The dildo, however, is another story. It is not just a nonhumming vibrator. Designed not for clitoral stimulation but for penetration, the dildo—worst of all—is meant to be strapped on and inserted. While both vibrators and dildos are often vaguely penile in shape, there is not much else one can do with a dildo besides put it in an orifice. In short, its purpose is solely perverse, and, when strapped on, this "mechanical device" supplants, visually and tactilely, the flesh-and-blood male member. Although the dildo gets all the attention—even in this essay—in a sense it is the harness that is decisive. Doubtless the crucial difference between dildos and vibrators is that the former can be attached to the wearer's body, strapped on as though it were a prosthetic penis. If the hand-held dildo or vibrator is a substitute for a "real man," the woman with the strap-on dildo is herself replacing the man; she becomes the man. In this sense, the anxiety of most lesbian sex advisors and academic theorists that the dildo is a "false penis" whose use in actual or represented lesbian sexual activity reduces the latter to "faked heterosexuality," as Judith Roof argues regarding the dildo scene in Anaïs Nin's

Henry and June, is well founded.[20] The dildo denies what Roof terms the "authenticity" of a purely female homosexuality, yet it also mocks the authenticity of the heterosexuality that it simulates.

The significance of the dildo is the manner in which it questions the nature of sexual difference, a difference that, in Jacques Lacan's memorable phrase, turns upon the difference between "being and . . . having" the phallus.[21] According to Lacan, relations between the sexes are structured by their differential relation to the phallus, a notably slippery term that, Lacan asserts, does not refer to an "organ" but is a "privileged signifier" of the alienation of desire in language (79–80). Lacan's disclaimer notwithstanding, Kaja Silverman has argued that the phallus "cannot . . . be rigorously distinguished from the penis";[22] indeed, the Lacanian phallus is, at various moments in his work, "the image of the penis," the symbol of castration, and the paternal metaphor or Name-of-the-Father. Because the penis and the phallus are inextricably entangled, for man to "have" the phallus is to possess the penis, despite his symbolic castration, while for woman to "be" the phallus is to be posited as the "Other," the mystified object of man's fantasy and the truth of his desire, despite (and because of) her lack of a penis.

Lacan's formulation is a revision of Freud's previous articulation of the normative positions of male and female in relation to the penis. As Elizabeth Grosz explains, the heterosexual, narcissistic, feminine woman, faced with the "fact" of her castration, is said by Freud to compensate for that fact, and thus at least partially to accept it, by "phallaciz[ing] her whole body, treating it as if it were the phallus."[23] According to Freud, women's "physical vanity" and "their [sensual] charms" are "a late compensation for their original sexual inferiority," or lack of a penis.[24] "Becoming a woman"—making oneself into the seductive, beautiful, and passive object of another's desire—is tantamount to "becoming the phallus." In truth, women can no more transform themselves into the phallus than men can possess it, and the vain belief that the man has the phallus by virtue of having the penis is only evidence of what Jane Gallop calls the pervasive and, in our society, "inevitable confusion between penis and phallus."[25] In orthodox Lacanian terms, the phallus is beyond gender, as the "attribute of power" (127); yet, according to Gallop, "*phallus* is always a reference to *penis*," and as a signifier is ineluctably dependent for its meaning and power upon its empirical reference to the penis, especially within a cultural "structure in which it seems reasonable that men have power and women do not" (127–28). If phallic potency boils down to the question of who has the penis, the dildo is a direct challenge to male possession of that instrument of authority. Turning the screw of interpretation further, the dildo exposes the penis as a deceptive, nonidentical double of the phallus—for the phallus is no more the "image of the penis" than of any other object so designated—and is thus an affront to our regime of sexual difference governed by the supposed identity between penis and phallus.

There is perhaps no more shameless instance of women's so-called penis envy than putting on the dildo. A dildo surely confirms the penis as the sign of masculine (phallic) power, and the woman who straps on a dildo thereby assumes that power, investing it as a fetish. Yet by taking it on, or taking possession of what she by rights does not or is not supposed to have, she openly challenges male proprietorship of the phallus, reducing it to only a dildo, capable of substitution and exchange—indeed, a commodity on sale for forty-nine dollars. The woman with the strap-on dildo thus at once "takes on" or defies male authority in its most obvious embodiment and "takes on" through identification the phallic symbol which will render her dildo as merely a prosthesis, never the "real thing," and hence her body as castrated.

The simultaneous avowal and disavowal of sexual difference inherent in the dildo renders it a fetish in the psychoanalytic sense. According to Freud, the fetishist disavows maternal castration. This denial contains an implicit affirmation—the fetishist "knows" the mother is castrated—so that the fetish constitutes an ambivalent, double utterance: on the one hand, that "woman doesn't have the phallus," and, on the other hand, that "woman does (or ought to) have the phallus."[26] The fetish object thus *implies* the mother's castration even as it *denies* her castration by acting as a substitute for the penis. Disavowing castration, the woman who straps on the phallic dildo fetishizes it—it becomes her phallus—but also thereby detaches the phallus from the penis. The dildo may be said to mark the difference between the phallus and the penis. But, as we know, the phallus and the penis are continually mistaken for each other, and so the dildo can at any moment be taken (on) either as a faithful substitute for the penis or as a parodic mime of its phallic pretensions. Like the fetish object in general, the dildo simultaneously acknowledges and rejects the equivalence of penis and phallus, paradoxically insisting upon the distinction between the two *at the same moment* that it proclaims or displays its resemblance to the penis as the "prototype of the fetish."

Strapping on a dildo could therefore be seen as *putting on the phallus* in several different ways: (1) In perhaps the most common sense, one puts on—and takes on—the dildo as an imitation penis, and thereby assumes or adopts or acquires the latter's phallic power. Here, dildo = (fake) penis = phallus. (2) When one "puts on" something, one wears it like a dress or makeup. The dildo is in this sense an article of clothing or costume, even of masquerade; a woman putting on a dildo is thus crossdressing in butch drag. (3) Finally, the dildo is a "put on," a joke, a fake taken not as the genuine article but precisely *as* an imitation; the joke here is on the penis, with its phallic aspirations.

The paradoxical double or triple gesture of the dildo parallels and repeats the paradox concerning gender difference that has troubled feminism in recent years, and that typically arises in debates between essentialists and social constructionists. This dilemma is the apparent necessity for feminists to insist upon gender difference or upon the specificity of "woman" in order to overthrow a system of gender oppression carried out on the basis of that difference—to the end, finally, of making that difference indifferent. The dildo rides on the horns of this dilemma, for it simultaneously affirms gender difference, marked by the phallus, and asserts the mutability and contingency of that difference. The scandal of the dildo, for feminists, is that it appears to collapse lesbianism into heterosexuality, while less obviously but no less portentously threatening to reduce the penis to a sex toy.

In a sense, the dildo confirms (in a reverse fashion) the widely shared feminist view that sexuality is determined by gender. Catharine MacKinnon's argument is representative: "If heterosexuality is the dominant gendered form of sexuality in a society where gender oppresses women through sex, sexuality and heterosexuality are essentially the same thing. This does not erase homosexuality, it merely means that sexuality in that form may be no less gendered."[27] Reiterating the now-familiar ideas of Luce Irigaray, Adrienne Rich, and others, this argument has had as one of its consequences the search for a specifically female homosexuality and a female subjectivity existing ambiguously, in Teresa de Lauretis's words, "on the margins of hegemonic discourses."[28] If lesbians are considered real women inasmuch as they refuse compulsory heterosexuality and identify wholly with women, then dildo-wearers are traitors to their gender. What the dildo enables us to consider is a gendered sexuality that is unfaithful to "woman," that betrays rather than embraces femininity, and that parodies while identifying with masculinity. Indeed, it confronts—and affronts—phallicism on its own turf. These problems in conceptualizing lesbian sexual practice also arise within the realm of lesbian sexual identity, specifically, within lesbian pornography.

A clear representation of the dildo's paradoxical avowal and disavowal of gender difference is a recurring advertisement in *On Our Backs*, the leading lesbian pornographic magazine in the United States, which frequently carries stories about and photographs of dildos as well as advertisements for them.[29] This particular ad features a photograph of two dildos (see Figure 8.1). One, placed on the left and slightly higher, is a life-like representation of a penis, complete with silicon rubber veins, arching upward in a full erection. The dildo on the right, slightly lower and a bit further back, is a curvaceous cylinder vaguely resembling a feminine figure. The latter may also be viewed as a finger and thus aligned with an eroticism of the hand. In the photograph, its edges are blurred, whereas the outline of the penile dildo is sharply defined. Both are resting on a platform in back of a round mirror angled toward the viewer. Above the photo is the inscription, "sabi: elegant simplicity, striving for something closer to nature than nature itself." Which one, you ask, is "closer to nature"? The ad suggests that the dildos it sells are more natural than real penises, the representation thus surpassing the putative original, but the representation is itself doubled into butch and femme models, reflecting the gendered "nature" it has allegedly surpassed. The arrangement of the two dildos gives priority to the anatomically correct model, while the femme version assures the viewer that she can enjoy penetration without explicit phallicism. The mirror in the lower foreground situates the viewer as both subject and object of the desire represented by the dildo; the appropriating gaze of the buyer is reflected back to her, implying her role as also the recipient of the dildo. Viewing the advertisement, she passes back and forth between both positions. In short, the advertisement naturalizes the dildo through appeals to gender difference as well as through advertising clichés borrowed from Madison Avenue (for example, "elegant simplicity"); but by placing the spectator in the oscillating role of subject and object of desire, the advertisement unsettles the naturalness it promotes.

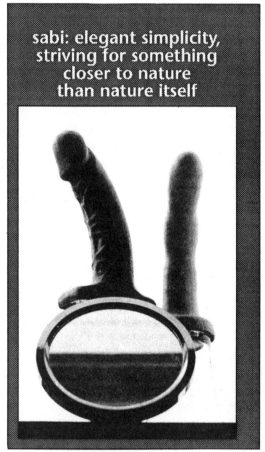

Consumers can choose between anatomically correct or digitlike dildos. Courtesy of Gosnell B. Duncan and Scorpio Novelty Products, Inc.

On Our Backs is laced with stories and photos that play out the doubleness of the dildo as a "put-on" of the phallus. Because these stories often situate their readers in a dual identification as both the desiring subject and the desired object—as both the lover and the beloved—the reader's position in these stories mirrors the complexity of their heroines' similarly doubled positions. "Packin' It" by Stud Edda from the March/April 1991 issue is typical of the dildo narrative.[30] Presented as a true-life story with all the fictional conventions of the genre, "Packin' It" opens with the heroine, rejected by a date, returning home to console herself by taking out her dildo, packing it into her pants, and strutting around her empty house admiring the bulge in her crotch. Turned on by this compensatory sense of power as well as by the dildo's friction against her clitoris, Stud strokes the bulge. "Stroked *myself*, as it . . . seemed. And the more I touched my dick, the more my clit grew. . . . The more I touched him/me through my pants, . . . the wetter I got" (15). Throughout the story, Stud's dildo is split into "him/ me" or just "him," whereas her clitoris remains "I" or "my clit." As she masturbates, the dildo articulates the subject/object sexual relation, the dildo becoming her objectified other through which she becomes the subject of her desire. Recalling one of her "dick dreams" in which she imagined having a penis and jacking off, Stud proceeds to unzip her pants, take out the dildo, and strap it into a harness. As she thrusts during her "floor-slapping air-fucking," Stud fantasizes hordes of women vying for favors from her "master dick" (32). So much for the date who spurned her.

At this moment of sexual triumph, when the dildo gives Stud complete power over the fantasied others, the story takes a turn: Stud decides to give "him/me to myself" (32). Having become the object of her own desires, Stud penetrates herself with the dildo and finally comes in "moaning spasms" (32). Her visibly *phallic* "prowess" (Stud's term) makes her *vaginal* pleasure all the more visible, as though her orgasm were a sort of combined "meat shot" and "money shot" of conventional pornography.[31] Now that Stud has discovered the "lone pleasure" she is capable of with the dildo, she can't wait to "try it out on someone else, and let her tell me the same," offering confirmation of her phallic abilities. A mere two days later, she "was proved right. And by a straight gal who was used to 'the real thing,'" Stud brags.

The dildo's relation to "the real thing" is the crux of many of On Our Back's dildo narratives. The dildo calls for proof of its authenticity—as an imitation it needs proving—yet, on the contrary, its power lies precisely in its specularity. The visibly erect dildo is both the sign of and the inducement to pleasure. The advantage of the dildo over the penis is that it is perpetually erect; in Stud's words, "that soft rubber . . . was gonna stay hard for good" (32). It would appear that the drawback of the dildo, and proof of its secondary, derivative status as "only" a simulacrum of the penis, is that the woman with the strap-on cannot feel any sensation in her rubber dildo. Yet this insensitivity permits even greater control and hence heightened phallicism, for the penetrator may remain untouched by the caresses and body of the penetrated.[32] The subject's pleasure is purely speculative, purely porno-graphic; as Linda Williams puts it, hers is "the frenzy of the visible" (35). The heroine of "The Shower," another story from the same issue of *On Our Backs,* describes this pleasure: "It was strangely tantalizing to see her caress that long, unfeeling device with her mouth. . . . As she flicked her agile tongue over the tip, I longed to feel it the way a man does, just for a moment. Still, *the image itself gave me considerable pleasure.*"[33] Such scenes of fellatio performed with a dildo—perhaps the most radical appropriation of phallicism in lesbian pornography—imply that, far from a pale imitation of its penile model, the dildo embodies the phallic ideal far better than a flesh-and-blood penis ever could.[34] The dildo's enactment of the phallic ideal in representations of cocksucking such as this from *On Our Backs* discloses the fact that the phallus is constituted through repeated performances that are always failed approximations of a phantasmatic "real thing."

The pleasure of the visible is what is believed to be difficult if not impossible to render in representations of female sexuality. Williams discusses the effort by hard-core film pornographers to overcome the problem of the "invisibility" of female orgasm within a regime dedicated to the visible confession of the flesh: "The animating male fantasy of hard-core cinema might therefore be described as the (impossible) attempt to capture visually this frenzy of the visible in a female body whose orgasmic excitement can never be objectively measured" (50). Rather than offering scenes of rape or ravishment, however, lesbian pornography confronts this "impossibility" by staging scenes in which female subjects express or confess their desire through various specular means, especially the use of dildos. Indeed, the recent popularity of the dildo may be due to the very spectacle it makes of female desire. For a better understanding of the operations of scopophilia and dildos, I will turn briefly to lesbian film theory.

The analysis of visual pleasure has come a long way since Laura Mulvey's famous 1975 article, which focused on the male gaze (directed toward women) and its two primary avenues of pleasure: fetishistic scopophilia and sadistic voyeurism. Critics of Mulvey have noted that she neglects or at best "masculinizes" the female spectator's pleasures;[35] they have instead concentrated on the pleasures of female identification with the images of women presented on the screen. Without going into the details of these debates, several points are relevant here. As Williams notes, within film theory "activity and passivity have been too vigorously assigned to separate gendered spectator positions with little examination of the mutability of male and female spectators' adoption of the other subject positions" (205). Taking up the question of the female spectator, de Lauretis has argued that "identification in women spectators alternates between . . . the subject and the object of the gaze."[36] Her work in *Alice Doesn't*, which stresses the possibility of alternate identifications by female spectators, seems a more fruitful way to approach the questions posed by the dildo. For the dildo, as the masquerade of phallic desire, implies that gender—those masculine and feminine identifications—is sexually performed.

In a sense, feminists have been saying this all along—that sex is the endorsement of gender—but usually with the assumption that gender is the stable, natural ground and origin of sexuality through which gender is expressed. The dildo and related sexual practices break the supposedly obligatory bond that derives sexuality from gender, so that sexual practices authorize provisional gender roles. In other words, by staging conventional *gender* difference within exchangeable *sexual* positions (for example, butch/femme, top/bottom, penetrator/penetrated), the dildo renders gender an obvious performance. The dildo produces meanings that pivot on gender difference, but without fixing sexuality to mandatorily gendered subject positions.

Most feminist film theorists have focused exclusively on female identification, claiming, like Annette Kuhn, that "seeing the woman in the picture as other . . . is a masculine position,"[37] an objectifying, desiring look that stems from men's fetishistic scopophilia or voyeurism. At bottom, these theorists wish to believe that women cannot be perverts, an assumption shared by Freud and cultural feminists. According to Naomi Schor, "it is an article of faith with Freud and Freudians that *fetishism is the male perversion par excellence*. The traditional psychoanalytic literature on the subject states over and over again that there are no female fetishists; female fetishism is . . . an oxymoron."[38] The dildo gives the lie to this denial of perverse viewing by women. Like the representations of the dildo in lesbian pornography, actual dildo practices permit avenues of pleasure heretofore foreclosed by the assumption that women are consigned to play the role of the object of another's desire. The replay of phallicism in the dildo denaturalizes and renders perverse its subject so that the dildo's representation must continue to provoke uneasiness, especially the uneasiness of the loss of a secure gender identity.

If *lesbian* refers to an open set of sexual practices whose performance constitutes a contingent, nonunified "lesbian" subject, we can view the spectacle of the dildo in "lesbian" sexual representation as a means of disrupting the heterosexist contract that grants sexual agency solely to the penis-as-phallus. However slight its narrative substance, "Packin' It" defies this contract on its own terms by asserting female phallicism. To be sure, the story repackages phallicism as much as or more than it mocks it; likewise, the dildo advertisement from *On Our Backs* reproduces the gendered nature it claims to surpass. Although neither text presents itself as parodic, and although they may not be read as such by their intended audiences, they nevertheless provide the occasion for reconfiguring sexual difference insofar as it is structured by the phallus. Because parody is dependent upon an appropriately ironic interpretation and thus is consigned to an infinite regress of ironic reframing in order to assure its validity, it is pointless to try to constrain the contingency of interpretation by claiming that the dildo, in any of these instances, constitutes a properly parodic repetition of the penis-as-phallus. Rather, these texts and others offer the opportunity of displacing and delegitimating phallic authority and sexual agency at the same moment as they claim such authority and agency for the dildo.

Finally, in this essay I have focused exclusively on the representation of dildos within indicatively lesbian contexts. Although the sex advice manuals and pornographic magazines that I have discussed are produced by and for self-identified lesbians, these texts imply, anxiously or happily, that the dildo renders the concept of lesbian identity in theory untenable and in practice unstable. A short story by Katherine Israel, "Midnight Blue," published in *Frighten the Horses,* a magazine which calls itself "a document of the sexual revolution" and which is aimed at an audience of both men and women of various sexual tastes, demonstrates the multiple directions of sexual desire that circulate through the dildo.[39] The heroine, a lesbian police officer, goes on a date with a fellow male officer named Paul, has torrid heterosexual intercourse with him, discovers afterwards that he is a transvestite woman, and ends up penetrating him/her with her own dildo. Such representations overtly call into question the nature of sexual difference.

The dildo has wide currency in nonlesbian contexts, notably in pornographic books, magazines, and films targeted at a straight male audience. The representation of female same-sex dildo practices within these contexts is generally assumed not to have the subversive effects that I have claimed for such representations within an indicatively lesbian context. On the contrary, the depiction of women engaged in sexual activity with a dildo in male heterosexual pornography is commonly believed to promote the hegemony of phallocentric heterosexuality. However, such representations are titillating because they play with the boundaries of masculine sexual control. To be sure, they almost invariably conclude with the insertion of a "real" penis that reinstates the phallic power that such representations temporarily concede. Rather than condemning straight male pornography for colonizing lesbianism though, we might acknowledge the allure of alterity that it encodes. If male heterosexuality is constituted, as Butler argues, by repeated performances of a phallic ideal to which such performances aspire but inevitably fail, the inclusion of so-called lesbian scenes within male heterosexual fantasy could signify more than just a challenge to be overcome—indeed, could signify the wish for an impossible fulfillment beyond the contingencies of any flesh-and-blood organ. In this sense, the recent appropriation of the dildo within lesbian pornography not only blurs the boundaries between straight male and lesbian sexual fantasy and practice, but also implies that heterosexuality and homosexuality share a cultural imaginary which they variously crave and pillage and even inadvertently mock. Notwithstanding the political and social conflicts between them, heterosexuality and homosexuality do not constitute discrete realms of gendered sexual desire. The contextual differences in the representation of "lesbian" dildo practices, while necessary for a critique of heterosexism, expose the radical interdependence of heterosexual desire with its abjected, homosexual other. Returning to the apparent contradiction raised by Butler's work, posed at the beginning of this essay, the inescapable dilemma of lesbian and gay studies is thus the need to attend aggressively and vigilantly to the specific difference of homosexuality to the end of subverting a heterosexist regime founded upon that difference.

A detachable part, the dildo humorously implies that the penis can be detached from its phallic burden—or that the phallus has spawned another symbol. Like simulacra in general, it is threatening and alluring in different contexts as a substitutive displacement of that which it represents. If the dildo has anything to reveal, perhaps it is that the phallus is a figure subject to and constructed through substitutions. By simultaneously avowing and disavowing the sexual difference signified by the phallus, the dildo ironically discredits the phallic power that it also assumes for itself. Not an *inherently* "subversive repetition," the dildo nevertheless offers, provisionally and contingently, a vision of the "lesbian" whose identity remains indeterminate and whose desires are not regulated by the hetero/homo division and enforced by the penis-as-phallus. The dildo, similar yet different from the penis, as a representation *goes both ways,* confirming *and* perverting its putative original in a double gesture which renders the phallus a malleable trope instead of a privileged signifier. The fabricated, figural status of the phallus is exposed through the act of "strapping it on."

NOTES

I owe warm thanks to Elisabeth Ladenson for her invaluable and gracious assistance on this essay.

1. Although there are sporadic earlier instances, the first widespread representation of dildos in Western literature occurred in seventeenth-century French libertine and satiric texts. The cosmopolitan Seigneur de Brantome cautioned women against using dildos in his *Lives of Fair and Gallant Ladies* (1665), and Claude le Petit, in his satiric poem "Aux Précieuses," attacked female intellectuals, advising them to roll up their books and use them as dildos. See Lillian Faderman, *Surpassing the Love of Men: Romantic Friendship and Love Between Women from the Renaissance to the Present* (New York: William Morrow, 1981), 31–32, 87. Further references will be included in the text.

Peter Wagner has documented the appearance of dildos in late seventeenth- and early eighteenth-century English erotica, such as Lord Rochester's poem "Signor Dildo" (1678), the mock epic *Dildoides* (1706), attributed to Samuel Butler, and the anonymous *Monsieur Thing's Origin: or Seignor D——o's Adventures in Britain* (1722), which describes the comic tribulations of a French dildo in England. See Wagner, "The Discourse on Sex—or Sex as Discourse: Eighteenth-Century Medical and Paramedical Erotica," in *Sexual*

Underworlds of the Enlightenment, ed. G. S. Rousseau and Roy Porter (Chapel Hill: University of North Carolina Press, 1988), 53–55. Henry Fielding's well-known pamphlet, *The Female Husband: or, The Surprising History of Mrs. Mary, alias Mr. George Hamilton* (1746), is a hostile account of the case of a cross-dressed woman who used an instrument "which decency forbids . . . even to mention" during sexual intercourse with her wife, but to which Fielding repeatedly alludes (37).

Terry Castle also discusses late eighteenth-century French obscene pamphlets that attacked Marie Antoinette by depicting her using a dildo on a female lover (*The Apparitional Lesbian: Female Homosexuality and Modern Culture* [New York: Columbia University Press, 1993], 129–30). This misogynistic, satiric tradition has persisted; Ronald Pearsall quotes doggerel by A. C. Swinburne (1870) that features Queen Victoria employing a dildo (*The Worm in the Bud: The World of Victorian Sexuality* [Harmondsworth: Penguin, 1969], 577).

2. The sixteenth-century Spanish theologian Antonio Gomez prescribed death by burning for women who employed dildos with each other, and the Italian cleric, Lodovico Maria Sinistrari, in *Peccatum Mutum* (1700), likewise declared that if a woman penetrated another woman they were both to be executed and burned (Faderman 36, 419).

Texas, along with Georgia and some other states, criminalizes the sale of dildos. Under the Texas Penal Code 43.21(a)(7) and 43.23(c)(1) and (f), it is an offense to "promote or possess with intent to promote any . . . obscene device," which is defined as "a device including a dildo or artificial vagina, designed or marketed as useful primarily for the stimulation of human genital organs." "A person who possesses six or more obscene devices . . . is presumed to possess them with intent to promote the same."

Historical evidence of dildo use consists largely of juridical and medical testimony produced after the exposure of women who had cross-dressed as men, often with disastrous consequences.

3. Good Vibrations in San Francisco and Eve's Garden in New York City—the largest sex toys shops in the United States that market specifically to women—report a substantial increase in the sale of dildos over the past fifteen years. According to Kathy Winks, the general manager of Good Vibrations, mail-order and over-the-counter sales of dildos at her store have grown between 20 and 25 percent annually for several years, and last year totaled 17,700.

4. Sheila Jeffreys, *The Lesbian Heresy: A Feminist Perspective on the Lesbian Sexual Revolution* (North Melbourne: Spinifex Press, 1993), 29. Further references will be included in the text.

5. Judith Butler, "Imitation and Gender Insubordination," in *Inside/Out: Lesbian Theories, Gay Theories,* ed. Diana Fuss (New York: Routledge, 1991), 17.

6. To be sure, Butler makes this point in *Gender Trouble: Feminism and the Subversion of Identity* (New York: Routledge, 1990): "The ideal of a coherent heterosexuality . . . is an impossible ideal" (122). She expands on the concept in

Bodies That Matter: On the Discursive Limits of "Sex" (New York: Routledge,
1993), where she argues that the "law" of ideal heterosexuality is "produced as
the law . . . by the very citations it is said to command" (14). Further references
will be included in the text.

7. See Butler's essay, "The Lesbian Phallus and the Morphological Imaginary," in *Bodies*, 57–91.

8. Havelock Ellis, *Studies in the Psychology of Sex*, vol. 1, part 4, *Sexual
Inversion* (New York: Random House, 1942), 258.

9. Mariana Valverde, *Sex, Power, and Pleasure* (Toronto: Women's Press,
1985), 98.

10. Sheila Jeffreys, *The Spinster and Her Enemies: Feminism and Sexuality
1880–1930* (London: Pandora, 1985), 109.

11. Karla Jay and Allen Young, *The Gay Report: Lesbians and Gay Men
Speak Out About Sexual Experiences and Lifestyles* (New York: Simon &
Schuster, 1979), 544.

12. Loulan's statistics on the dildo are derived from responses to a question-
naire she distributed on her lecture tours and at women's resource centers
between 1985 and 1987, and are therefore from women who presumably take
an active interest in lesbian sexuality. See JoAnn Loulan, *Lesbian Passion:
Loving Ourselves and Each Other* (San Francisco: Spinsters Ink, 1987), 173–
218. Further references will be included in the text.

13. Sophie Schmuckler, "How I Learned to Stop Worrying and Love My
Dildo," in *Coming to Power*, 3rd. ed., ed. Samois (Boston: Alyson, 1987), 103.

14. *Eve's Garden Catalogue* (1992), 14.

15. Celeste West, *A Lesbian Love Advisor* (San Francisco: Cleis Press, 1989),
47. Further references will be included in the text.

16. Pat Califia, *Sapphistry: The Book of Lesbian Sexuality*, 3rd ed. (Tallahassee, FL: Naiad, 1988), 51. I quote from the most recent edition. Further
references will be included in the text.

17. Susie Bright, *Susie Sexpert's Lesbian Sex World* (Pittsburgh: Cleis Press,
1992), 30. Further references will be included in the text.

18. See Laura Doan, ed., *The Lesbian Postmodern* (New York: Columbia
University Press, 1994).

19. This is also where the State of Texas, among others, draws the line
between legal, "hard" vibrators (such as Hitachi's "Magic Wand") and illegal,
"soft" or pliable vibrators.

20. Judith Roof, *A Lure of Knowledge: Lesbian Sexuality and Theory* (New
York: Columbia University Press, 1991), 1.

21. Jacques Lacan, "The Meaning of the Phallus," in *Feminine Sexuality:
Jacques Lacan and the Ecole Freudienne*, ed. Juliet Mitchell and Jacqueline
Rose, trans. Rose (New York: Norton, 1985), 83. Further references will be
included in the text.

22. Kaja Silverman, "The Lacanian Phallus," *differences* 4, no. 1 (1992):
96.

23. Elizabeth Grosz, "Lesbian Fetishism?" *differences* 3, no. 2 (1991): 48. Further references will be included in the text.

24. Sigmund Freud, "Femininity," in *New Introductory Lectures on Psychoanalysis*, ed. James Strachey (New York: Norton, 1965), 117.

25. Jane Gallop, *Thinking Through the Body* (New York: Columbia University Press, 1988), 131. Further references will be included in the text.

26. Grosz, 50–54. See Sigmund Freud, "Fetishism," in *Sexuality and the Psychology of Love*, ed. Philip Rieff (New York: Collier, 1963), 215–16.

27. Catharine MacKinnon, *Feminism Unmodified: Discourses on Life and Law* (Cambridge: Harvard University Press, 1987), 60.

28. Teresa de Lauretis, *Technologies of Gender: Essays on Theory, Film, and Fiction* (Bloomington: Indiana University Press, 1987), 25.

29. *On Our Backs,* which began publishing in 1984, now has a circulation of approximately 30,000 paid subscribers in addition to its bookstore distribution, making it by far the largest lesbian pornographic magazine in the United States in terms of readership, sales, and commercial success.

30. Stud Edda, "Packin' It," *On Our Backs* (March/April 1991): 15ff. Further references will be included in the text.

31. As Linda Williams explains, the "meat shot" is a close-up of penile penetration of the vagina; the "money shot" (so called because it costs more money to shoot) is a close-up of penile ejaculation (*Hard Core: Power, Pleasure, and the "Frenzy of the Visible"* [Berkeley: University of California Press, 1989], 93–94). Further references will be included in the text.

32. The pressure of the dildo on the clitoris may be intensely stimulating. Strictly speaking, the dildo is itself insensate, yet its very insensible, unflagging firmness renders it phallic par excellence. I am indebted to Elisabeth Ladenson and Joseph Valente for conversations on this matter.

33. Anna Conchita Senos, "The Shower," *On Our Backs* (July/August 1991): 42 (emphasis mine).

34. In his attempt to detach the penis from the phallus, Charles Bernheimer argues that the corporeal penis, subject to failure and flaccidity, challenges the claim of the phallus to transcendent potency. "A phallic penis is impersonal and unchanging, always erect, impervious to differences in desire—whether the other's or one's own. To bring the phallus into the scene of erotic exchange is to freeze that scene outside of time and to require the body to become an inexhaustible performative machine. For a penis to be phallic the blood would have to be drained from it and replaced by an enduring artificial substance. *It would have to become a dildo*" ("Penile Reference in Phallic Theory," *differences* 4, no. 1 [1992]: 120 [emphasis mine]).

35. Teresa de Lauretis, "Film and the Visible," in *How Do I Look: Queer Film and Video*, ed. Bad Object-Choices (Seattle: Bay Press, 1991), 247.

36. Teresa de Lauretis, *Alice Doesn't: Feminism, Semiotics, Cinema* (Bloomington: Indiana University Press, 1984), 142.

37. Annette Kuhn, *The Power of the Image: Essays on Representation and Sexuality* (London: Routledge, 1985), 31.

38. Naomi Schor, "Female Fetishism: The Case of George Sand," in *The Female Body in Western Culture: Contemporary Perspectives,* ed. Susan Rubin Suleiman (Cambridge: Harvard University Press, 1986), 365 (emphasis Schor's).

39. Katherine Israel, "Midnight Blue," *Frighten the Horses* 11 (Winter 1993): 32–35.

NINE

Recasting Receptivity: Femme Sexualities

ANN CVETKOVICH

What is the experience of "being fucked" for lesbians? That's one version of the question this chapter explores, but my ability to name my topic is hampered by problems of vocabulary; even when used more literally to mean, for example, "being penetrated," "being fucked" has come to signify being dominated, being made weak, or being passive, giving rise to the rich range of figurative uses that seem inseparable from the more specifically sexual acts signified by the "passive" form of the verb "to fuck." The term sometimes seems so thoroughly associated with degradation as to be irredeemable, making it impossible to describe being fucked as a pleasurable experience without renaming it. I will thus sometimes focus on sexual "receptivity," in order to investigate lesbian representations of getting fucked or receiving sexual attention that give the experience a better name. But the advantage of the term "receptivity" is also its hazard; necessarily vague, it can resolve too quickly the questions rendered visible by the concept of "fucking," which sustains the tensions between the literal and the figurative, the physical and the psychic, and the sexual and the social that complicate any investigation of sexual experience. (As for the term "lesbian" in my first sentence: my focus is ultimately on sexual acts, not sexual identities, but I am interested in how the sexual act[s] of "being fucked" are represented by lesbians, whose experiences suggest possibilities that need not be exclusive to either self-identified lesbians or women fucking other women.)

I turn to accounts of femme lesbianism, especially those by self-identified femmes and the butches who fuck them, as an important resource for lesbian representations of the experience of getting fucked.

One of the ways that being fucked gets stigmatized is through its association with femininity, and in the process of revising understandings of
"feminine" lesbianism, femme lesbians also recast notions of "receptivity." My interest in "femme" sexualities was inspired by the "stone
butches" described and given voice by Elizabeth Lapovsky Kennedy and
Madeline Davis's oral history of the lesbian community in Buffalo in the
1940s and 1950s. I was struck by the figure of the "stone butch" who,
far from dominating her lover in a "masculine" way, seeks to remain
"untouchable" because of a fear of the vulnerability that comes with
receiving sexual attention or being fucked.[1] "Untouchability" seemed in
these butch accounts to be both a source of pleasure, making way for
the power of giving attention to a lover's desire, *and* a response to fear
and hesitation. I find this ambiguity a compelling one, among other
things a significant and largely unacknowledged challenge to equations
of butch identity with stereotypes about masculinity. Furthermore, the
complexities of butch untouchability ultimately led to my fascination
with the experiences of self-identified femme lesbians, who, unlike the
stone butches, seemed to welcome touch and the pleasures of allowing
themselves to be fucked or to receive sexual attention.

For a dyke fascinated by butch/femme, the past few years have provided a lot of good reading material, with the publication of not only
Kennedy and Davis's book but also Joan Nestle's edited collection, *The
Persistent Desire* (see Figure 9.1), among others.[2] Both Nestle's own
writing and the collection *The Persistent Desire* give voice to and document femme sexuality, not only correcting the historical record about
butch/femme, but recasting theories of both gender and sexuality.

My interest in these texts, however, has been less historical than
sexual. As an appropriator of the history of 1940s' and 1950s' butch/
femme and its now burgeoning textual legacy, I represent a particular
kind of 1990s' dyke. Whether I agree with them or not, I'm immersed in
theories that celebrate butch/femme as a parodic inversion of gender
rather than a repetition of misogynist stereotypes.[3] And I live in the
cultures of gender fuck, glamour dykes, and pro-sex debates about s/m
and power that have led to a renewed interest in pre-Stonewall butch/
femme culture, and a new respect for practices that had often been
dismissed by lesbian feminism as passé or sexist or a product of internalized homophobia.[4] *The Persistent Desire,* from which many of my
examples will be drawn, is not "new"; some of it has been previously

Cover photograph from The Persistent Desire. *Copyright © Morgan Gwenwald. Courtesy of Morgan Gwenwald.*

published in important collections from the sex debates of the 1980s, but the issues it raises are newly visible within the context of both academic and public discussions about new forms of gay and lesbian and "queer" identities and politics that draw inspiration from and re-frame pre-Stonewall history. [5]

This chapter is not a historical record. It is not, ultimately, about pre-Stonewall lesbian culture. Women like Elizabeth Kennedy, Madeline Davis, and Joan Nestle have done the important work of documenting a subculture that plays a crucial role in pre-Stonewall gay and lesbian history. Their work has many implications, not least of which is its addition to the still sketchy historical record of sexual identities and experiences; but, it also facilitates the reclamation of that history for the present and enables the articulation of contemporary experiences and identities that may differ from those of the past even as they make reference to them. I hope to honor the voices whose testimony I wish to address here. I do so, though, through appropriation, itself a way of sustaining traditions. Rather than remaining sealed in the past, the documents and testimonies I read here, which are so much about touch and receptivity, touch me in the present as they expand and transform my vocabularies and experiences.

Since this chapter is partly about role models and how texts provide them, I will begin with a reading of a reading, Christine Cassidy's construction of Walt Whitman as a "model femme" (PD, 392). That she invokes Whitman, a fellow "queer," but one who is as likely to be gendered "masculine" as "feminine," to express her own sexual identity suggests how butch-femme lesbianism might serve as inspiration for a variety of forms of cross-identification with unpredictable effects.[6] Cassidy admires Whitman because his "strength lay in receptivity" (PD, 392). Through his example, she redeems the femme as powerful in her capacity to embrace the world, to be open to the touch of things both material and immaterial. Receptivity stems from a capacity to live inside the body, and Cassidy contrasts Whitman's "passionate belief in the power of the body" with Emily Dickinson's "ethereal, completely of the mind" sensibility (PD, 392). She constructs the distinction between Whitman and Dickinson as a distinction between public and private selves, between a "flamboyant" search for connection with the world and a "cloistered" rejection of it. More salient than the sexual identities or practices of Whitman and Dickinson are their social identities. Through the construction of Whitman's democratic and public urges as the essence of femme behavior, Cassidy challenges the stigmatization of the "femme" as weak or passive. Central to this enterprise is her description of Whitman's engagement with the world as "active receptivity," which she defines as "passionate curiosity, that hunger insatiable—for knowledge, for touch, for power received and transformed" (PD, 393).

Whitman's social power operates through the erotic and sexual power of the body. Cassidy literalizes the receptivity that characterizes the femme's "hunger" for the world, her willingness, like Whitman, to embrace the world, when she suggests that "for me to really understand anything, I have to take it into my body" (PD, 393). Although she is referring to a metaphorical openness to the world, exemplified by Whitman's grand claim in *Leaves of Grass* that "To me the converging objects of the universe perpetually flow,/ All are written to me, and I must get what the writing means" (quoted in PD, 393), Cassidy (and Whitman) also invoke more overtly physical and sexual acts, such as being penetrated, or taking the body parts of others inside of the body, as a means to explore and know the world. Sexual relations physicalize or embody social relations, at once making them literal and providing a metaphor for those relations. Thus, sexual acts are only one dimension of femme identity. Cassidy's femme sensibility expresses itself not just through sexual acts but through other creative endeavors—it is Whitman's power as a poet, not just his identity as a social and sexual subject, that makes him such an appropriate role model for Cassidy's sexuality and her writing.

To discuss receptivity or getting fucked, then, involves considering how ideologies of sexuality construct the body, but also how the body and its materiality embody and thus construct ideologies of sexuality. Both Whitman, and Cassidy borrowing from Whitman, understand "receptivity" to be both a sexual and social concept, both a literal and figurative process. Just as another form of taking things into the body, the penetration of anus or vagina by the penis, has been construed as a metaphor for domination (so successfully that its status as metaphor has been effaced), so Cassidy constructs meanings out of sexual acts. For Cassidy, being penetrated or taking things into the body means something other than being dominated; it provides access to power, and not just sexual power but creative and social power. Redefining penetration through a notion of active receptivity, she suggests the power of femme sexuality to challenge conventional understandings of the links between the sexualized body and power.

The Femme

Redefining "receptivity" as a quality that is not "feminine," in the negative sense of "passive," is only one of the many obstacles that femme discourse has to overcome to combat the stigmatized conceptions of "femininity" that not only pervade a misogynist dominant culture, but constitute a significant strand of thinking within feminism. The connection between being penetrated and being feminized is a powerful one, evident, for example, in homophobic constructions of anal penetration as a form of humiliating emasculation. Adding still greater force to this charged combination are conceptions of activity and passivity; both the social construct, femininity, and the physical act, being penetrated, are constructed as passive. The assumption that a bodily orifice receiving an object or body part must either be passive or be rendered passive when penetrated does not seem credible at a strictly biological level. Thus the only way to understand being penetrated as linked to a negative passivity or femininity is to consider it to be a social construction at its origin. In other words, this association is not the result of some prediscursive physical process being made available for social meaning; the social meaning constructs the physical process of penetration at the same time as social meanings are brought into being through their embodiment or materialization.

Many self-identified femmes challenge the idea that getting fucked is a negative experience, by testifying to their active and eager desire to be fucked. Madeline Davis refers to "that hunger, that desperate need, that desire to be 'fucked senseless' and to know that we have, do, and would put up with some incredible shit to get it" (PD, 268). Amber Hollibaugh describes the femme's self-definition in terms of an ability to name and take her pleasure: "But I want to come and I want certain things to happen. I am real defined by how I want to be fucked" (PD, 263). In an essay titled, "Re-Collecting History, Renaming Lives: Femme Stigma and the Feminist Seventies and Eighties," Lyndall MacCowan characterizes getting fucked as a "loss of control" that is enabled by a butch lover's willingness to read and respond to her desire:

> It is butch women who made wanting sex okay, who never said I wanted it "too much" or thought I got too wet. With so many other women I was either "an ironing board" or "a slut"; it was butch women who taught me about multiple orgasms and the incredible high of fisting, who made it okay to want to be made love to until I was too spent to move. It was butch women who made it right to give by responding rather than reciprocating, to make love by moving beneath them instead of using my tongue or hands. It was butch women who gave me permission to not be in control at all times, and butch women who didn't think it vain that I wanted to be pretty, who, indeed, made me feel beautiful. (PD, 320)

MacCowan characterizes getting fucked and losing control as a hard-won privilege, made possible by butch women who are willing to give her the luxury of "responding" rather than having to use her "tongue or hands" to engage with them more overtly. She articulates the stigma against expressing the desire to be fucked that has to be overcome by the persistent attention of her butch lovers. For all these women, femme sexuality is about voracious desire for which no apologies are necessary because it can be accepted and fulfilled by another's attentions.

Central to femme discourse about being the recipient of a lover's sexual attention is the recurrent need to counter the notion that this position is a passive one. Nestle and other self-identified femmes insist that the femme is active rather than passive in her sexual relation to her lover and to her own desire. Moving beneath her lover's body, for example, MacCowan redefines responsiveness as a physical *activity* and hence not as the state of physical passivity that enables "getting fucked" to serve as a metaphor for weakness, powerlessness, or submissiveness. Many femmes stress the power and the labor of receptivity, a term that replaces "passivity" so as to make the role of "bottom" less stigmatized. In an essay whose title, "Butchy Femme," itself indicates a redefinition of femme power, Mykel Johnson makes this discursive and conceptual move:[7]

> My femme eroticism was not passivity but receptivity. Being good in bed as a femme meant communicating my responses. Moaning, talking, breathing, shifting, letting her know the effect her lovemaking had on me, letting her know what I wanted. To be femme with her meant to be vulnerable, to open to her the thoughts and feelings of my imagination, to let her know the inner recesses of my mind as well as my body. (PD, 396)

Johnson characterizes the femme's receptivity as active, as she gives her lover physical signals of the effects of her lovemaking. "Communicating [her] responses" is work, as is allowing herself to be "vulnerable" enough to enable her lover to "know" her. The text hints that making oneself "open" is a physical process of, for example, allowing oneself to be penetrated, but "the inner recesses" of not just her body, but her mind, are made available to her lover. Far from being passively taken, Johnson must actively engage with and return her lover's attentions, and in return for the work of letting her lover know what she wants, she gets what she wants. If making one's desires known requires effort, the value of a butch lover who can read those desires is considerable.

In addition to casting the power to receive sexual pleasure as desirable, Johnson indicates that it is a difficult, and thus precious, power to obtain, further challenging negative constructions of being fucked. Like Lyndall MacCowan, she describes her appreciation of the attention she receives from her butch lovers, who allow her to forget her concerns about taking too long to come or demanding too much from them. "What had been a liability was transformed in her eyes into an asset" (PD, 396). This kind of fear of getting fucked is rather different from that often associated with acts of penetration, where the bottom is constructed as humiliated by or used for the pleasure of the person doing the fucking or penetrating. If femme (or butch) lesbians have problems with being made love to, being taken advantage of is not necessarily one of them. If anything, they seem to fear too much attention rather than too little.

Amber Hollibaugh is right when she says, "It's hard to talk about things like giving up power without it sounding passive."[8] So impoverished is the language of sexual power, especially loss of sexual power, that it can only be translated into an active/passive dichotomy, where passivity is always stigmatized. In a dialogue with Cherríe Moraga, "What We're Rollin Around in Bed With," a crucial contribution to 1980s' sex debates, Hollibaugh articulates a notion of femme sexuality that echoes Johnson's and MacCowan's insistence on the pleasures of making oneself open to a lover and of the agency involved in the process of being desired.

> I am willing to give myself over to a woman equal to her amount of wanting. I expose myself for her to appreciate. I open myself out for her to see what's possible for her to love in me that's female. I want her to respond to it. I may not be doing something active with my body, but more eroticizing her need that I feel in her hands as she touches me.[9]

Like the butch who focuses on her partner's pleasure, the femme emphasizes the way in which her pleasure emerges in response to her partner's desire. Hollibaugh suggests that she need not be physically active to be responsive, that she acts by "eroticizing" the "need" that is manifest in her lover's touch. Allowing oneself to be touched can be an action just as much as doing the touching is.

At stake in these descriptions of femme desire and femme sexuality are assumptions about the physical, sexual, and social hierarchies embodied by sexual acts. The vocabulary of sexual "relation" or "intercourse" often consists of binary distinctions that map the bodies of (usually two) sexual partners onto social hierarchies and vice versa. These include relatively abstract dichotomies, such as "giving/receiving," which can name a range of physical and psychic exchanges, and more graphic oppositions, such as "fucking/being fucked," which signifies both more specific physical acts and more specific power relations (although perhaps with no greater precision than "giving/receiving"). Other sexualized dichotomies for describing power relations emerge out of the vocabulary of different sexual subcultures, including "butch/femme" as terms for specific sexual role-playing, and the language of s/m, such as "top/bottom" and "dominant/submissive."[10] Such terms do not necessarily announce what specific sexual acts constitute a particular role.

In the writing of this chapter, I have found it difficult to choose between terms such as "butch/femme," "top/bottom," "fucking/being fucked," and "penetrating/being penetrated." Yet this inconsistency of vocabulary is potentially unavoidable given the variety of links and disconnections among and between these terms. The discourse of femmes undoes assumptions about any simple relation or analogy between these binarisms and makes it difficult to reduce them to any single master binarism, such as "masculine/feminine" or "active/passive." For example, fucking or topping can involve literal or physical penetration, but it need not. Similarly, being penetrated need not always represent being topped or dominated. Furthermore, different kinds of penetration *mean* different things, a complexity sometimes effaced in a phallocentric culture that assumes that only penises do the penetrating, or that only vaginas are meant to be penetrated (thus, for example, rendering the anus/asshole a suspect orifice). Lesbian sexuality requires a language for penetration with dildos, fingers, or fists, and it faces the challenge of expanding the erotics of penetrating objects or body parts, which is too often limited to a focus on penises or phallic substitutes.[11] By the same token, an erotics of how different orifices, such as anuses, vaginas, mouths, get fucked would be useful in order to reveal the wide range of ways that getting penetrated is experienced, both physically and symbolically. It would then be impossible to appeal to some biological common ground to explain the meaning of penetration, but even more importantly, new social and sexual imaginaries could be enabled.

Not only are the physical dynamics of fucking and receptivity extraordinarily diverse, but receptivity as a psychic or emotional, and not just physical, process further complicates any analysis of sexual acts. The lack of physical or literal specificity in the term "receptivity" indicates how femme discourse articulates both sexual and emotional receptivity, both physical and nonphysical forms of being "touched." Using a more overtly sexual vocabulary to express the power dynamics of fucking and being fucked, such as "penetrating/being penetrated," may not be adequate to the task of representing its emotional qualities.

Nor will the distinction between "top" and "bottom," which might seem to characterize the relation between the butch who gives pleasure and the femme who receives it, resolve the problem of terminology. (The use of the terms "femme top" and "butch bottom" reveals that they are not equivalent distinctions.) If the "bottom" is understood to be the partner who receives pleasure, that term might more accurately reflect the nature of femme sexuality than the term "being fucked," if the latter vocabulary presumes penis-in-vagina or penetration of an orifice. The connection and disconnection between "top/bottom" and "penetrating/ being penetrated" creates the potential for confusion, however. If the "top" penetrates the bottom with a penis, then the "top's" sexual pleasure might be assumed to be central. In contrast, if the "top" penetrates with a finger, fist, dildo, or other nonorgasmic object, then the bottom might be considered to be the partner whose sexual pleasure is the primary goal. In descriptions of butch/femme sexuality, receiving pleasure or achieving orgasm is the bottom's role, not the top's. One can be penetrated both in order to receive pleasure and in order to give pleasure, and different terms might be used to indicate which is primary. "Receptivity" can be used to signify both an openness to one's own pleasure and a willingness to give someone else pleasure, although the former is foregrounded in femme discourse. These ambiguities are often effaced when penises, penetration, and topping converge, and it can be assumed (not necessarily correctly) that the top's pleasure (of orgasm) is both desired and easy to achieve. When the bottom is being penetrated and the goal is his/her pleasure, these assumptions may be confounded, especially since many femmes, for example, emphasize the difficulty of achieving or receiving pleasure (since it involves the active support and desire of a butch top to allow her to lose control).

Rather than fucking being constructed as a situation where one person takes pleasure and the other person gets no pleasure (or endures the process), butch/femme sexuality focuses on giving pleasure and receiving pleasure as separate but mutual pleasures. The dynamics in which an unequal distribution of power creates a rigid binary distinction where only one partner is presumed to be getting or receiving pleasure are replaced by a dynamic in which both the giver and the receiver experience pleasure. That the pleasure is mutual, however, does not necessarily mean that it is the same in each case, as indicated by the possibility, for example, that only one partner will expect to experience the pleasure of genital orgasm. (Whether this kind of pleasure should be privileged as primary or central to sexual activity would also be a question to consider.) When conceived in terms of domination and submission, sexual interaction is often represented as a win-lose economy (although this may well be an inaccurate assumption); lesbian butch/femme, however, by emphasizing, for example, the butch's pleasure in giving her lover pleasure, does not depend on this assumption. Articulating the nature of femme sexuality makes it possible to challenge assumptions about being the "bottom" that pervade not only representations of lesbianism but representations of heterosexuality and gay male sexuality.

The complex connections and disconnections between "butch/ femme," "top/bottom," and "penetrating/being penetrated" suggest that correct vocabulary alone will not resolve the issues at stake here. Appeals to biology or anatomy to determine who is getting pleasure or who is on top do not hold up in any systematic way because the experience of pleasure and the possession of power are not inherent features of any particular sexual act. There are unpredictable linkages between the oppositions that describe the physical and psychological features of sexual relations. Thus, I focus on one rather vague term, "receptivity," and one more charged term, "getting fucked," to describe the locus of my concerns. The assumptions about gender and power that map onto these terms are malleable, and the "feminized" experience of "getting fucked" or of being sexually "receptive" cannot be reduced to a single consistent meaning.

There has been a conspicuous silence about the experience of "getting fucked," which has often been construed from the "top's" point of view as one of being violated, emasculated, or dominated. While it is relatively easy (although long overlooked) in the case of the lesbian femme bottom to assert that getting fucked is about getting pleasure, attention to this case suggests that others like it need to be reconceptualized. One reason for this lack of understanding is the slippage between "femme," "bottom," "getting fucked," and "being penetrated" facilitated by the persistent connection between domination and penetration. It is possible to be a femme, a bottom, or the one who gets fucked without being penetrated but assumptions about penetration tend to affect the meanings of those terms. Why assume, though, that there is no pleasure involved in making oneself available to oral, anal, or vaginal penetration, or other acts of "receptivity," a pleasure that may include, but cannot be reduced to, the pleasure of orgasm?

Penetration and Male Homosexuality

This question is not, unfortunately, a merely rhetorical one, given the pervasiveness of the assumption that being penetrated and/or being fucked constitutes being dominated and/or being feminized. The linkage between penetration and domination that is challenged by some, but by no means all, discourses of lesbian sexuality stands as a counterweight to the tremendous power of cultural constructions of heterosexuality, and of male homosexuality as well. The penetration of the anus is perhaps even more culturally freighted as a signifier of power than the penetration of the vagina; one indication of its cultural power is the frequency and virulence with which anal penetration and male homosexuality have been mutually defining.

It thus seems worth considering how constructions of anal receptivity and/or male homosexuality compare with the positive constructions of receptivity found in discussions of lesbian sexuality. Because, even when open to challenge, the construction of heterosexual penetration as domination by both patriarchal ideology and by feminist critiques seems understandable, constructions of male homosexual relations seem like a more likely source for discussions of the pleasures of "receptivity" or of being penetrated.

Or so one might expect. In fact, though, the connection between penetration and domination remains quite evident in a variety of constructions of male homoeroticism and homosexuality. In addition to providing accounts of forms of sexuality ignored and repudiated by heterocentric theory and history, recent studies of homosexual relations between men have dramatically demonstrated the constructed nature of sexuality and have shown how power and social relations are propped on (in the Freudian sense of anaclisis) the physical configurations of intercourse. Studies such as those by David Halperin on Greek sexuality and Tomas Almaguer on male homosexuality in Chicano and Latino cultures have the enormously powerful effect of unhinging penetration and heterosexuality in order better to illuminate the complex relations between sexual acts and sexual, gender, and social identities.[12] Yet, although different in many respects, in each of the cultures that Halperin and Almaguer describe, the relation between penetration and domination remains intact, a construction facilitated by a gendered binary in which the penetrator is cast as masculine and the person being penetrated is cast as feminine, or in which one is active and the other is passive. It is peculiar that scholarship designed to suggest the variability of the social meanings attached to sexual acts should have the unintentional effect of leaving the impression that penetration signifies domination and feminization, if not universally, then remarkably extensively.

In search of external confirmation to the femme premise that penetration does not have to mean domination, I have found myself drawn to the attractions of receptivity as articulated by Leo Bersani's "Is the Rectum a Grave?" In a "perverse" way, Bersani's essay is a celebration of anal receptivity, or more accurately, a celebration of the psychic experience of "self-shattering" that being fucked enables. "Perverse" because Bersani's professed desire to argue for the value of "powerlessness" is intended as a theoretical challenge to what he dubs "pastoral" and "redemptive" sex-positive theories. In its most colloquial form, Bersani's underlying premise is that "most people don't like [sex]" and that its value lies in its "anticommunal, antiegalitarian, antinurturing, antiloving" aspects.[13] Ultimately turning to psychoanalytic theory to ground his claims, Bersani recommends getting fucked for its capacity to produce "self-shattering," which is not strictly reducible to the physical experience of being penetrated, but is a more profoundly psychic experience.[14]

It is unclear whether Bersani defends the sexual experience of "self-shattering" in order to challenge universalizing and naturalizing assumptions about the "innate" positivity of sex or whether he posits his own form of sexual essentialism. In its former, more modest form, Bersani's claim is strategically useful for, and compatible with, theories of lesbian sexuality that seek to challenge the idea that any sexual relation marked by power is problematic. He attempts to confront the conceptual dilemma of theories that ultimately romanticize or utopianize sex in order to declare that relations of domination can be pleasurable. According to him, these conceptual frameworks beg the question of unpleasure by reinscribing it within the economy of the pleasure principle. Seeking to avoid this charge, Bersani qualifies his advocacy for the "strong appeal of powerlessness, of the loss of control" by adding, "I don't mean the value of gentleness, or nonaggressiveness, or even of passivity, but rather of a more radical disintegration and humiliation of the self."[15] In order to sustain his argument against sex-positivity, Bersani must preserve the negative dimensions of getting fucked. The specter of the grave can never leave the rectum because of the work of the death drive.[16]

I would argue that the negativity Bersani wishes to preserve is more available and more various in its forms than he supposes. Moreover, they may be more susceptible to historicization than his invocations of a monolithic psychoanalytic theory suggest. A fuller account of sexual experiences of powerlessness, to which femme discussions of getting fucked have a great deal to contribute, can offer different versions of sex-negativity from Bersani's. Femme lesbians also value "loss of control," and they don't prettify powerlessness as Bersani claims sex-positive celebrations of s/m by theorists such as Gayle Rubin and Pat Califia do. It's hard to say whether femmes describe "radical disintegration" and "humiliation of the self," especially since those two states are not necessarily the same; I wonder, though, if Bersani's use of those terms emerges in the context of how a specifically *masculine* self is humiliated, and hence threatened with disintegration, by anal penetration. But even if "radical disintegration" and "humiliation" don't adequately characterize the negative affects that both butch and femme lesbians associate with being fucked, that doesn't mean their accounts romanticize it either. Lesbians, for example, describe a rather different fear—not the fear that comes with getting fucked but the fear that *prevents* one from getting fucked. Bersani's counterintuitive premise that people don't like to have sex is less startling in the case of women, for whom the dangers and discomforts of sexuality (whether pregnancy, rape, or an inability to attend to their own pleasure) have been all too readily apparent.

Like David Halperin's analysis of Greek sexuality, as well as those of other historians and theorists of male homosexuality, Bersani's discussion helps to separate sexual hierarchies from gendered ones by focusing on same-sex relations. Analyzing how men in different cultures have desired and made meanings out of being penetrated is important as a way of historicizing the fear of penetration. It has also been important to disconnect male receptivity to penetration from gay, and even homosexual, identity. Furthermore, Bersani's argument that men not only want to be penetrated but want to "get fucked" may constitute a more powerful claim for its attractions than saying that (straight) women want to get fucked, which can more easily be attributed to prescribed gender roles. Yet the fact that men like to get fucked only seems counter-intuitive (or "queer"), if it is assumed that everyone really wants to be "masculine" and on top. [17]

Giving and Taking: Femme Receptivity

Femme accounts of receptivity avoid a redemptive reading of sex, insisting on the fear, pain, and difficulty that can block the way to and be conjured up by making oneself physically and emotionally vulnerable or receptive. Furthermore, the negative affects attached to particular acts cannot be attributed to problems to be resolved by "better" sex, such as nonhierarchical sex, sex without penetration, sex in a culture without homophobia, or any number of other utopian solutions to eliminate "perversion" or pain. An ongoing problem with lesbian/feminist critiques of butch/femme sexuality, now being addressed by revisionist attention to the pre-Stonewall period, has been the assumption that the supposedly perverse or dysfunctional aspects of earlier cultures can and should be resolved by overcoming internalized homophobia or sexism.[18] I would suggest that this reform is neither possible nor necessarily desirable and that there might be something to be learned from the persistent presence of negativity in sexuality. What's required is a sex-positivity that can embrace negativity.[19]

The painful and difficult aspects of femme sexuality, which are also some of its most powerful qualities, are explored in Joan Nestle's essay "The Gift of Taking." At least as vivid as the language of "fucking/being fucked," "top/bottom," and "penetrating/being penetrated" is Nestle's use of the terms "giving" and "taking." She is most immediately describing the process of being penetrated digitally:

> She takes me into her hand, pushing, squeezing, opening. She slips one finger into me. I gasp at how she fills me with that one thrust when I have taken so much and will again, but still the first entry has all the joy, the surprise of her power. . . . I can match her demanding with my giving, her hand with my insides. . . . She is a total force over me, and yet all her power is giving me myself.[20]

While her lover "takes" her by slipping a finger inside of her, Nestle describes herself as also "taking" her lover's hand inside of her. "Taking" is thus used to mean both receptivity to another and possession of another. Furthermore, as butch and femme each take, they give as well. Nestle's lover is giving attention, a body part, and a demand, but she herself is also giving back, as her "insides" respond to her lover's hand. The femme thus both gives and takes in a process of being penetrated that allows her to "match her [lover's] demanding with my giving, her hand with my insides." In this act of simultaneous giving and taking, Nestle claims that the butch's "power" to take gives "me myself," quite a different conception of power (and exchange) from that implied by the construction of penetration as an act that destroys the selfhood of the person being penetrated. The butch top definitely has power over Nestle, though; she is not simply servicing Nestle's femme desires in a way that ultimately makes Nestle the top. As bottom, Nestle experiences her own forms of power and pleasure. Ultimately the exchange of power seems more important than the actual physical acts; although Nestle seems to be describing digital penetration, what is more important than the actual body parts is the "appropriation of the body" (to use David Halperin's term) to signify the intersubjective dynamics of giving and taking.[21] Given the complex interdependence of the physical and the psychic, a more explicit naming of the body would not help to represent the sexual act more accurately.

Important to Nestle's account of the pleasures of being taken is her description of the difficult aspects of being "taken" or fucked by her lover. As her lover enters her body, "the pain is sweet; it destroys the years of numbness" (Gift, 128). Feeling is contrasted with numbness; even pain is preferable to no feeling at all. Her lover's attention destroys the numbness created by an inability to express desire. Submission to the demands of her lover's touch involves a difficult admission of her own desire: "I want to scream out to her, 'Now, please take me now,' but I can't, even in this dream. . . . I want to. I need to. For so many years I have not screamed, for so many years the world was not safe enough, or there was no one there to hear it" (Gift, 129).

Nestle's account highlights the context within which sexual experience takes place—an often homophobic and variously deadening culture that threatens to destroy the self that is precariously brought into being through sexual activity. The pleasure of being fucked, but also its difficulty, compensates for the self-erasure and "self-hatred" that are otherwise all too pervasive:

I know this woman, my friend, will bring my body to light, will make me use it and hear it, will strain it to its fullest, and she will help me through her demands and her pleasure to forget self-hatred. Through her gift of taking, I will be given back to myself, a self that must live in this body and thus desperately needs reconciliation. (Gift, 128)

Through the "gift of taking," Nestle is able to live with her body, which comes to represent herself. More important than the actual physical acts, but inseparable from them, are the psychic effects of receiving attention. Nestle's language of "giving" and "taking" need not be translated into more explicit or graphic terms because the body is already a metaphor for psychic and social states. She constructs penetration, however, as a metaphor that signifies not domination but something else. In celebrating the process of getting fucked, though, Nestle does not deny that a kind of "taking" is going on as she gives over power to her lover. The resistance, the pain, and the vulnerability that Nestle articulates suggest that "receptivity" is a difficult experience.

Joan Nestle's affirmation of sexuality, and more specifically receptivity and femme sexualities, does not exclude fear or emotional pain. She acknowledges the pleasures of power and powerlessness and makes no attempt to disavow the hierarchy that structures the giving and taking of pleasure. She provides a language of sexuality, and of fucking and being fucked, that is dramatically different from the model of penetration and domination that makes getting fucked a process of submission to the other and fucking a process of domination.

Why does this matter? It is important not only to make other sexualities visible, but to find new ways of imagining the body and its meanings, or the body *as* meanings. Femme conceptions of receptivity and of "getting fucked" redefine and render flexible the relations between bodies and meanings that feminists questioning the relation between penis and phallus have called for. Many kinds of significance can be attached to femme "receptivity," just as butch/femme currently represents many different theories. Yet, before meanings are made, attention must be paid to that which is said to have meaning, and "receptivity," even in its ostensibly literal or graphic forms, defies easy description.

NOTES

For helpful readings at various stages, I'd like to thank Lisa Moore, Jorie Woods, and Susan Lurie. Thanks to Colleen Lamos for the invitation to present some of this material at Rice University, and to Paul Smith and the Institute on Culture and Society participants for hearing me out yet again. I learned from the audience of my workshop on these issues at the Michigan Womyn's Music Festival. For discussion of Walt Whitman, thanks to Chris Newfield and Brian Bremen. I took more than I can say from Kay Turner, who gives me so much with her own work (and who, along with Laurie [Ella] Gant, gave me my first chance to air these ideas in the video *Get It Girl*). Thanks above all to Gretchen Phillips, who gave me not only a lot of ideas but a lot of experience.

1. See Elizabeth Lapovsky Kennedy and Madeline D. Davis, "Oral History and the Study of Sexuality in the Lesbian Community," in *Hidden From History: Reclaiming the Gay and Lesbian Past*, ed. Martin Bauml Duberman, Martha Vicinus, and George Chauncey, Jr. (New York: Meridian Press, 1989), 426–40. Kennedy and Davis's work has since been published in book form as *Boots of Leather, Slippers of Gold* (New York: Routledge, 1993), a monumental achievement not only in chronicling gay and lesbian history but in challenging, through its use of oral testimony, the way history is written.

2. Joan Nestle, ed., *The Persistent Desire: A Femme-Butch Reader* (Boston: Alyson Press, 1992). Quotations from this anthology will be cited in the text as PD.

3. For revisionist analyses of butch/femme, see, for example, Sue-Ellen Case, "Toward a Butch-Femme Aesthetic," *Discourse* 11:1 (Fall 1988/Winter 1989): 55–73; and Judith Butler, *Gender Trouble: Feminism and the Subversion of Identity* (New York: Routledge, 1990): 122–24, 136–39; and "Imitation and Gender Insubordination," in *Inside/Out: Lesbian Theories, Gay Theories*, ed. Diana Fuss (New York: Routledge, 1991), especially p. 25. While my essay also "appropriates" butch/femme for its own theoretical and political agendas, one of those implicit agendas is to suggest that Butler's and Case's uses of butch/femme, by taking it as a figure, miss some of the specificity of the sexual and social practices themselves. I am not, though, suggesting that such figurative uses are mistaken, only that the use of butch/femme to deconstruct gender (Butler) or postmodern theory (Case) is a gesture that itself requires attention, and one that draws on only a small portion of its complex meanings. I'm interested in expanding the range of meanings that butch/femme discourse makes available for generalization, not least of which are its implications for the logic of abstraction and embodiment.

4. For discussions of this cultural formation, see Arlene Stein, ed., *Sisters, Sexperts, Queers: Beyond the Lesbian Nation* (New York: Plume, 1993), and "Sisters and Queers: The Decentering of Lesbian Feminism," *Socialist Review* 22:1 (January/March 1992): 33–55; Lisa Duggan, "Making It Perfectly Queer," *Socialist Review* 22:1 (January/March 1992): 11–32; Michael Warner, ed., *Fear of a Queer Planet* (Minneapolis: University of Minnesota Press, 1993). For the expression of pro-sex feminist practice, see Susie Bright, *Susie Sexpert's Lesbian Sex World* (Pittsburgh: Cleis Press, 1990). For recent work on lesbian sexuality that extends and reframes the discussions of the 1980s, see Colleen Lamos,

"Taking on the Phallus" (in this volume); Heather Findlay, "Freud's 'Fetishism' and the Lesbian Dildo Debates," *Feminist Studies* 18:3 (Fall 1992): 563–80; June Reich, "Genderfuck: The Law of the Dildo," *Discourse* 15:1 (Fall 1992): 112–27; Lisa Henderson, "Lesbian Pornography: Cultural Transgression and Sexual Demystification," in *New Lesbian Criticism: Literary and Cultural Readings,* ed. Sally Munt (New York: Columbia University Press, 1992), 173–91; Julia Creet, "Daughter of the Movement: The Psychodynamics of Lesbian S/M Fantasy," *differences* 3:2 (Summer 1991): 135–59.

5. For discussion of the 1980s' debates about sexuality, see Ann Snitow, Christine Stansell, and Sharon Thompson, eds., *Powers of Desire: The Politics of Sexuality* (New York: Monthly Review Press, 1983), and Carole S. Vance, ed., *Pleasure and Danger: Exploring Female Sexuality* (Boston: Routledge, 1984). Some of the contributions from these collections are reprinted in Nestle's collection, and some of the same writers reappear in the more recent work as well. In addition, Joan Nestle's own writing has been collected in *A Restricted Country* (Ithaca: Firebrand Press, 1987), and other contributors to *The Persistent Desire,* such as Leslie Feinberg, Pat Califia, Esther Newton, Dorothy Allison, and Cherríe Moraga, have published important books. The appearance of these writers together in a single volume forges connections among them and both refigures and consolidates some of the trends in lesbian writing about sexuality in the decade since the publication of the 1980s' anthologies.

6. The relations between lesbian sexuality and male homosexuality can by no means be taken for granted, especially since each of these categories is itself complex, particularly in its various relations to gender. It should not, for example, be presumed that Whitman's availability as a "model femme" must necessarily stem from any "femininity" on his part. For more on Whitman's gender identity and the relation between his sexual politics and democratic ideals, see Christopher Newfield, "Democracy and Male Homoeroticism," *Yale Journal of Criticism* 6:2 (1993): 29–62. For discussions of Whitman's work in the context of theories of gender and sexuality, see also Eve Kosofsky Sedgwick, *Between Men: English Literature and Male Homosocial Desire* (New York: Columbia University Press, 1985), and Michael Moon, "Disseminating Whitman," in *Displacing Homophobia: Gay Male Perspectives in Literature and Culture,* ed. Ronald R. Butters, John M. Clum, and Michael Moon (Durham: Duke University Press, 1989).

7. Writing about coming out in the 1980s, Johnson adapts the categories of 1940s' and 1950s' butch/femme and appreciates this history as it contributes to her own erotic self-definition. (And she sees butch/femme first and foremost as an erotic, "more than a gender or political understanding" [PD, 396].) She claims butch/femme without feeling the need to choose one role over the other or to choose between making love to or being made love to. Her self-identification as a femme is described as the end point of a process of at first aspiring to be butch and desiring butch lovers. That she both identifies with and desires the butch position suggests that butch and femme need not be opposed. As her title indicates, femme power can have its butch elements.

8. Amber Hollibaugh and Cherríe Moraga, "What We're Rollin Around in Bed With: Sexual Silences in Feminism," in *Powers of Desire*, 398. This essay is also reprinted in *The Persistent Desire*, 243–53.

9. Hollibaugh and Moraga, "What We're Rollin Around in Bed With," 398.

10. For further discussions of this vocabulary, see Esther Newton and Shirley Walton, "The Misunderstanding: Toward a More Precise Sexual Vocabulary," in *Pleasure and Danger*, 242–50; and Mark Thompson, ed., *Leatherfolk: Radical Sex, People, Politics, and Practice* (Boston: Alyson Press, 1991).

11. Eve Kosofsky Sedgwick's work on the poetics of fisting and the erotics of the anus as orifice is an example of such work. In addition to attending to how the specificity of the anus as the orifice being entered and the hand or fist as the penetrating object challenges assumptions about penetration and sexuality, her work also makes important theoretical claims about the variability of sexual acts across gender and sexual identity. See "Queer Performativity: Henry James's *The Art of the Novel*," *GLQ* 1:1 (1993): 1–16, and "Is the Rectum Straight?: Identification and Identity in *The Wings of the Dove*," in *Tendencies* (Durham: Duke University Press, 1993), 73–103. The attention that Sedgwick devotes to the erotics of fisting is also warranted by the erotics of digital penetration. For example, such an investigation could shed new light on debates about the lesbian dildo, which have tended to consider it as a substitute for the penis or phallus, not for the fingers.

12. See David Halperin, *One Hundred Years of Homosexuality* (New York: Routledge, 1990), for discussion of ancient Greek sexuality. For discussion of Chicano and Latino male homosexual practices, see Tomas Almaguer, "Chicano Men: A Cartography of Homosexual Identity and Behavior," *differences* 3:2 (Summer 1991): 75–100; and Ana Maria Alonso and Maria Teresa Koreck, "Silences: 'Hispanics,' AIDS, and Sexual Practices," *differences* 1:1 (Winter 1989): 101–24.

13. Leo Bersani, "Is the Rectum a Grave?" *AIDS: Cultural Analysis, Cultural Activism*, ed. Douglas Crimp (Cambridge: MIT Press, 1987), 195, 215.

14. Bersani is not entirely clear about the distinction between self-shattering as a psychic experience and self-shattering as a physical experience. His emphasis on the psychic rather than the physical raises a variety of unanswered questions about the cultural construction of "self-shattering," which, even as a psychic category, should not be universalized. Bersani's argument would seem to depend on a variable or contingent relation between the psychic and the physical, since it would be a problematic universalization to assume that any particular physical act necessarily produces psychic experiences of self-shattering. For example, even very "minor" forms of touching or penetration can potentially be highly threatening. And it is in relation to particular cultural constructions of gender and sexuality that the anus and penetration of it become so highly charged that anal penetration produces "self-shattering." Thus, a concept such as "self-shattering" raises an array of questions about the construction of the relations among body, psyche, and culture.

15. Bersani, 217.

16. Bersani, like many of the critics of dominant-submissive sexuality that he would otherwise disagree with, seems to accept the premise that sex that is about power or that is nonegalitarian is about pain, not pleasure. He posits the experience of a self-shattering masochism as central to a sexuality based on pain rather than pleasure. (For a fuller account of Bersani's reading of Freudian notions of the death drive and masochism, see *The Freudian Body*.) His argument about the value of self-shattering (or getting fucked) rests on the assumption that a coherent self is necessary and desirable and dependent on avoiding the violation of penetration. His argument could easily take a different direction here, using claims about the value of self-rent selfhood and its dependence on bodily self-sufficiency and to argue that these are by no means universal values. Instead, Bersani reverses the erotic affect attached to a hierarchy that remains established by models of heterosexuality and masculinity that are grounded in constructions of penetrating and being penetrated. Gay male sexuality and anal penetration thus derive their meanings from heterosexuality and straight masculinity; in Bersani's view, getting fucked is always for gay men a process of emasculation or feminization which is humiliating even when it is pleasurable. Even if this were generally true within the present cultural construction of gay male sexuality, it would by no means be a universal fact about male homosexuality or anal penetration. (I am grateful to David Halperin for clarifying and confirming these issues for me in a very helpful conversation.)

17. The potentially misogynist underpinnings of Bersani's assumption that getting fucked results in an undesirable feminization are related to other aspects of his argument that have been critiqued by feminist critics, who have noted the misogyny of his remarks about camp and effeminate gay male behavior. See Carole-Anne Tyler, "Boys Will Be Girls: The Politics of Gay Drag," in *Inside/Out*, 38–40; and Teresa de Lauretis, "Film and the Visible," in *How Do I Look? Queer Film and Video*, ed. Bad Object-Choices (Seattle: Bay Press, 1991), 246–47.

18. An example of this kind of analysis is Lillian Faderman's discussion of butch/femme bar culture in *Odd Girls and Twilight Lovers*, in which she attributes the violent aspects of bar culture to alcoholism. Bars emerge as a breeding ground of addiction and dysfunctionality in her account, which lends itself to a moralizing and judgmental assessment of butch/femme. See *Odd Girls and Twilight Lovers: A History of Lesbian Life in Twentieth-Century America* (New York: Viking Penguin, 1991), 159–87.

19. Current usage of the term "queer" might be understood as sustaining and articulating this apparent contradiction. For example, Eve Sedgwick's discussions of the centrality of shame to "queer" sexual and cultural practices represents an effort to preserve their negativity and to see it as a potentially "positive" political and cultural resource. See "Queer Performativity."

20. Joan Nestle, "The Gift of Taking," in *A Restricted Country*, 129–30. Other citations will be included in the text as "Gift."

21. In "The Lesbian Phallus and the Morphological Imaginary," *differences* 4:1 (Spring 1992): 133–71, Judith Butler addresses this issue as it emerges in psychoanalytic theory, emphasizing how the concept of the "phallus" speaks to the contingent or historically specific processes by which parts of the body are zoned as meaningful in order to create, for example, concepts of sexuality or power. Butler notes the way in which what we might think of as a body that precedes social construction is in fact constituted by those constructions. See also "Bodies That Matter," in *Bodies That Matter* (New York: Routledge, 1993), 27–56, in which the above article is also reprinted.

TEN

Clits in Court: *Salome,* Sodomy, and the Lesbian "Sadist"

JENNIFER TRAVIS

In 1918, Maud Allan, star of Oscar Wilde's play *Salome,* began a libel suit against Noel Pemberton-Billing, MP, for his accusation of her "lesbianism" and "sadism" and the paragraph entitled "The Cult of the Clitoris" that he printed in his paper, the *Vigilante.* Although Billing was the defendant in what became a criminal libel trial, Allan became the sexual subject under investigation. The unsuccessful libel suit brought by Allan against Billing in 1918 was the first time in England that "lesbianism" as a category of sexual identity was the subject of legal discourse.[1] The accusation against Allan by Billing and the subsequent trial echoed Wilde's tragic fate twenty-three years earlier. It was the 1885 Criminal Law Amendment Act under which Wilde became the embodiment of "homosexual" identity that acted as a kind of phantom precedent in Allan's failed action.[2] Because there was no legislation with regard to women's "acts of gross indecency" with other women, however, Allan, unlike Wilde, did not suffer a criminal prosecution.

Although the action initiated by Allan would appear to mirror the circumstances of its infamous precursor, Wilde's and Allan's cases mark substantial differences in the articulation of lesbian and gay identities. With the 1885 Criminal Law Amendment Act, the long history of the regulation of sodomy had changed from punishing the sin of nonprocreative sexual practices to prosecuting the sexual crime of sexual identity.[3] The ratification of Section 11, the Labouchere Amendment, meant sexual "crimes" between men no longer required direct proof of the sexual activity but could be proven by the relationship of the accused. In other words, the use of the legal phrase "acts of gross indecency" enabled possible prosecution for a range of behaviors, including those which were not necessarily solely sexual in nature, as long as those acts involved two or more men. The Labouchere Amendment allowed for same-sex intimacy between men, rather than particular sexual practices and proof of penetration that were required of previous statutes, finally to be defined as sex. Indeed, sexual object choice became an operable or the operable category with regard to male sexuality. The legal definitions of female *sensuality,* in England, however, had remained confined to and obscured by the only imaginable sexual object available to women: men. Because sexual acts between women were largely undefined in the English law, "homosexuality" for women took on very different meanings in that law. To ask how the law produced "lesbians" and why the law often ignores lesbians is to critique the groundwork for the multiple articulations (and silences) of lesbian identity and lesbian *sensuality* today.

In February 1918, Noel Pemberton-Billing's right-wing propaganda paper, *Vigilante,* ran a story called "The Cult of the Clitoris" which contained a coded attack on Maud Allan:

> *The Cult of the Clitoris*
> To be a member of Maud Allan's private performances in Oscar Wilde's *Salome* one has to apply to a Miss Valetta, of 9, Duke Street, Adelphi, W.C. If Scotland Yard were to seize the list of these members I have no doubt they would secure the names of several thousand of the first 47,000. [4]

Billing had been developing a story about a black book which he claimed contained the names of 47,000 German sympathizers. According to Billing these conspirators, comprised of a cross-section of the population, everyone from members of Parliament to the London bordellos, sought to infiltrate England with "homosexuals." [5] In conjunction with this story, Billing targeted *Salome,* a play that previously had been banned from performance and was now playing to an audience of subscribers. [6] Oscar Wilde was its author and the most famous convicted "sodomite" in English history; the lead role was played by Maud Allan, a Canadian-born, unmarried, avant-garde dancer. Allan was celebrated for her performance of "The Vision of Salome," which she danced across Europe, the United States, India, Asia, and Australia. She was notorious for her exotic costume and "scorching" sexuality, appearing as Salome with bare legs and painted toenails.[7] Allan cultivated her sexual persona as a means of enhancing her public recognition, and she was rumored to have had numerous lovers, male and female, in the years before the Billing trial. In those years, Allan enjoyed both success as a dancer and prominence as a member of London society.

Her renown in London and abroad had also familiarized her with legal methods well before the Billing suit; she had taken legal measures against a London review of "The Vision of Salome" that she believed misrepresented her performance, and she had also appeared in an Australian court for breach of contract.[8] For Billing, Allan was the perfect subject upon which to initiate his allegations. Whether or not Billing was privy to Allan's previous court dealings, her sexual infamy could assure Billing a well-publicized event. When Allan read the paragraph that appeared in the *Vigilante* on 16 February 1918, she immediately began a libel action against Noel Pemberton-Billing. Like Oscar Wilde twenty-three years earlier, charged with "posing as a Somdomite [*sic*]," Allan saw no other course of action but legal proceedings.[9]

Prosecution for the "performance" of sexuality had already been legalized by the 1895 Wilde trials. The Marquis of Queensbury's argument concerning Wilde, however tenuous, had succeeded: "I do not say that you are it [a 'sodomite'], but you look it, and you pose at it, which is just as bad."[10] Sex, according to Queensbury's accusation, was not an act with particular meaning, but a distinct identity that could be constituted apart from any act.[11] The act was in the appearance. With the passage of the 1885 Criminal Law Amendment Act under which Wilde was tried, the law criminalized such appearances, although it nevertheless labeled them "acts of gross indecency."[12] The legal phenomenon that followed the accusation of Wilde's *appearance* as a "sodomite" established within legal reasoning that a verdict of guilt indeed might be obtained without proof of the act. Indeed, the performance of "sexual identity" that initiated and subsequently substantiated Wilde's conviction as a sodomite may have suggested to Billing, some years later, that Maud Allan's willingness to perform the part of Salome revealed and played out her essential sexuality. Allan, Billing would try to prove, was a perverse, sadistic lesbian, who was a threat to national security. But "lesbians" were not, or as yet had not been, the subjects of juridical discourse. (Section 11 under which Wilde was tried specifically referred to male subjects and acts.) On trial were the gendered assumptions about what female sexuality entailed. Gender was visible; "lesbianism" was invisible. Thus when the charge of "lesbianism" was dropped at the very end of the legal proceedings (a matter I will discuss later), the jury went into deliberation asking not whether "The Cult of the Clitoris" and Billing's accusations regarding this cult's lesbianism had been proven, but whether Allan had transgressed a normative gender role.

Noel Pemberton-Billing was charged with obscene and defamatory libel, both criminal charges to be prosecuted by the Crown. The mixture of political intrigue implied by the mention of some 47,000 in the *Vigilante* paragraph, as well as the allusion to "unnatural" sexuality in the paragraph's title, was found to be a threat to public order. Yet rather than an interrogation of Billing's interpretation of the play, the trial became the occasion to investigate Allan. Indeed, the trial played out women's subjection to male law and rehearsed how women were defined as sexual objects by it. Allan's reputation as the risqué Salome dancer, her uncertain sexual status, and her fearless initiation of the libel suit itself, all helped to define her as "unwomanly," and indeed, finally a threat, in the eyes of the law. The trial publicly proclaimed female *sensuality* a political threat because it was not sexually definable in terms of the rules of gender. I am substituting the word "sensuality" where "sexuality" might otherwise be used because what constituted sexuality with regard to "lesbianism" (as this trial makes clear) was not yet definable. [13] The Allan case suggests how lesbians became the conspicuous subjects of legal reasoning and what finally defined lesbianism in the language of early twentieth-century English law.

Producing "The Cult"

The Billing case brought into the courtroom the debate between what could be considered the congenital nature and constructed practices of women's sexual activity and sought to define what constituted sexual pleasure for women. The Wilde trials had stripped male persons suspected of "perversity" of their "privacy" through what became the revelatory discourse of "private" letters. The Billing trial, however, made the publicness of the trial itself and Allan's initiation of a libel action against the paragraph titled "The Cult of the Clitoris" the very matter of her guilt. Her professed knowledge of a discourse that women were supposed to be ignorant of was, according to the defendant, and ultimately the jury, a sure sign of her sadism, and subsequently, lesbianism.

The criminal libel trial of Noel Pemberton-Billing opened on 29 May 1918. Maud Allan's counsel, Ellis Hume Williams and Travers Humphreys (Humphreys had been Wilde's counsel) sought to prove that not only was Allan libeled, but also that the libel could constitute a breach of peace and should be punishable by a penalty for Billing of two years' imprisonment. Billing's plea of justification sought to demonstrate that there was truth in the paragraph, that what Allan called libel was published for the public's benefit. Indeed, Billing's argument was that the sexual display in *Salome* was demoralizing and perverting the British public. Maud Allan, according to Billing, was a "lewd, unchaste, and immoral woman" and her private performances of *Salome* were "designed as to foster and encourage obscene and unnatural practices among women." Billing submitted to the court that all the defamatory matters concerning Maud Allan that were alleged in his indictment were true, including the charge that Allan was intimate with persons "addicted to obscene and unnatural practices."[14]

Since Oscar Wilde's trials, the public intervention and social control of male sexuality had become a central political concern. Billing, in fact, stressed Wilde's authorship of *Salome* throughout the trial. He repeatedly invoked the name of Wilde, "a well known monster"[15] to suggest Allan's participation in particular "perverse" sexual acts. Yet Billing sought to prove at the outset of the trial that Maud Allan was not simply a "consensual pervert"; that is, she knew about and was indoctrinated into such "practices," however undefined these "practices" may be. He also claimed that her condition was congenital. Taking his cue from the Wilde trial, Billing thought he could prove Maud Allan's participation in lesbian acts despite the fact that those acts remained undefined. Since lesbian acts have no such history within the legal system, the articulation of lesbian identity was being constructed by Billing, despite the conspicuous absence of discourse about what lesbian sexuality would entail.

Billing's research led him to William Henry Theodore Durrant, an infamous criminal in San Francisco, and the brother of Maud Allan. On the first day of the trial Billing handed Maud Allan *Celebrated Criminal Cases of America* (1910), which had been published by the San Francisco Police Department. He asked her to identify her brother pictured therein. Durrant had been executed in 1898 for murder of and necrophilia with two girls in San Francisco. It was because of Durrant's indictment, trial, and imprisonment that Isabell Durrant, Maud Allan's mother, insisted that her daughter remain in Europe. In her exile from her family and home, Allan initiated a dancing career; it also permitted Allan to distance herself from a family disgrace. The Billing trial became the occasion to resurface the Durrant family's past. Billing, acting as his own counsel, whispered to the judge his intent to prove that Allan's performance as Salome was a sign of her hereditary sadism, indeed, that Allan's "sadism"—and by implication, her "lesbianism"—was congenital. It seemed that Billing wished to limit the acts of "sadism" that Salome performed to the acts that Allan's brother had committed. But if vices were truly hereditary, how could Billing prove that the presentation of vice in the form of the play *Salome* would produce "perverts" rather than repel good people? How, in turn, do these acts of "sadism" correspond, according to Billing, to "lesbianism"?

Like the trials of Oscar Wilde, the suit brought by Maud Allan helped popularize and institutionalize the medico/legal definitions of sexual identity. The Labouchere Amendment of 1885 that made "acts of gross indecency" a crime for men, established within legal reasoning that a wider scope of acts could be prosecuted as sex. It also suggested that not all behavior considered sexual in a political sense is physiologically sexual. As Michel Foucault proclaimed in *The History of Sexuality,* "the homosexual was now a species."[16] Men could "be" homosexuals, therefore, by *desiring* other men, without necessarily participating in acts that were previously defined as "sexual" with other men. For women, however, sexual identity was defined by their availability to and for men. Maud Allan's "lesbianism" was not constituted according to the legal reasoning under which Wilde became the embodiment of "homosexuality," that is, desire for a same-sex sexual partner. If Billing's defense during the trial sought to conflate Allan's sexuality with those acts performed in her role as Salome, how could this be considered lesbian? Salome's sexual preference according to the interpretations of the play during the trial was clearly "heterosexual."[17] That is, Salome's actions that were thought to exhibit her sexuality (and those which were focused on for the purposes of the defense) were directed at the prophet, Jokanaan. In fact, at issue during the trial was not Salome's sexual desire for women, but her longing for and eventual revenge upon Jokanaan. What constituted Salome's (and, in turn, Allan's) "lesbianism," according to this trial, was the "violence" of her sexual arousal.

> Do you really wish the gentlemen of the jury to understand that that illustrates the course of beautiful and pure love for a man? Do you wish the jury to understand that any pure-minded woman would demand for her own sensual satisfaction the head of a man she loved, and would toy with it?[18]

Billing sought again and again with his repertoire of expert witnesses to define the acts of the play as sexually "sadistic," and Miss Allan an accomplice to such "perversity." The defense contended that Maud Allan performed "unnatural practices" playing the part of Salome, and that she was associated with people who enjoyed and celebrated such practices. One of Billing's key witnesses, Captain Spencer, named these "vices" sodomy and lesbianism, and claimed they catered to and were sponsored by German spies. Spencer argued that sodomy was a clear "criminal offense," and lesbianism was an "unnatural vice" that required exposure and prosecution because it posed a danger to the nation. Billing agreed with Spencer that "only perverts . . . practice these vices."[19] Yet in order to implant an image of vice, and the names and faces of the perverse in the minds of the jury, Billing had to define such practices. Sodomy was apparently easy: all Billing had to do was throw around the name of Oscar Wilde and the "cult of sodomy" was implied.[20] Lesbianism, however, was more difficult to prove. Noel Pemberton-Billing, with Captain Spencer's and Dr. Serrell Cooke's help, devised a strategy in which he contended that "sadism" was the "unnatural vice" thematized throughout Oscar Wilde's play. It was the violent sexual arousal induced by sadistic acts that Billing hoped would imply the practices of lesbianism.

"Sadism," Dr. Cooke testified, is "the most monstrous of all the sexual perversions. Lust and sexual excitement are brought about by cruel acts and violence. It is not necessary to perform these acts; these passions may be brought about by simply thinking of the bare idea of them; imagination may bring them about."[21] Salome, however, was intended for performance, not the imagination, and in it, Billing contended that a young girl murdered in order to satisfy her sexual lust. Would performing acts of "sadism" make Allan a sadist herself? Dr.

Cooke seemed to think so: "a person performing the part of Salome must be a sadist."[22] Billing would try to validate this absurd attack when Allan took the witness stand:

BILLING: When you were toying with what the play portrays as the bleeding head of John the Baptist, you were committing an act of sadism in pantomime; do you understand that?

MISS ALLAN: No, I do not understand it.

BILLING: I mean that when you hinted, or said, or endeavored to convey to the audience that you were going to bite those lips through, you were committing an act of sadism; do you understand that?

MISS ALLAN: No, I do not.

BILLING: Do you know what sadism is?

MISS ALLAN: Yes, I do.

BILLING: You say that it was with a knowledge of actual sadism that you still persist—

MISS ALLAN: I do not say I have a knowledge of actual sadism; I said I know what is meant by the word sadism.

BILLING: And you say there is not evidence of it in this play?

MISS ALLAN: There is no evidence of it any more than there is in any other play or opera where passion is portrayed; otherwise every play is a sadic play and every opera is a sadic opera.

BILLING: Do you know of any other play where the head of a man is used as a means of generating sexual excitement in a young girl? . . . You tell me, with your artistic experience and knowledge generally, that you see no signs of sexual excitement in the last act of that tragedy?

MISS ALLAN: Not in the way in which you wish to imply it.[23]

Photographs survive of both Wilde and Allan "posing" as Salome in the moment described above, perhaps the most controversial scene of the play. Their poses mimic each other. Both are full body shots in left profile; they both are kneeling. Wilde reaches down longingly for the head of Jokanaan placed upon a silver platter, while Allan holds the head up between her hands, close to her face, as she is about to seal the "sadistic" kiss. Wilde considered *Salome* the expression of his artistic essence, and both his and Allan's postures as Salome dramatize the performance of identities that challenge the "knowledge" of authentic sexuality. Yet not even the fictive constructions (or costumes) of sexual-

Oscar Wilde in costume as Salome. Collection Guillot de Saxe, Roger-Viollet, Paris.

ity could escape the charge of "knowing" posed by the medical and legal establishments. In the above exchange at the trial, Billing tries to manipulate Allan's understanding of sadism to imply that even her "knowledge" of the word *sadism* is evidence of her participation in

Maud Allan as Salome, 1908. Courtesy of the Raymond Mander and Joe Mitch-enson Theatre Collection Ltd.

sadistic acts. It is this manner of argument made with reference to medical knowledge about women's bodies that would eventually win Billing the case.

Policing Pleasure

The veiled woman at the fin de siècle was a figure of sexual secrecy.[24] In Salome's dance of the seven veils, Salome's unveiling is the dance that seduces Herod and simultaneously shrouds her deathly intentions for Jokanaan. Yet Noel Pemberton-Billing's question to Maud Allan initiates another role for the veiled woman. According to Billing, certain words, terms associated with women's bodies, are only unveiled and revealed to those initiated into sexually subversive acts. Billing, therefore, made repeated reference to the "unveiled" medical naming of the female body in an effort to convince the jury that Allan was one of those initiated. His defense against the charge of criminal libel was that Maud Allan's knowledge of what the medical name "clitoris" referred to made her guilty of the acts themselves, although the trial never makes clear just what "lesbian" acts would consist of. According to Captain Spencer, a self-proclaimed military and medical "authority," the "clitoris" is "what remains of the male organ in the female."[25] His definition implies that a knowledge of the clitoris may make for a masculinized woman, but not necessarily a woman who seeks erotic acts with other women. Billing informed Allan that twenty-four people, including many professional men, had been shown the paragraph in question, and of that number, only one, a lawyer, understood what it meant. Whether any of those twenty-four was a woman is never known; however, Billing could be sure that the members of the all-male jury would ask themselves whether they knew what *clitoris* meant. The "reification of ignorance," as Eve Kosofsky Sedgwick makes brutally clear in *Epistemology of the Closet,* is a powerful tool.[26]

The recourse to medical "knowledge" as a way to implement racial, social, and political discrimination was a familiar and successful tactic. Sexologists, scientists, and medical doctors in the nineteenth and twentieth centuries developed a medical model by which to study and interpret behaviors that were earlier considered social or ethical. Influenced by white middle-class morality, "objective" medical evidence was used in Wilde's trials, for instance, to make discriminations in the moral, political, and aesthetic quality of his written work. Similarly, medical professionals provided evidence in cases which opposed the growing feminist movement (particularly women's suffrage) in England and the United States.[27] Indeed, the libel trials brought by Wilde and Allan are evidence of the many roles that medicine and the law have played in circumscribing normative sexuality and gender behavior.

On the last day of the trial, before the jury was to go into deliberation, the judge decided that the real libel to Allan was limited to the title and first sentence of the *Vigilante* paragraph. This meant that Billing, whose defense strategy had described Allan as a sexually sadistic, perverse performer, who posed a threat to the English nation, was merely responsible for the act of name calling. Judge Darling decided that the libel was contained by the title of the paragraph "The Cult of the Clitoris," stating, "It has been given in evidence what that means; it means these vices which are compendiously described as the lesbian vices; they are described in the play as vices of women with women, and so on, and enlarged by sadism, and so on."[28] At no time during the trial did anyone venture a clear definition or explanation of what was to be understood as "lesbianism" (the judge articulated it here for the first time as "vices of women with women, and so on"). The judge's "and so on" here seems to me roughly the rhetorical equivalent of the 1885 Criminal Law Amendment Act's "and other purposes" that forms part of that Act's title. The phrase "and other purposes" with regard to the Criminal Law Amendment Act allowed the Labouchere Amendment to prosecute sexual relations, or indeed, sexual desire between men in an Act aimed at protecting young women from male heterosexual violence. To criminalize same-sex sexual desire was the "other purpose" of the Act. In Judge Darling's summary for the jury, his use of the phrase "and so on" dangerously broadens the range of actions, identities, and desires that women have that might potentially be labeled among the "perverse." The Allan trial, like the Wilde trial, marked important moments in the production and prosecution of sexualities. The language employed in these particular cases made clear the extent to which legal reasoning circumscribed sexualities. Indeed, in Billing's closing statements the judge permitted him to withdraw the charges of lesbianism that began the proceedings and claim his defense via another tactic. According to Billing, "by the mere act of watching this sadism, the sexual impulse of the audience, of the pervert, is aroused. *Clitoris* is an anatomical term . . . the word was calculated to be here understood only by those people who would refer to these things."[29] If Allan is not "guilty" of "vices of women with women, and so on," she certainly is guilty of understanding an implicit accusation leveled against her, one which only the guilty, according to Billing, might understand. Thus lesbian sexuality is developed within legal reasoning as that which implies some claim to a kind of knowledge that one is not supposed to "know." Indeed, lesbian sexuality is constructed within the early twentieth-century English legal system as acutely caught up with and dependent upon access to knowledge. With nothing but Oscar Wilde's authorship, their ignorance of the play, Allan's brother's crime, and Allan's knowledge of her own body by which to decide the case, the jury returned in one and one-half hours with a verdict of not guilty for Billing. Billing's accusations were not considered libelous, and Maud Allan remained, if not in the courtroom, then to the public beyond it, a lesbian sadist.

In his summary at the end of the trial, Justice Darling noted that women, for the first time in England, would be able to have influence upon legislation by way of the vote. Indeed, for the first time in England this trial subjected lesbianism to legal discourse at a moment when women were not even recognized within the law as full citizens: women did not have voting rights, although activists for political rights were within immediate reach of a victory on this front. The judge stated his hope that women's suffrage would encourage more purity in art, implying that dramas such as *Salome* might no longer be written or performed. Although the judge makes clear the causal relationship he posits between politics and the production of sexualities, he also clarifies the heterosexist presumptions of the court when he intimates that lesbianism must end when women have access to power. Although the judge's statements suggest he was sympathetic to the cause of women's suffrage, the cost, finally, is the restraint of female sexuality.

Allan did not suffer a criminal trial due to the decision of the court, since the accusations of lesbianism were dropped and there was no legislation with regard to nor definition of this practice. Because Billing's accusations that Maud Allan was a "lewd, unchaste, and immoral woman" were not found libelous by the jury, and were, in fact, celebrated in the press, Maud Allan slipped out the back of the courtroom and into relative obscurity.[30] It was only *after* the trial brought by Maud Allan that a 1921 proposal to add a new clause to the Criminal Law Amendment Act was introduced in Parliament. The framers of the proposal sought to mimic the 1885 Labouchere Amendment with a clause that referred specifically to "Acts of Gross Indecency by Females."[31] Because English legislators could not agree that sexual relations between women were possible, it was never ratified.[32]

Nonetheless, the early twentieth-century classifications as to what constituted "lesbianism" differed from the homosexual/heterosexual model of sexual identity articulated by Foucault, and which has been the subject of much discussion and debate since.[33] Lesbianism, according to the legal reasoning advanced in the Billing trial, did not depend upon sexual object choice. For Allan, who did not at this time choose to call herself a lesbian, yet was labeled a lesbian within the English legal system, the Billing trial suggested that the body became the site for the production of sexual identity.[34] It was not, finally, sexual desire for women by a woman, but Allan's apparent knowledge of what the medical discourse about her own body entailed that constituted her participation in the cult of the clitoris, or rather her position as its "master." Billing, of course, was never subject to the same interrogation for his understanding of language; he successfully argued that his language and the paragraph titled "The Cult of the Clitoris" benefited the public, while Allan's understanding of his language perverted the public. Indeed, it was Allan's inability to claim ignorance about the meaning of certain words and the domain of her own body that cemented her guilt. The trial's substantiation of legal reasoning that defines knowledge as a lack of ignorance had tremendous ramifications for the designation and prosecution of sexual identities. It continues to be legally sanctioned ignorance that legitimizes and often perpetuates violence against those subjects today.

NOTES

I would like to thank both Paul Morrison and Wai Chee Dimock for their enthusiasm for this project and their thoughtful comments on previous drafts of this paper, and especially Michael Malone for providing expert legal advice.

1. Although female same-sex sodomy was not recognized in England, it was a capital offense in several other European countries. See Louis Crompton, "The Myth of Lesbian Impunity: Capital Laws from 1270–1791," *Journal of Homosexuality* 6:1–2 (Fall/Winter 1980–81): 11–25, and Judith C. Brown, "Lesbian Sexuality in Medieval and Early Modern Europe," *Hidden From History: Reclaiming the Gay and Lesbian Past,* ed. Martin Bauml Duberman,

Martha Vicinus and George Chauncey, Jr. (New York: Meridian Press, 1989), 67–75.

My thanks to Nancy Goldstein for these references as well as for allowing me to read her fine essay, "Discipline and Publish: Henry Fielding's Policing of 'Lesbian' Sexuality in *The Female Husband*," MS: Boston, MA.

2. Oscar Wilde was tried, convicted, and sentenced to two years' imprisonment under the Criminal Law Amendment Act of 1885. The Act was entitled "An Act to make further provision for the Protection of Women and Girls, the suppression of brothels, and other purposes." Of the twenty separate provisions that comprised the Act, most claimed to limit the sexual availability to men of women under the age of sixteen. The final phrase of the Act's title made clear, however, that the "protection" of young women from male heterosexual violence was not its sole purpose. The Labouchere Amendment (Section 11) was designed to produce and then prosecute "homosexual" men:

> Any male person who, in public or private, commits, or is a party to the commission of, or procures or attempts to procure the commission by any male person of any acts of gross indecency with another male person, shall be guilty of a misdemeanor, and being convicted thereof shall be liable at the discretion of the court to be imprisoned for any term not exceeding two years, with or without hard labor. (Criminal Law Amendment Act, 1885, 48 & 49 Vict., ch. 69, § 11)

3. For a legal history of sodomy, see Ed Cohen, "Legislating the Norm: From Sodomy to Gross Indecency," *South Atlantic Quarterly* 88: 1–2 (1989): 181–221.

4. This paragraph was written by Captain Spencer for Billing's paper, *Vigilante*. Quoted in Michael Kettle, *Salome's Last Veil: The Libel Case of the Century* (London: Granada Publishing, 1977), 18–19. My analysis of the trial is indebted to the transcript of the court proceedings that are published in Kettle's book.

5. Neither Billing's black book nor his accusations were furthering his unstated aim: to overthrow the coalition government and stop peace talks with the Germans. For a discussion of the international politics involved in the trial, see Kettle.

Because my primary focus in this chapter is the trial itself, my characterizations of Noel Pemberton-Billing and Maud Allan are, at best, brief. See the biography of Maud Allan for a fuller discussion of the works written on or about her: Felix Cherniavsky, *The Salome Dancer* (Toronto: McCelland & Stewart, 1991).

For a brief summary of the events of the trial see: Regina Gagnier, Appendix A "Art as Propaganda in Wartime," in *Idylls of the Marketplace: Oscar Wilde and the Victorian Public* (Stanford: Stanford University Press, 1986), 199–206, and Elaine Showalter, *Sexual Anarchy* (New York: Penguin Books, 1990), 162.

6. The play was banned from public performance by the London Lord Chamberlain's office for representing a biblical subject. Wilde never saw his play performed. For a brief history of the play, see Showalter, 149–50.

7. See W. T. Titterton's review of Allan's performance, "The Maud Allan Myth," *New Age*, quoted in Cherniavsky, 174.

8. Cherniavsky, 173, 222.

9. Richard Ellman, *Oscar Wilde* (New York: Vintage Books, 1988), 438.

10. The Marquis of Queensbury quoted in Ellman, 447.

11. Wilde's participation in anal intercourse, which was suggested by the accusation, was unsubstantiated. (This is the act, however, about which most homophobic discourse revolves.) Ibid., 461.

12. The Criminal Law Amendment Act, 1885, 48 & 49 Vict., ch. 69, § 11.

13. See Claudia Card, "Intimacy and Responsibility: What Lesbians Do," in *At The Boundaries of Law: Feminism and Legal Theory,* ed. Martha Albertson Fineman and Nancy Sweet Thomadsen (New York: Routledge, 1991), 72–90. Card's discussion of lesbian "sensuality" has been helpful for my thinking about what constitutes sexuality and how sexualities are defined. My analysis is not meant to suggest that lesbianism was more acceptable; women's sexual relations with other women were merely more unthinkable within the English political and legal systems.

According to historian Lillian Faderman, women did not conceive of themselves by the identity "lesbian" until sexologists at the turn of the century diagnosed "female inversion." See Lillian Faderman, *Odd Girls and Twilight Lovers: A History of Lesbian Life in Twentieth Century America* (New York: Penguin, 1991), 10–61.

14. These statements are part of the criminal indictment of Billing submitted to the court by Allan's counsel. In Billing's plea of justification, Billing confirms the counsel's interpretation of the intentions of the paragraph titled "The Cult of the Clitoris." Essentially, Billing claims that these descriptions of Maud Allan are "true." See Kettle, 65, 229, 246, 259.

15. Dr. Serrell Cooke quoted in Kettle, 152.

16. Michel Foucault, *The History of Sexuality,* vol. 1 (New York: Vintage Books, 1990), 43.

17. I warily invoke sexual "preference" here (which I believe implies an element of choice) to the extent that this category is meaningful when "homosexuality" is illegal and women do not have full "rights" under the law.

18. Billing quoted in Kettle, 74.

19. Kettle, 115.

20. Ibid., 233.

21. Cooke quoted in Kettle, 151.

22. Ibid., 164.

23. See Kettle, 81.

24. See Showalter, 144.

25. Spencer quoted in Kettle, 144.

26. Eve Kosofsky Sedgwick, *Epistemology of the Closet* (Berkeley: University of California Press, 1990), 7.
27. Jane Marcus, "Salome: The Jewish Princess was a New Woman," *Bulletin of the New York Public Library* (1974), 111.
28. Judge Darling quoted in Kettle, 219.
29. Billing quoted in Kettle, 229.
30. Cherniavsky describes her final years as sad and sour; Allan worked in an aircraft factory and taught deportment to Jane Wyman, Reagan's first wife. Cherniavsky, 242–60.
31. Jeffrey Weeks, *Coming Out: Homosexual Politics in Britain from the Nineteenth Century to the Present* (London: Quartet Books, 1977), 105–7.
32. I do not intend this analysis to suggest that such an amendment was necessary for recognizing lesbians, nor do I wish to imply that sexual relations between women were permissible in English culture. I would argue, however, that the erasure of women's sexual agency is systemic, and that this helps sustain the cultural subordination of women and the violence against women.
33. Homosexuality, Foucault argues, was constructed to be a "sexual sensibility, a certain way of inverting the masculine and the feminine in oneself. Homosexuality appeared as one of the forms of sexuality when it was transposed from the practice of sodomy onto a kind of interior androgyny, a hermaphroditism of the soul. The sodomite had been a temporary aberration; the homosexual was now a species." Foucault, 43.
34. Foucault argues that the body is a site of power, and many feminist critics share this idea with Foucault. He describes the discursive construction of women's bodies as:

A hysterization of women's bodies: a threefold process whereby the feminine body was analyzed, qualified and disqualified as being thoroughly saturated with sexuality; whereby it was integrated into the sphere of medical practices, by reason of a pathology intrinsic to it; whereby, finally, it was placed in organic communication with the social body (whose regulated fecundity it was supposed to ensure). (104)

What is interesting, among many things, about the Billing case is that lesbianism was understood as Allan's inexplicable access to the medical discourses in which the "hysterization" of "women's" bodies was constructed.

ELEVEN

The Regulation of Lesbian Sexuality Through Erasure: The Case of Jennifer Saunders

ANNA MARIE SMITH

Jennifer Saunders is a young woman from Yorkshire who was tried and convicted for indecent assault. The charges stemmed from sexual relationships which Saunders had had at the ages of sixteen and seventeen with two women aged fifteen and sixteen years old. The Crown prosecution successfully argued that she had secured the consent of her partners under false pretenses in that she had passed as a man throughout the two relationships. The court heard allegations from her partners that Saunders had used a strap-on dildo in penetrative sex with them, that she had convinced them that her dildo was a penis, and that she had produced elaborate medical stories to account for her feminine breasts and to dissuade her partners from touching her "penis."

Saunders pleaded not guilty to the charges. In letters to her supporters and in interviews with the lesbian and gay press, she countered that her partners were lying. She admitted that she had passed as a man when she had been in the company of her partners' relatives and friends. She nevertheless maintained that both of her partners had always known that she was a woman. There are two particularly significant aspects to her case: first, that it was heard in a court of law in September 1991, and second, that she was indeed convicted of indecent assault and sentenced to six years' imprisonment. In other words, this case reveals much about the status of lesbian sexuality in contemporary official discourse in Britain. We cannot understand its significance until we consider the case in terms of its historical and discursive context.

Saunders's own story has been published in the lesbian and gay press. In a letter written to her supporters in the lesbian and gay direct action group, OutRage!, she stated that one of the two relationships had lasted eighteen months and that she had only passed as a man at the request of her partner. Saunders wrote:

> She knew I was a bird and that she was a lesbian. But her mom and dad were middle-class and snotty, so she told her family I was a man to make herself clear, if you know what I mean. . . . I couldn't believe it when I was arrested. I went along with all the stupid things she was saying as I loved her more than anything in the world. I couldn't hurt her. So I promised to say nothing. [1]

After spending almost nine months in prison, Saunders won her High Court appeal, had her sentence reduced to two years' probation, and was immediately released. Lesbian journalist Cherry Smyth interviewed Saunders directly after the judges handed down their decision. Smyth published her interview with Saunders in two lesbian and gay publications, *Capital Gay*, a London weekly newspaper, and the *Advocate*, an American monthly magazine. In the interview, Saunders commented on the conditions in prison and on her earlier sexual relationships.

> "The prison's full of dykes. They all come in and turn. I've had a girlfriend there for nine months. It's like Paradise City in Styal [Prison]. They all kept joking about my dildo." And where pray in Yorkshire did she get the strap on we all read about. She laughed. "There never was no dildo. They thought there had to be a penis involved so they said that about the dildo." She paused and grinned. "My tongue was good enough." [2]

This interpretation of the relationships between Saunders and her two partners was certainly not shared by the courts. In his sentencing remarks, Judge Crabtree of the Doncaster Crown Court stated that Saunders's alleged assaults constituted an offense that was far more serious than heterosexual rape because Saunders had violated not only the sanctity of her alleged victims' bodies, but their heterosexual identities as well. Judge Crabtree stated:

> You have called into question their whole sexual identity and I suspect both those girls would rather have been actually raped by some young

man than have happened to them what you did. At least that way, given time and counselling, those girls might have been able to forget it more easily than I suspect they will forget the obvious disgust they now feel at what has happened to them.[3]

The fact that Judge Crabtree not only accepted the impossible accounts of Saunders's partners as perfectly credible evidence, but aiso viewed Saunders's alleged deception as more serious than the brutal crime of rape, reveals the sexist and homophobic character of his standpoint on the case. Judge Crabtree should not be regarded as a maverick judge who deviated from British judicial norms. I will demonstrate that his standpoint actually reflects the hegemonic tendency within official discourse on lesbian sexuality.

Judge Crabtree's six-year sentence for the alleged indecent assaults was intended not only to discipline Saunders, but also as a warning to other lesbian and bisexual women. He stated:

Apart from the possible risk to the public I take the view these offences are far and away too serious to be dealt with in any other way than by a long custodial sentence. . . . Also, in these days of sexual openness about lesbianism and bisexual behaviour, I think I have to ensure that anybody else who is tempted to try and copy what you did will, first of all, count the cost of it.[4]

Judge Crabtree's comments indicate that for all the unique aspects of Saunders's case, he associated her behavior with the dangerously subversive advance of the feminist and sexual liberation movements. The fact that the rights of women, lesbians, and gay men have actually come under increasing attack through the 1980s and 1990s in Britain is irrelevant to Crabtree's perceptions. Like many other British officials, Judge Crabtree viewed these gains as dangerous steps on a "slippery slope" toward the destruction of heterosexual and patriarchal norms. From his perspective, then, Saunders's sentence had to be addressed not only to her but also to other nonheterosexual women, who, by their perverted nature, would probably reproduce Saunders's alleged crime. As I will argue below, lesbians are rarely represented as dangerous sexual predators; we are usually sanitized to support homophobic attacks on gay men, and, when we are specifically demonized, it is usually with reference to some additional aspect of our identities. Judge Crabtree's anticipation of women's imitation of Saunders' alleged deception constitutes an important exception to this general tendency.

However, his use of an imitation trope in his remarks is not purely accidental. After the prosecution argued that Saunders had deceived her partners by imitating a male heterosexual, Judge Crabtree re-articulated the equation of lesbianism and imitation in his judgment. From a homophobic and sexist perspective, lesbianism is nothing but a deceptive imitation, nothing but a masquerade. From sexist pornographic images which reduce lesbian sex to supplementary foreplay which merely prepares the way for male heterosexual pleasure, to Section 28 of the Local Government Act, 1987–88, which describes lesbian parenting as a "pretend family relationship," lesbianism is represented as a pale shadow of the "real thing"—male heterosexuality and the patriarchal control of women's sexuality. If Saunders had passed as a man and then had had sex with men, or if Saunders had been male, passed as a woman, and then had had sex with women, her trial would have never taken place, for the seriousness of her crime was directly proportional to the value of the norms which she had displaced through masquerade. Certainly no British judge would have interpreted a woman's imitation of a gay man or a man's imitation of a lesbian as a crime that was more serious than rape. For the courts, Saunders's gender and that of her partners was of crucial importance in the case. Her crime did not simply consist in deception in a sexual relationship, for it was a gender-specific crime framed within a heterosexist value system, namely the crime of realizing the subversive potential of lesbian masquerade: the displacement of the male heterosexual.

The evidence against Saunders was reviewed in the Court of Appeal. It is clear from the Court of Appeal judgment that the three presiding judges fully accepted the Crown prosecution's version of Saunders's relationships, namely that she had had consensual sex with two women, but that both partners had believed that she was male. The "facts" of the case, Lord Justice Staughton stated, were that Saunders had successfully misrepresented a dildo as a penis in penetrative sex with one woman on twenty different occasions across a two-month period. Without a trace of irony, Lord Justice Staughton noted, "Oral sex occurred between them both ways."[5] The judges also accepted the basic logic of Judge Crabtree's original sentence. They agreed that the alleged indecent assaults had caused "damage to these girls and very serious damage to the mother of one of them." They only differed with Judge Crabtree on two points. First, they stated that, given the fact that Saunders was sixteen and seventeen years old at the time of the alleged offenses, the sentence was "substantially too long." Second, they did not challenge Judge Crabtree's use of the sentence as a warning to other women, but questioned its effectiveness. Lord Justice Staughton stated:

> There is only one respect in which we would question what [Judge Crabtree] said. That is when he said . . . that he wished the sentence imposed on Miss Saunders to be a deterrent to others who might otherwise be minded to commit such offences. We question whether it would, in practice, have that effect. [6]

Even with the Court of Appeal's reduction of Saunders's sentence, then, the Crown's interpretation of her actions was preserved in the official record.

For both courts, a virtually impossible story of gender impersonation was accepted as a credible account. Saunders's interpretation of the facts—namely that her partners had indeed known that she was a woman, had had sexual relationships with her on the basis of informed consent, but had produced their narratives of Saunders's deception under tremendous homophobic parental pressure—was ruled out as incredible. We might usefully begin our attempt to understand the logic of the courts' interpretation by examining another case in which a woman was not believed, namely the Anita Hill/Clarence Thomas hearings. Kimberlé Crenshaw argues that Anita Hill's testimony was dismissed as untrue not because of its specific content, nor because of Hill's individual identity, but because it was already de-authorized within the hegemonic framework of contemporary American legal discourse. Black women's credibility is sharply limited because their narratives do not fit within the parameters of officially recognized narratives. Gender discrimination narratives have obtained some degree of official credibility, but official interpretations of these narratives tend to presuppose a white woman complainant. In the case of racial discrimination narratives, official interpretations presuppose a black male complainant. As a black woman, Anita Hill's credibility was already greatly diminished even before the hearings began because there was no authorized position from which she could speak. Black women are represented in official discourse as a social problem, as an object of social control strategies rather than a subject who is capable of producing her own coherent versions of official discourse. [7]

This is of course precisely the way in which hegemonic erasure operates. Hegemony does not take the form of brute domination; it entails instead the delimitation of the intelligible, the naturalization of one specific discursive field as the only coherent discursive field.[8] To be subjected to a hegemonic strategy does not mean that one is forced to believe a certain ideology; it means that the extent of one's credibility is directly proportional to one's occupation of a legitimized position. In the case of Anita Hill, the combined effects of hegemonic sexist and racist codes were such that her black woman's sexual harassment narrative was relegated to the sphere of the unintelligible. Her narrative was consequently framed in terms of hostile perspectives such that Hill was transformed into a psychologically deranged woman and a victim of a white feminist plot. Without these hegemonic reconstructions, Hill's narrative would have failed to conform to the rules of coherence which had been installed as the only possible rules of coherence.[9]

Hegemonic discourse regulates subjectivity, then, by preparing a table of legitimate positions in advance; although no one ever fully occupies any one position, some subjects "fit into" the prefabricated positions better than others. To fail to achieve an adequate "fit" within an officially recognized position is to be de-authorized—to be denied recognition as an author of a text, and to have one's text dismissed from the start as incoherent, illegitimate, or unbelievable. Hegemonic discourse also regulates subjectivity insofar as it authorizes each of the legitimized positions only through the exclusion of other positions.[10] Viewed in terms of a strategic discursive analysis, the de-authorization of Anita Hill's discourse is not an isolated event or an historical accident; it is instead the effect of a whole complex set of hegemonic strategies.

The analogy between the erasures of Hill and Saunders is not a perfect one; while Hill was de-authorized because of her blackness, in spite of her heterosexuality, upper middle-class professional status, and conservative political credentials, Saunders was de-authorized because of her youth, working-class background, lesbianism, and criminal status, in spite of her whiteness. Saunders faced several criminal charges in addition to the sexual assault charge. At her trial, Saunders pleaded guilty to charges relating to the receipt of stolen property, the burglary of a school, the burglary of a private home, the theft of a vehicle, and an assault. From the court documents and Smyth's interview with Saunders, it is not at all clear whether the police discovered Saunders's criminal behavior during the investigation of her alleged sexual deception, or vice

versa. We can nevertheless suggest that the connections between these
two different groups of charges were significant. For the courts, Saunders was a juvenile delinquent whose correction depended upon the
gathering of detailed information about that aspect of her life which—
in the case of a law-abiding, middle-class, heterosexual man—would
have been regarded as private conduct. In Foucaultian terms, the courts'
interrogation of Saunders's sexual practices was entirely "normal" when
considered in terms of the modern disciplinary tradition. The establishment of this tradition entailed the subjection of underclasses and social
demon figures to the observations, individualizations, and minute descriptions which had been previously reserved for the heroization of the
elite.[11] In other words, officials in another time and culture would
have never bothered to investigate the mundane practices of Jennifer
Saunders; such attention would have been reserved solely for the docu-
mentation of the everyday life of the social elite. In a modern British
setting, however, it was indeed very much the court's business to establish a complete psychological profile of Saunders. As a working-class
delinquent—and, even worse, a female delinquent—Saunders became
just one more legitimate target of hierarchical surveillance, normalizing
judgment, and disciplinary techniques.

The courts' representation of Saunders's sexual practices was also
framed within a specific historical tradition, namely the representation
of lesbianism in British legal discourse. To analyze the representation of
the lesbian in this discourse is to perform an archaeology of erasure.
Lesbian practices were not referred to in Henry VIII's 1533 law on
sodomy, the 1861 and 1885 laws on sodomy and gross indecency,
the 1898 Vagrancy Act which dealt with female prostitution and male
homosexuality, the 1967 Sexual Offences Act which decriminalized a
narrowly defined set of male homosexual practices, or Section 25 of the
1991 Criminal Justice Act which increased the severity of sentences for
"public" sexual offenses.[12] These absences do not reflect some particularly benevolent attitude toward lesbians; on the contrary, they are the
products of deeply misogynist ideas about women's sexuality. When
attempts were made in 1921 to include lesbian practices in the category
of gross indecency, Lord Desart argued that this inclusion would be
inappropriate in that it would only bring lesbian sex "to the notice of
women who [had] never heard of it, never thought of it, never dreamed
of it."[13]

This erasure of lesbianism in official criminal discourse is the product of two representational strategies. First, lesbianism is defined with reference to hegemonic conceptions of women's "feminine" nature, and, second, femininity is equated with sexual passivity. Many feminist theorists, most notably Gayle Rubin, reject the conflation of gender and sexuality in hegemonic discourse. They contend that no one's gender naturally determines their sexuality. Both the assumption that female physiology necessarily produces feminine behavior and the equation of feminine behavior with sexual passivity are illegitimate. The same is true for biological males, masculine behavior, and men's sexual practices. The linkage or articulation between biological bodies, gendered behavior, sexual practices, and sexual object choice is, in theory, purely undetermined. If some articulations become more "normal" than others, this is only because oppressive institutions such as sexism, heterosexism, and sexual demonizations consistently reward conformity to the norm and impose heavy socioeconomic penalties on deviants.[14]

Read from a feminist perspective, the logic behind the erasure of lesbianism is problematic on three counts. It is simply not true that all women are feminine and all men are masculine; indeed, the very terms, "feminine" and "masculine" are constantly being redefined through subversive "gender-bending" practices. Second, only sexist discourse equates femininity with absolutely passive behavior; as many feminine men and women have shown, there is no contradiction between femininity and assertiveness. Indeed, this colonization of women within the so-called natural category of passive helplessness legitimates the deauthorization of women's discourse, such that our self-representation is displaced by paternal control. Finally, the articulation between an individual's gender identity—her/his femininity, masculinity, or some other gendering—and her/his sexuality—her/his active or passive role-playing; her/his heterosexuality, bisexuality, or homosexuality; her/his "straightness" or "kinkiness"; and so on—is entirely contingent. As the lesbian saying goes, one can be "butch in the streets and femme in the sheets"; we simply cannot predict the ways in which gender and sexuality will coincide in any particular performance.

The strategies at work behind the erasure of lesbianism—the conflation of gender and sexuality and the reduction of women to absolutely passive beings—are not accidental maneuvers. Their arguments conform to the much wider patriarchal discourse in which women are treated as commodities which are exchanged between men in the constitution of their cultural relationships.[15] In Western cultures, for example, women are passed from father to husband in the marriage ritual, and the marriage establishes a whole new set of bonds between previously unrelated individuals. Patriarchal discourse protects the commodification of women by erasing the very possibility that women could be the subjects of our sexual practices. The naturalization of the idea that women are incapable of assertive sexual practices therefore plays a central role in patriarchal relations, for it legitimates the treatment of women as the sexual property of men.

The general erasure of women's sexual subjectivity has ambiguous effects: some lesbians have successfully escaped from the criminalization of our sexual practices precisely because their practices have been relegated to the sphere of the impossible. In the parliamentary debates on Section 28 of the Local Government Act, 1987–88, which prohibited the promotion of homosexuality by local governments, it was for the most part gay male sexuality which was represented as a threat to the social order. Supporters of the Section consistently invoked an image of what I have called the "good homosexual," a law-abiding, self-contained, invisible, and apolitical subject who keeps herself/himself behind closet doors. Like the supporters of President Bill Clinton's "don't ask, don't tell" policy on lesbians and gays in the American military, the supporters of Section 28 promised that as long as lesbians and gays conformed to the standards of the "good homosexual," we would win full social acceptance. The point is that no one can actually occupy the position of the "good homosexual" because the standards of self-discipline for this imaginary figure are impossibly strict—and they are, of course, much stricter than the standards of the "good heterosexual." The supporters of Section 28 developed the image of the "good homosexual" to clarify their real target, the "dangerous homosexual." Through intensely homophobic arguments, they depicted virtually every lesbian and gay man who failed to conform to the standards of the "good homosexual" as a "dangerous homosexual": a diseased, self-promoting leftist subject who preyed upon innocent children and flaunted his/her perversion in public at every opportunity.

For our purposes, it should be noted that the good homosexual and dangerous homosexual were also differentiated in terms of gender. Lord Halsbury argued, for example, that in contrast to the dangerous excesses of gay male sexuality, lesbians are "not a problem": "They do not molest little girls. They do not indulge in disgusting and unnatural acts like buggery. They are not wildly promiscuous and do not spread venereal disease."[16] He further claimed that gay men attempt to conceal their dangerous practices by placing the term "lesbian" before the term "gay" in the names of community groups, such that the "relatively harmless lesbian leads on to the vicious gay."[17] There were two exceptions to this total sanitization of the lesbian in official homophobic discourse—black lesbians were identified as dangerous political activists and lesbian mothers were depicted as perverted parents. But, for the most part, the lesbian simply did not exist in the parliamentary debates—she only made explicit appearances as a de-sexualized "good homosexual" to support the demonization of the dangerous gay man.

Understood in terms of this tradition of erasure, the courts' reaction to Saunders's case becomes coherent. The courts had to construct an account which both accommodated Saunders's sexual subjectivity as a possible phenomenon and obeyed the limits of the official tradition. The judges recognized that the three women had had several sexual interactions and that Saunders had initiated these interactions. However, with their recognition of Saunders's sexual subjectivity, the judges in effect ruled out Saunders's lesbianism, for, as an active sexual subject, she had clearly violated the conditions which governed the representation of the lesbian in official discourse. There were only three pre-authorized positions in legal discourse which could have accommodated Saunders's sexual subjectivity—the heterosexual male, the dangerous gay man, and the heterosexual female prostitute. The heterosexual female prostitute is of course one of the very few women figures who are recognized as sexual subjects in official discourse; she owes her specificity precisely to the fact that she threatens to disrupt the exchange of women between men along patriarchal familial lines.

Like Anita Hill, Saunders could not be believed because she did not adequately "fit" into a pre-authorized position. Saunders could not speak in court as a sexually active lesbian because that position had been already hegemonically erased. The courts also did not invest Saunders— a white English woman—with the dangerous agency of the black lesbian figure; their treatment of this case probably would have been radically different if the accused had been African British or Afro-Caribbean British. Saunders's practices were therefore understood as the key to her deception: since she was a white English woman who had taken an active and explicitly sexual role in relationships with women, she must have been passing as a heterosexual man. Her masquerade as a man was interpreted as the condition of possibility for her sexual practices: the courts reasoned that without her male appearance, and without the imaginary penis that was imposed upon her, she would have never successfully persuaded her two partners to have sex with her. With the prosecution of gay men, by contrast, it would be quite unusual for the court to assume that a gay man must have passed as a woman if he had engaged in consensual sex with another man.

The courts' interpretation of Saunders's gender performance is of course a cruel misreading. Her masquerade was indeed the condition of possibility of her relationships—not because of the impossibility of lesbian sexuality in and of itself, but because of the fact that with the tremendous pressures of homophobic bigotry which Saunders faced, she had had to conceal her lesbianism, and the lesbianism of her partners, behind her gender masquerade. With their interpretation, the courts' antilesbian erasure came full circle: Saunders's own resistance to homophobia was taken as proof of her deception of the very women that she was trying to protect.

The courts' use of a rape charge against Saunders, and Judge Crabtree's original six-year sentence, which is much longer than that of most convicted rapists, are also significant. The relative value of the victim, determined from the point of view of the courts, is a primary factor in rape cases. The rapes of working-class women, prostitutes, women of color, and foreign women are not taken as seriously as the rapes of white European middle-class or upper-class women. According to the sexist logic which is still hegemonic in criminal discourse, the real plaintiffs in a rape case are the persons—usually male—who have lost social standing because of the devaluation of the woman victim.[18] Saunders had had two women partners, and one of them came from a middle-class family. The parents of the latter woman played an active part in Saunders's prosecution. In Saunders's case, they were the real plaintiffs. The rape charge against Saunders was intended to rescue the social value of her middle-class partner, to restore not only her honor but that of her parents as well. For the courts and the parents, there was no question that Saunders's middle-class partner had been "violated" by Saunders's lesbian practices. Given their homophobia, the restoration of the partner's value necessitated the construction of the fiction of her heterosexuality, and, in turn, the transformation of Saunders into a pseudo-male. Whereas Judge Crabtree explicitly concluded that the middle-class partner would have been better off raped by a man, he also implicitly concluded that she would also be better off if she emerged from the whole ordeal as an incredibly naive victim of deception rather than an active lesbian lover.

The apparatus of erasure was therefore deployed, above all, against the lesbian desires of Saunders's partner. Her relatively high social value as a white "heterosexual" middle-class English woman was the major stake in the case. The case would have been handled differently if the accused had been black, but there would have been no trial at all if the alleged victims had been black, working-class, juvenile delinquents or sex trade workers. There would have been no wrong to address because a rape charge presupposes the despoiling of a valuable commodity and none of these women would have been recognized as valuable commodities by the courts. The courts' erasure of the lesbianism of Saunders's partners was also relatively easy given her specific identity. It is simply not true that all lesbians are equally "invisible." Black lesbians, working-class butches, and lesbian prison inmates pay a very high price for their extraordinary visibility. If we could imagine a lesbian visibility/invisibility continuum, these women would be located at the far end of the visibility scale. At the opposite end, we would find—for radically different reasons—Asian lesbians and white English upper-class lesbians. The race and class structure of lesbian erasure had in this sense already prepared the way for the courts' misinterpretation of Saunders's narrative.

The conflation of gender and sexuality in sexist discourse is also structured in terms of race and class differences. Asian women and white upper-class women are supposed to exhibit exemplary forms of femininity. The upper-class white woman possesses exemplary femininity for sexist discourse since its very notion of femininity is in essence a racist and bourgeois construct which passes as a universal category. In racist discourse, Asian women, Asian gay men, Asian heterosexual men, and indeed the Orient itself are equally represented as feminine, irrational, passive, and open to penetration. Viewed from the Orientalist perspective which informs virtually every Western perception of Asian culture, to be Asian is to be incoherent and helpless without the intervention of the white male European.[19] If lesbianism is generally erased wherever it is articulated with a sexist conception of femininity, then it is erased most effectively in the case of white upper-class women and Asian women. Lesbians who are, by contrast, working class, black, and/ or delinquent acquire much more visibility because they are women who, by their racial, class, and criminal status, cannot possess exemplary forms of femininity.

The relative invisibility of lesbian desire in the white middle-class English lesbian is therefore the product of a complex intersection of gender, race, class, and sexual differences. Wherever she actually benefits from her relative invisibility, she does so only within a structure which penalizes her working-class, black, and criminalized counterparts all the more severely. For every privileged woman with lesbian desires who disappears in a visual sense back into heterosexuality with relative ease, there is always some "other" woman who is subjected to increased surveillance. If Saunders's middle-class partner's lesbianism was going to be erased, such that the status of her parents could be restored, someone else had to pay the price. The actual exchange which took place in Saunders's case—the normalization of her partner in return for her imprisonment—can in this sense be read as a symbolic metaphor for a much more general relationship in which working-class, black, and/or delinquent lesbians carry a disproportionate burden of demonization on behalf of their privileged counterparts. Paying the price and carrying the burden for her privileged partner meant, for Saunders, being trans- formed into a pseudo-male and a rapist of her lover. The transformation of Saunders for the courts was not that difficult; as a working-class delinquent, she was already a poor specimen of femininity. Her passage from working-class delinquent woman to aggressive rapist masculinity was, for the courts, a relatively short journey.

Ironically enough, Saunders herself was caught up in another bour- geois tradition, that of romantic love and male-defined heroic sacrifice for a helpless woman lover. In her letter from prison, the spirit of self- negation for the sake of her lover's protection moves though her text : "I went along with all the stupid things she was saying as I loved her more than anything in the world. I couldn't hurt her. So I promised to say nothing." The male-defined heroic "lover" is supposed to prove his "love" by paying the price of self-dissolution in exchange for the love object's pleasure. Above all, he expects no heroic behavior on the part of the rescued woman; as a passive victim of fate, she is absolved of all responsibility for her own discourse. Taking on the role of the romantic male hero, Saunders does not blame her partner for condemning her to the painful experience of prosecution and incarceration. In a truly queer twist of fate, Saunders's expression of devotion can be misread as tacit consent for the class-differentiated exchange relationship which resulted in her prison sentence. Saunders speaks as if she went to jail out of love for her partner, but the courts never actually recognized her status as a lesbian lover.

Saunders's case clearly raises problems for the debates on gender parody which are currently quite prominent in American lesbian, gay, and bisexual studies. Judith Butler's own insistence on contextualizing gender performances within specific configurations of power relations and hegemonic traditions[20] is often lost in the voluntarist "I-can-be-anyone-I-want-to-be" tendency within these debates. The imposition by the courts of their interpretation of Saunders's gender performance as the only possible interpretation serves as a timely reminder of the fact that hegemonic institutions and traditions can often redefine the practices and resistances of oppressed peoples against their intentions.

This analysis of the Saunders case also raises various methodological questions which cannot be fully dealt with here. Saunders's own interpretation of her relationships which was published in the lesbian and gay press constitutes a typical example of what James Scott calls a "hidden transcript" of resistance.[21] The official transcript of her case does not include any mention of Saunders's version of her relationships. Judge Crabtree only referred to her laughter and "boasting" in court, interventions which he interpreted as contempt. Saunders's account therefore constitutes a "hidden transcript" in that it is an unauthorized narrative which refuses to obey the logic of the hegemonic framework. However, it would be misleading to suggest that invisible lesbian relationships are simply hidden from view, and that they remain purely unaffected by the processes through which they are brought to light. Joan Scott rightly warns us that when we claim that we are merely "uncovering" invisible relationships, we actually de-historicize identity. She urges us to pay close attention to the fact that identity claims are contextually constructed and, as such, are always being reformed, broken down, and reconstructed.[22]

Saunders's lesbianism, then, was not simply there all along, waiting to be recognized. Given her comments on her prison experience, it is highly probable that her nine-month incarceration in Styal Prison—a detention which was meant to block further lesbian imitations—actually reconstructed her lesbian identity after the trauma of the first trial. A solidarity campaign in support of Saunders was organized by LABIA (Lesbians Answer Back in Anger), the lesbian subgroup within the direct action lesbian and gay group, OutRage! LABIA's campaign was also performative in that it gave lesbian activists a valuable rallying point. Gay male activism in Britain predominantly takes the form of resistance to the legal persecution of gay men;[23] the Saunders case provided LABIA with a rare opportunity to put lesbian sexuality on the gay rights agenda. Before we take pleasure in these unintended outcomes, and before we indulge in the apparently innocent enjoyment which comes with every discovery of a concealed text, we need to count the cost of the courts' regulation of lesbian sexuality through erasure. To whom do we send the bill?

NOTES

I would like to acknowledge the invaluable assistance of Cherry Smyth who shared her resources on the Jennifer Saunders case with me. I presented the original version of this chapter at the 1993 Berkshire Conference on the History of Women. My thanks to Carolyn Dean and Brenda Marston for their helpful comments as respondent and chair of our "Lesbian Erasures" panel.

1. Quoted in Cherry Smyth, "Out News," *City Limits* (Nov. 21–28, 1991): 52.

2. Cherry Smyth, "Judge Frees Jailed Lesbian," *Capital Gay* (19 June 1992): 1. To my knowledge, Saunders has only been interviewed for publication by Smyth. Although the tabloid press did publish various stories on the case, Smyth's interview and Saunders's letter constitute the only reliable sources which describe the case from Saunders's point of view.

3. Judge Crabtree, Sentence, *Regina v. Jennifer Lynne Saunders,* Crown Court at Doncaster (20 September 1991): 1–2.

4. Crabtree, Sentence, 2.

5. Lord Justice Staughton, Mr. Justice McKinnon, and Mr. Justice Potter, Judgment, *Regina v. Jennifer Lynne Saunders,* Court of Appeal, Criminal Division, Royal Courts of Justice (12 June 1992): 3.

6. Staughton, McKinnon, and Potter, Judgment, 7.

7. Kimberlé Crenshaw, "Whose Story Is It, Anyway? Feminist and Antiracist Appropriations of Anita Hill," *Race-ing Justice, En-Gendering Power,* ed. Toni Morrison (New York: Pantheon Books, 1992), 402–40. In the wake of the two trials of the Los Angeles police officers who beat Rodney King, we should also

note the almost total de-authorization in American legal discourse of black men who have a criminal record.

8. Ernesto Laclau and Chantal Mouffe, *Hegemony and Socialist Strategy* (London: Verso, 1985); Judith Butler, *Gender Trouble* (New York: Routledge, 1990).

9. For other examples of this type of hegemonic de-authorization and erasure, see Edward Said, *Orientalism* (New York: Percgrine Books, 1985); and Zakia Pathak and Rajeswari Sunder Rajan, " 'Shahbano,' " in *Feminists Theorize the Political*, ed. Judith Butler and Joan Scott (New York: Routledge, 1992), 257–79.

10. Judith Butler, "Contingent Foundations: Feminism and the Question of 'Postmodernism,' " in *Feminists Theorize the Political*, 13.

11. Michel Foucault, *Discipline and Punish* (New York: Random House, 1979), 191–92.

12. For a more detailed historical discussion of the erasure of lesbianism in Europe, see Judith Brown, "Lesbian Sexuality in Medieval and Early Modern Europe", in *Hidden From History: Reclaiming the Gay and Lesbian Past*, ed. Martin Bauml Duberman, Martha Vicinus, and George Chauncey, Jr. (New York, Meridian, 1993), 67–75.

13. Quoted in Jeffrey Weeks, *Coming Out: Homosexual Politics in Britain From the Nineteenth Century to the Present* (London: Quartet, 1977), 106–7.

14. Gayle Rubin, "Thinking Sex," in Carole Vance, ed., *Pleasure and Danger* (New York: Routledge, 1984), 267–319.

15. Gayle Rubin, "The Traffic in Women: Notes on the 'Political Economy' of Sex," in *Toward an Anthropology of Women*, ed. Rayna Reiter (New York: Monthly Review Press, 1975), 157–210.

16. *Official Report*, House of Lords (18 December 1986), 310.

17. Ibid., 310.

18. Angela Davis, *Women, Race and Class* (New York: Random House, 1981), 172–201.

19. Said, *Orientalism;* Sunil Gupta, "Black, *Brown* and White," in *Coming On Strong: Gay Politics and Culture*, ed. S. Shepherd and M. Wallis (London: Unwin Hyman, 1989), 163–79; Pratibha Parmar, "Gender, Race and Class: Asian Women in Resistance," in *The Empire Strikes Back: Race and Racism in 1970s Britain*, Centre for Contemporary Cultural Studies (London: Hutchinson, 1982), 212–35.

20. Butler, *Gender Trouble*.

21. James Scott, *Domination and the Arts of Resistance* (New Haven: Yale University Press, 1990).

22. Joan Scott, "Experience," in *Feminists Theorize the Political*, 22–40.

23. Anna Marie Smith, "Resisting the Erasure of Lesbianism: A Challenge for Queer Activism," in *Modern Homosexualities: Fragments of Lesbian and Gay Experience*, ed. Ken Plummer (London: Routledge, 1992), 200–216.

PART III

Lesbian Erotics in Film and Literature

TWELVE

She Must Be Seeing Things Differently: The Limits of Butch/Femme

KARIN QUIMBY

Toward the middle of Sheila McLaughlin's film *She Must Be Seeing Things,* Agatha, Jo's lesbian lover, steps from behind a curtain dressed in a man's suit and tie with her hair combed back looking like the quintessential butch. This dramatic change of clothing is apparently a jealous response to Jo's admission that she will be having lunch with a male colleague. Agatha then proceeds secretly to follow and watch Jo on her lunch date and eventually imagines or hallucinates that Jo is having sex with this man in the backseat of a car. While her jealousy may have some foundation given Jo's heterosexual past, what is striking about this scene is that Agatha dons male or butch attire to represent, somehow, her desire for Jo. As in several other erotic scenes in the film, Jo and Agatha's desire for one another is also represented through butch/femme roles or performances which might lead us to suspect that the erotics of their relationship functions primarily through these identities.

Shortly before the scene in which Agatha changes into a suit, she arrives at a sex shop one evening in search of a "realistic" dildo which, like the butch/femme scenes, renders the desire between Jo and Agatha as gendered; that is, in terms that can be traced, despite their possible subversion of these models, to heterosexuality or sexual difference. Although Agatha eventually decides against any of the plastic or rubbery models placed on the counter by the clerk, this scene not only underscores the terms of lesbian desire in the film, which relies on gendered models of identification such as butch/femme, but encapsulates the recent fixation on dildos in lesbian culture and theory.

These "erotic" moments dramatize the very debate within the lesbian community between lesbians who define themselves as sex-positive and who practice any form of lesbian sex they want (which includes dildos, s/m, butch/femme, and watching, buying, making pornography), and those who remain committed to more traditional, or what is sometimes called "vanilla," sex. Agatha's trip to the sex shop represents ambivalence toward the two sides of this debate; she decides not to purchase the dildo, but she has, after all, made the trip. It is not surprising that *She Must Be Seeing Things* has been taken up in lesbian feminist theory as an important film about lesbian desire because it so distinctly examines the erotics of butch/femme roles or postures. The centrality of butch/femme in this film indeed represents the extreme shift in lesbian/ feminist thought from twenty years ago when these identities were considered retrograde because of their apparent mimicry of heterosexuality. Today butch/femme is affirmed not because it replicates a heterosexual model, but because while appearing to affirm it, it actually subverts it. This kind of thinking perhaps invokes the scene in the porn shop, where one might have one's dildo and leave it, too.

Given the fact that lesbian theorists have eagerly taken up analysis of how butch/femme subverts heterosexual models in an attempt to theorize autonomous lesbian desire, it is interesting that much controversy erupted from the lesbian community around the focus on heterosexuality in this film as if it were simply affirming—rather than simultaneously subverting—relationships to heterosexuality. While it remains important to theorize what are and have been central models of lesbian attraction such as butch/femme, this interpretive conflict also might signal the need to explore new paradigms of lesbian desire. Sue-Ellen Case's article "Toward a Butch-Femme Aesthetic" has largely defined the theoretical terms of the contemporary debate regarding butch/ femme. She emphasizes for instance that the butch/femme couple disrupts the hetero, patriarchal order by playing "*on* the phallic economy rather than *to* it."[1] Lesbian desire thus is not wholly outside a heterosexual order, but plays off of it in a particular way that destroys its dominant meanings, and encodes instead an autonomous lesbian desire. June Reich argues similarly that in lesbian sex the dildo has potential to upset gender categories, an argument which exemplifies the concern with playing *on* and not *to* the phallic. The dildo represents, she says, "the arbitrariness of the hegemonic phallus = penis construction, while attending to the rigid logic of the phallic economy."[2] Thus, according to Reich, the dildo paradoxically holds the potential both to acknowledge and destabilize sexual difference.

The problem of course is that dominant codes of representation insist on reading or seeing the dildo, whether attached to the lesbian body or not, as confirming masculinity and thus the very sexual difference it is also supposedly subverting. The same has been said about the butch/femme couple. The point, to me, is that despite the degree to which we may play *on* the phallic economy (rather than *to* it), by using such paradigms we always reconfirm a single male libido no matter how much we also call it into question.[3] Given the circularity of this argument, perhaps it would be more useful at this point in lesbian sexuality studies to articulate other possible paradigms of lesbian desire: ones not based exclusively on the possible subversion of heterosexuality.

The erotic lure of butch/femme has frequently been located in its play with difference in power and gender, which both carry the potential to excite desire. However, we might consider how other kinds of differences between lesbians may draw them together. While the desire between Jo and Agatha in the film seems to be represented mainly through butch/femme identifications, I think this film also notably shows that the attraction between Jo and Agatha hinges on the differences in their sexual orientations. Examining *this* difference might in fact allow us to theorize another paradigm of lesbian desire that does not entirely depend on playing with or subverting gender identifications. Shifting our attention from complete focus on butch/femme and dildo desire in lesbian theory and practice will, I hope, encourage studies of how other equally important differences between lesbians function to attract them to one another.

Imagining other varieties of lesbian desire does not mean refusing what have been and continue to be important erotic configurations between women; it *does* mean resisting an easy return to seeing these erotics *only* in terms of gendered difference such as butch/femme. While McLaughlin's film takes up (and even questions) the traditional butch/femme model on the one hand, it also makes the complex relationship between Jo and Agatha visible by strongly scripting their sexual histories, and it is a story about the involved ways in which they experience these differences in their relationship. Jo has had many male lovers in the past, which we learn about from Agatha's discovery and reading of Jo's journal. In contrast, Agatha has identified as a lesbian from an early age. We learn this fact not only from her psychoanalytic admission that she preferred identifying with her father rather than falling in love with him, but also because she is identified in Jo's mind with Catalina—the seventeenth-century nun who rebelled and lived her life cross-dressed as a man. Catalina is the central character in a movie Jo is making. Catalina's story, this film within the film, serves in part to represent Jo's complicated desire for Agatha.

Teresa de Lauretis's important article on *She Must Be Seeing Things,* "Film and the Visible," explores how the film might encode an autonomous form of lesbian desire and subjectivity through its fantasy scenes between Jo and Agatha.[4] Given the way the male gaze constructs what is visible, as many feminist film theorists have pointed out, de Lauretis poses the difficult question of lesbian desire and representation: "what can be seen, and eroticized?"[5] In questioning the possibility of an autonomous lesbian desire and subjectivity she bases her theory on the relationship of desire to fantasy. De Lauretis defines a lesbian fantasy (and subjectivity) as that in which the scene of fantasy itself functions as the originary moment of lesbian subjectivity—thus when Agatha and Jo together watch the "primal scene" in the film Jo is making they are constituted, according to de Lauretis, as lesbians. The emphasis here is in these two women sharing the moment together rather than their fantasy being directed toward or in response to any particular object (like another lesbian).

Although de Lauretis's project is to theorize how lesbians might see and desire one another outside of a patriarchal system of representation, it may be equally useful, I think, to examine in this film how Jo and Agatha actually fantasize about each other which itself might lead us to recognize new, or perhaps strangely familiar configurations of lesbian desire. By focusing primarily on the *scene* of desire in her analysis of lesbian fantasy and representation (rather than on the actual women), de Lauretis seems to assume a generic lesbian (or a generic lesbian couple) which risks ignoring the racial, cultural, and class differences between Jo and Agatha. I think it is important to maintain an emphasis on lesbian identification when discussing lesbian desire because not only might women bring significantly different cultural, class, and gendered experiences and identities to a relationship, but also the various ways women have arrived psychically and materially at their lesbian identities may as well inform how they desire one another.

Both the film and de Lauretis's analysis provide important insights into lesbian desire and invite us to look more deeply into the models of attraction for lesbian erotic identification. My project is to look beyond the familiar paradigms of lesbian desire and to pose another model through which we might examine how the differences in lesbians' sexual orientation—that is *how* and *when* they come out—might excite desire between women. While it appears to adhere to fairly traditional gendered forms of lesbian erotics as I have pointed out, McLaughlin's film also in fact strikingly represents the complexity of desire between Agatha and Jo based on the differences in their sexual orientation. And, as de Lauretis herself says of this film: "other visible representations of lesbian subjectivity and desire are already there for all to see, if only we know how to look."[6]

Lesbian psychologist and theorist Beverly Burch invokes Melanie Klein's work in object relations to theorize ways in which and the age at which women begin identifying as lesbians might inform *how* they desire other lesbians. Burch discusses the importance of examining sexual orientation differences between women and suggests that the psychic draw between lesbians who have identified as such from an early age and those who may have had significant relationships with men in the past may indicate as substantial an attraction as lesbian desire represented in butch/femme. Burch states:

> All women who call themselves lesbians share an identity, but they do not necessarily share the same desires, fantasies, and inclinations, nor do they have the same history. Some feel their internal experiences are more bisexual in nature, some feel theirs are more truly woman-centered. This is a difference that matters.[7]

Much of the narrative tension in the film clearly involves the fact that Agatha and Jo do not perceive (hetero)sexual relationships in the same way because they have come from such different sexual backgrounds. Although Agatha seems mostly jealous about Jo's heterosexual past, her response to a friend's warning of "what do you expect getting involved with a woman whose sexual history has been mostly with men?" reveals her simultaneous desire for Jo despite—or even because of—this difference. In a characteristically rebellious reply, Agatha says: "All my life I've been told what's right and what's wrong—from my father, by nuns, by priests, and finally I discover something that gives me great pleasure [Jo] and there's another ideology that's telling me that it's wrong. Do you know what I think about that?" The dilemma Agatha experiences in her desire for Jo is exactly the point at which we ought to focus in order to begin to articulate other (common) paradigms of lesbian desire. Her refusal simply to dismiss Jo because of her past, and her resolution to continue to work through these vexed questions of her desire signal the psychic, sexual, and emotional draw Jo holds for Agatha. If one were to pose the question of autonomous lesbian desire, perhaps this moment could even serve as an example, for what other combination of genders and sexualities must confront these exact experiences?

Burch and de Lauretis approach the question of lesbian desire from opposing psychoanalytic positions, yet interestingly they both locate the crux of their analysis within the sphere of fantasy between two women. Both theoretical positions locate the liminal region between fantasy and material reality as a possible site or condition of lesbian subjectivity and desire. Burch defines this space through the Kleinian definition of projective identification, a concept specifically linked to object relations, whereby one person projects her fears or fantasies onto another: "Imaginative elaborations on reality . . . occur as the boundary between 'me' and 'not-me' is transcended. Here, unconscious illusion exists without the interference of reality, yet paradoxically it does not deny reality either." [8]

De Lauretis attempts to arrive at a place of lesbian definition or subjectivity through a reading of the fantasy scenes in McLaughlin's film which produce, she argues, new ways of seeing. In an effort to define an originary (or autonomous) lesbian subjectivity and sexuality, de Lauretis focuses her discussion on Jo and Agatha sharing a fantasy together— that is, what defines Jo and Agatha (or their gaze) as lesbian is not them looking at or considering each other, but looking together at something else. De Lauretis agrees with Jean Laplanche and Jean-Bertrand Pontalis's definition of fantasy in which they assert that "in this discourse no longer addressed to anyone, all distinction between subject and object has been lost." [9] Importantly, this space minimizes if not ignores material conditions between lesbian lovers. Because McLaughlin's film deals explicitly with voyeurism and fantasy, it offers the ideal vehicle to explore both de Lauretis's and Burch's theories.

By locating her definition of lesbian fantasy within intrapsychic phenomenon, de Lauretis specifically refuses object relations in the Kleinian sense because she rejects the interrelatedness of fantasy and objects. Specifically, de Lauretis invokes the terms of fantasy that Laplanche and Pontalis define as such: "Fantasy . . . is not the object of desire, but its setting. In fantasy the subject does not pursue the object or its sign: [s]he appears caught up [her]self in the sequence of images."[10] In the film, de Lauretis locates the important moments of fantasy during the times when Jo and Agatha together watch "the primal scene" which occurs in "the film within the film" that Jo is shooting. Thus it is the scene of their sharing a fantasy that defines both their lesbian identity or subjectivity, and their desire: "This is a film about two women who share a common fantasy, a lesbian fantasy, and if 'the origin of the subject [her]self' is located 'in the field of fantasy,' . . . then this very fantasy, which they share, constitutes them as a lesbian subject."[11]

Thus, de Lauretis not only moves her discussion of fantasy into intrapsychic phenomena (an objectless scene), but in so doing effectively eliminates actual women (with their attendant histories and identities) from the definition of lesbian fantasy and subjectivity. Fantasy, however, can also be understood through a Kleinian approach of object relations which, in contrast, would locate lesbian desire both within material reality and intrapsychic phenomena. Burch's study shows how the concept of projective identification might explain the ways that individuals "both apprehend and make use of another's subjectivity, especially at unconscious levels."[12] She defines projective identification as "an integration of projection with identification process[es]. In the combined unconscious transaction one person projects an aspect of her . . . mental functioning—thoughts, feelings, and impulses—onto another and thereby comes to identify with that person."[13] Jo and Agatha clearly project their fantasies, fears, and desires onto each other, and because they identify differently as lesbians I believe these projections represent the complexity of their attraction to one another.

In the film, Jo and Agatha negotiate their desire for one another through imagining and confronting how they are different. The narrative overtly represents their dissimilarity in such trivial (yet potentially irritating) habits as housekeeping, while also raising other more significant differences in their identities and experiences such as their diverse cultural backgrounds and the different ways they identify as lesbians (with Jo veering more toward a bisexual identification). Although not her main point, de Lauretis herself directs attention to the way Jo perceives Agatha's differences: "It is clear that Catalina represents Agatha, or better, represents what Jo finds attractive in Agatha—her rebelliousness against a repressive, Catholic upbringing; her jealousy and anger at God's and men's claim of exclusive access to women; *her lesbian difference;* her pain and her defiance." [14] Among the other characteristics that distinguish Agatha from Jo, Jo importantly perceives, projects, and is attracted to the way that Agatha identifies differently from her as a lesbian.

Because of her history as a woman who has had significant relationships with men, Jo's fascination with Agatha's "lesbian difference" suggests an interest in a woman who has developed in primary sexual and emotional relationship to women. As de Lauretis suggests, we can read Agatha's "history" in the figure of Catalina, who represents a woman who has rebelled against religious and sexual norms. Through this association between Catalina and Agatha we might understand how Jo imagines Agatha's psychosexual past. Frequent cutting between Agatha's and Catalina's scenes, and more importantly, the way Jo fashions Catalina's history, signifies the terms of her fantasy surrounding Agatha.

Notably, Agatha's psychosexual history gets displaced significantly onto a "foreign" historical figure which emphasizes Agatha's cultural and racial difference as a black Brazilian lesbian. This association with Catalina certainly raises another crucial question as to the nature of Jo's desire, which may depend as much on Agatha's "cultural" or racial difference as on her "lesbian difference." Indeed, because Agatha is so closely associated with Catalina, and Jo desires both Agatha and Catalina, the erotic economy in the film operates at least partially through Agatha's cultural and racial otherness. Issac Julien critiques this aspect of the film: "In terms of racial difference, Agatha was masquerading as Eurasia, becoming a mythologized, fetishized black subject within the narrative." [15] Reducing Agatha to a "fetishized black subject" however fails to account for the possible way that Jo's desire for Agatha's racial or cultural difference operates complicatedly in tandem with her desire for Agatha's lesbian difference.

Jo's sexual history is also extensively scripted in the film by the focus on her journal which lists and describes (along with Polaroids of male faces and genitals) the many male lovers she has had. Agatha's focus on Jo's diary through much of the film reveals the significance for her of

Jo's heterosexual past. The film begins with Agatha's discovery of the journal which she then reads and carries around with her imagining, at various stages, through Jo's words and images, what it might mean to be with a man, or to be a man, or for Jo to be with a man. She is visibly compelled in the film to contemplate Jo's difference in sexual orientation, to imagine psychically what this difference means to her and to their relationship. Through Jo, Agatha must explore, in a way we assume she has not before, her own relationship to heterosexuality, or more specifically, to the complicated ways her own identity as a lesbian now operates with a woman who has a bisexual past. Projection and fantasy play a crucial part in Agatha's process of attempting to understand her relationship to Jo, and to both of their sexual orientations.

Agatha's contemplation of her own shifting identity and desire is also demonstrated in the film. For instance, when playing on the beach, Agatha captures Jo and ties her hands behind her asking, "Did men ever do that to you?" Jo replies, "I did it with Paul . . . it's different with you." Later, while alone, Agatha reviews Jo's journal reciting names of men as she turns the pages until she reaches Paul's name at which she pauses, visibly struggling with the significance, for her, of Jo's (hetero)-sexual past.

Thus, Agatha's desire for Jo is clearly, and I would argue primarily, informed by Jo's different sexual orientation and this desire engages her in an intrapsychic relation to Jo which she addresses and confronts through projective identification which is, as Burch suggests, a way to "both apprehend and make use of another's subjectivity."[16] While, on the one hand, this projective identification might provide a way to explore lesbian desire that results in a richer and more complex understanding of a particular relationship, Agatha's frequent fantasies, in which she imagines Jo being sexual with men or being brutally murdered, raise, on the other hand, important issues and consequences of lesbian existence and desire. That is, Jo's difference in sexual orientation also produces much anxiety, jealousy, and fear in Agatha, and for good reason given the often violent and always obnoxious nature of heterosexual male prerogative in Agatha's eyes.

Concerns with gender identity and difference, or butch/femme parody, however, tend to mask these other complicated differences that inform Jo's and Agatha's desires. For example, in one much-discussed erotic moment in the film, Jo performs a femme "masquerade" for

Agatha. While de Lauretis describes this erotic moment as an ironic performance of femininity, I believe desire may be located as significantly in the scene leading up to it as in the "subversive" performance itself. Agatha arrives at Jo's apartment one evening to find Jo drunk and her apartment a mess with money strewn about it. After some frustrated and angry questioning from Agatha, who has spent time cleaning the apartment, Jo replies: "I'm not interested in your Catholic self-sacrificing martyr trip. It's boring." Her apparent hostility toward Agatha's "cultural difference," which she has paradoxically shown such fascination with through the film she is making about Catalina, signals the complexity of the desire that is operating between the two lovers. The tension from this exchange is immediately channeled into a butch/femme performance, thus instantly shifting the strain of acknowledging their differences into an eroticized gender parody. The involved negotiation of their desire thus is translated into actions that gender its terms and it is easy to remain focused here when analyzing lesbian erotics.

Although the film clearly represents these other complex terms of

Agatha and Jo looking awry. From She Must Be Seeing Things. *Courtesy of Sheila McLaughlin and First Run Features.*

attraction between Jo and Agatha, the crucial differences in sexual orientation between the two women are represented as well *through* gender parody as in the scene I first mentioned in which Agatha suddenly appears in full butch regalia: a coat, tie, and greased hair. Agatha is understandably threatened by Jo's plans and says to herself, "You just want to add him to your list. Slut." Her appearance in drag at this instance genders the terms of her jealousy or of her psychic struggle with the difference in Jo's sexual orientation. Her change into butch attire, in which she dons the signifiers of (heterosexual) male privilege, could signal her wish to be someone she thinks Jo desires. But she may also be visibly claiming her already acknowledged identification as a lesbian. As a response to Jo's sexuality, Agatha signals her evolving (and difficult) psychic relationship to Jo by changing into butch attire. The complex position Agatha occupies is signified further when she later follows Jo and her male colleague to the restaurant and gazes at them from outside. This position indicates the degree to which she is outside the hetero economy, but her voyeuristic gaze, which eventually results in her hallucinating Jo having sex with the man, also signifies how she is experiencing (or introjecting) this heterosexual existence through Jo. Her butch clothing represents (just as when she momentarily considers the dildo) a significant contemplation of the complicated terms of lesbian identification and desire.

It is crucial not to deny the ways in which gender parody may inform desire (an idea central to butch/femme relations), but to consider how gender might also mask or even inspire other kinds of attraction that are also apparent and certainly "at play" in lesbian erotics. We might end up considering not simply how gender affects lesbian erotics (butch/femme) but how we have come to identify as lesbians first, and then the way *that* identity (or those identities) function variously in lesbian desire. Indeed, while McLaughlin's film appears at first to locate its representation of lesbian erotics primarily within the traditional gendered models of butch/femme, it also strikingly articulates these other important ways lesbians are attracted to one another. The stake in pointing out these differences is to encourage lesbians to look more closely at the nuances of our desire and to articulate them in ways which cannot be appropriated, colonized, or recuperated into a sexual difference binary that prevents us from defining our own terms of existence, and our own textured forms of desire. Insistence on seeing lesbian erotics outside of these binaries then, it seems to me, is both an important and subversive project.

We might return, finally, to a scene rarely mentioned in discussions of McLaughlin's film, and that is the exchange that takes place between Jo and Agatha on the boardwalk while they are gazing down to the beach below observing the abundance of heterosexuals kissing and fondling each other. While Agatha looks on in partial horror and disgust at the hetero couples, Jo responds: "Come on. It's no big deal. They all come here to make out," to which Agatha exclaims, "But will you look at them. They are everywhere!" Perhaps this, rather than the "primal scene," on which de Lauretis bases her analysis of lesbian fantasy and subjectivity, is a more germane moment at which to pause in order to realize the complexity of the desire and identification between these two lesbians. While they clearly are faced again with the heterosexuality that defines the primal scene, rather than sharing a common fantasy here, their vastly different interpretations of *this* scene point out the very uncommonality of their sexual histories and identities which, I have argued, inform their desire for one another. So while they may be looking together at the same scenario, what they actually see is different, and this is a difference that matters.

NOTES

1. Sue-Ellen Case, "Toward a Butch-Femme Aesthetic," *Discourse* 11:1 (Fall 1988/Winter 1989): 64.

2. June Reich, "Genderfuck: The Law of the Dildo," *Discourse* 15:1 (Fall 1992): 121.

3. Jill Dolan presents a similar position to Reich's arguing for the subversive potential in playing *on* and not *to* the phallic economy in her discussion of public lesbian performance and pornography. She suggests that the lesbian context of these performances disrupts traditional gender meanings and hence opens up a space to rearticulate gender and sexuality. See Jill Dolan, "The Dynamics of Desire: Sexuality and Gender in Pornography and Performance," *Theatre Journal* 39:2 (May 1987): 156–74.

4. Teresa de Lauretis, "Film and the Visible," in *How Do I Look: Queer Film and Video,* ed. Bad Object-Choices (Seattle: Bay Press, 1991), 223–76.

5. Ibid., 255.

6. Ibid., 263.

7. Beverly Burch, *On Intimate Terms: The Psychology of Difference in Lesbian Relationships* (Urbana: University of Illinois Press, 1993), 36.

8. Burch, 56.

9. Jean Laplanche and Jean-Bertrand Pontalis, "Fantasy and the Origins of Sexuality," in *Formations of Fantasy,* ed. Victor Burgin, James Donald, and Cora Kaplan (New York: Methuen, 1986), 26.

10. Ibid., 26, pronominal gender altered.

11. De Lauretis, 232.

12. Burch, 61.

13. Ibid.

14. De Lauretis, 228.

15. Julien responded thus to de Lauretis's suggestion that Agatha's racial difference is presented, but not addressed, in the film. See de Lauretis, 271.

16. Burch, 61.

THIRTEEN

Dracula's Daughter: Cinema, Hypnosis, and the Erotics of Lesbianism

BONNIE BURNS

I.

One might have predicted that *Dracula's Daughter* (1936), the sequel to the classic Bela Lugosi vampire movie *Dracula* (1931), would concern itself with the erotic appetites of its villain, the exquisitely sophisticated Countess Marya Zaleska.[1] Given the film's debt to a literary and cinematic tradition that has coded vampires as threateningly like and unlike their human prey, one might also have predicted that such a film would raise provocative questions about classic cinema's constructions of female sexuality and its relation to difference, especially sexual difference as it is articulated in the visual realm. The film, however, raises these issues in explicit relation to *lesbian* desire, and to the perturbing effects that this desire produces in the representational machinery of classic Hollywood cinema.[2] Indeed, *Dracula's Daughter* is an astonishingly provocative exploration of the operations of gaze, look, and image with which feminist film theory has been preoccupied in the last decade. It offers an especially canny analysis of the fraught relation between lesbianism and the logic of the visible that establishes and sustains our culture's notions of sexual difference—and sexual sameness.

Historically, of course, the relationship of lesbianism to notions of visibility has been a vexed one. Valerie Traub's analysis of the emergence of the lesbian as a figure of sexual (in)significance in England in the early modern period, and Terry Castle's account of the "apparitional" lesbian in literary history since the Enlightenment are two recent examples of work in lesbian theory that point to the problem of locating the lesbian in the social text, a text from which she has been notoriously absent.[3] Perhaps more significantly, however, this work also suggests that lesbianism has been represented at the limit of the visible, or indeed, *as* the limit of the visible, in order to serve a particular ideological agenda at a particular historical moment.

With the advent of film in the early twentieth century, the figure of the lesbian as a liminal one could be deployed in startling new ways that both confirmed and complicated the authority of the visible. In many ways, classic Hollywood cinema constructed a version of the lesbian virtually in its own image; *Dracula's Daughter,* for instance, represents both lesbianism *and* the cinema as dangerously seductive and hypnotic. Lesbianism manifests itself in this film either as the ravishing spectacle which we have come to associate with the ephemeral images flickering on a movie screen, or as the machine of projection itself, the source of light from which these images emanate. In other words, lesbianism emerges in this representational system not only *through* the apparatus of the cinema, but *as* the apparatus of the cinema itself.

In order to understand why the figure of the lesbian is so insistently entangled with the technologies of vision as they were defined by the cinema in the early part of the twentieth century, we need to consider the ways in which heterosexual culture repeatedly reconfirmed its authority through the body of the lesbian. *Dracula's Daughter* is a pivotal example of American film's ability to reestablish the representational authority of heterosexual culture through the regime of the visible. Catching a vampire, after all, requires a system of detection that can distinguish the masquerade of the undead from the authenticity of the living, a system, in other words, that can articulate the difference between imaginary and symbolic realms.

The film begins where the Lugosi film left off, immediately after the death of Count Dracula whom the local police discover in London with a stake through his heart. Countess Marya Zaleska, Dracula's daughter, has inherited the curse of the Draculas but believes that her father's death and proper burial will provide her with release from "the shadows of the dead." Unsuccessful in her attempt to find release, however, the Countess resumes luring her victims, men and women, into the orbit of her influence by entrancing them with her extraordinary gaze. With the aid of a rather spectacular antique ring, she induces in them a peculiar state which Jeffrey Garth, the psychiatrist from whom the Countess seeks help and who will eventually expose her as a vampire, labels "forced hypnosis," a condition and diagnosis which will come to define both lesbian desire and the cinematic apparatus in this film. After Garth's attempts at "sympathetic treatment" fail and he finally recognizes the Countess's vampiric compulsions, she flees London for her father's castle in Transylvania, but not before abducting Garth's assistant, Janet. Garth, of course, pursues them, and the Countess is eventually destroyed with an arrow through her heart. Garth and Janet are reunited with the promise of an eventual marriage. The film ends with a close-up of the Countess's properly "inanimate" face; her eyes are open in a fixed stare. A conversation between men redefines not so much her life as her death: "The woman is beautiful," remarks the Scotland Yard inspector, to which Professor Von Helsing replies: "She was beautiful when she died, a hundred years ago." [4]

The profound concern the film exhibits in relation to the figure of the lesbian becomes apparent in the odd camera work that introduces the figure of the Countess at the local jail where she has gone to retrieve the body of Dracula. The moment before she enters, the camera tracks in on a constable's face as he looks toward a door that we hear opening off-screen to the left. Rather than following his look toward the door, however, the camera seems to make a mistake by panning to the right toward the room where Dracula's corpse lies. Almost immediately, though, it swings back to the left of the screen to reveal Countess Zaleska standing erect and veiled, with only her eyes exposed; the door swings shut behind her, echoing the movement of the camera. This particular shot, which will be repeated later in the film when the camera pans away from the Countess's coffin lid swinging open only to pan back a moment later to find the Countess standing perfectly composed and still, suggests that something crucial about the camera's ability to "see" and its inability to "look" literally *hinges* on the status of the Countess's body as spectacle. In effect, the camera discovers its own impossible position when confronted not with Dracula, but with Dracula's daughter, the embodiment of a contradictory and disruptive spectacle, a spectacle that upsets the cinematic conventions that define and sustain heterosexual hegemonies.

The Countess appears for the first time in the film, after all, as a spectacle that produces an array of startling and often shocking effects on the bodies of those that behold her. Immediately after her dramatic entrance, the Countess commands the unfortunate constable, Albert, who has been left behind to look after Dracula's corpse, to look, instead, at her. Entranced initially by her gaze, and then by the hypnotic quality of her ring, the constable gradually relinquishes his will to the Countess, becoming like and unlike her. When his sergeant returns, he finds Albert sitting rigidly in a chair with his eyes fixed and staring, mirroring the characteristics exhibited by the Countess at her entrance, though in a degraded and comic form. His look is devoid of animation, and, when the sergeant taps his shoulder for some response, his body slumps loosely to the floor. Having already been chided by his sergeant for being "worse than an old woman" about the presence of rats in Whitby jail and subsequently reminded that "HhEngland hhexpects hhevery man to do his duty," Albert's position as a comic foil is secure.[5] But the constable's easy fall into the passivity of trance raises anxious doubts about the ability of the law to perform *its* duty, especially when confronted by a female spectacle that, in effect, seizes the authority of the gaze. By placing the constable in a trance which reproduces him as a degraded copy of her own more potent phallicism, the Countess reverses the image of the feminine as a mere shadow of masculine authority, reproducing the constable as the literal, material, and above all, inanimate, object of her gaze.

The function of the gaze in the production of subjects under the law is, of course, a primary concern in the theoretical discourse of Jacques Lacan.[6] As many film critics have pointed out, though Lacan's descriptions of the gaze and its effects are expressed through a number of different metaphors, one of the most striking of these represents the gaze and its functions as similar to the apparatus of the camera:

> What determines me, at the most profound level, in the visible, is the gaze that is outside. It is through the gaze that I enter light and it is from the gaze that I receive its effects. Hence it comes about that the gaze is the instrument through which light is embodied and through which—if you will allow me to use a word, as I often do, in a fragmented form—I am photo-graphed. (Lacan 106)

The gaze, which Lacan has suggested elsewhere "participates in the ambiguity of the jewel" in its ability to focus and disperse light, is strikingly emblematized by the ability of the Countess's ring to produce the effect of hypnotic fascination from a single point of light, to entrance, at the same time that it seems to photograph, its subjects (Lacan 96). In drawing an analogy between the hypnotic effect of the Countess's gaze and the ring which she uses to lure her victims, the film announces its preoccupation not only with the instrumentality of the gaze—its ability to produce subjects, or more to the point, objects—but also with its status *as* an instrument, as, in Kaja Silverman's apt phrase, "the *imaginary* apparatus through which light is projected onto the subject" (my emphasis).[7]

The final images of *Dracula's Daughter* suggest that the Countess undergoes a deadly return to the realm of spectacle in spite of her ability to lay claim to the power of the gaze throughout the film. This return of the Countess to the "proper" visual register—that of an inanimate spectacle—works to restore the illusion of coherence to the symbolic realm through the relentless fetishization of the female body into an image that compensates for the horror of castration; the image of the Countess's beautifully lifeless face evokes just such a process of fetishization. The return of the Countess at the end of the film to an embodiment of the reassuringly beautiful, rather than the provokingly monstrous, occurs at the expense of the "animate," and, I want to suggest, the "animating" woman. However, though she is named as "beautiful" and returned to a realm where she secures male heterosexual privilege by the end of the film, the status of the Countess's gaze in the closing frames raises a perplexing question. What is the difference, after all, between her look at the beginning of the film, a close-up of her brilliantly seductive eyes, and her look at the end of the film, in which virtually the same image is repeated? In response to this dilemma, the film proposes to offer a properly symbolic gaze—one that is manifested through the apparatus of the cinema itself—in order to establish its authority to determine the difference between these two dangerously similar looks. Though it pursues this distinction as relentlessly as Jeffrey Garth pursues Countess Zaleska to her death, the difference between these two "looks" is precisely what threatens to exceed the camera's ability to see.

II.

In her astute reading of Lacan, Kaja Silverman points out that "all subjects, male or female, rely for their identity upon [a] repertoire of culturally available images, and upon a gaze which, radically exceeding the libidinally vulnerable look, is not theirs to deploy" (153). Silverman, following Lacan, attempts to distinguish between the look and the gaze by locating the gaze outside of the agency of individual subjectivities. To suggest that any individual can command a gaze which is by definition "other" is to confuse a libidinally invested "look" with the "gaze" that produces us as subjects. But of course, it is precisely this confusion that produces heterosexual masculinity as the proper site of the gaze, an "imposture," Silverman has argued in a slightly different context, "made possible only through the propping of the look upon the gaze" (129). In other words, if, in answer to the question posed by feminist film theory, the gaze *is* male (and heterosexual), it is only able to masquerade as such through the agency of the *look*. This imposture, of course, is what, in classic Hollywood cinema, the camera hopes to effect, which is why the "look," in its capacity as prop or prosthetic to the gaze, needs to be returned to Jeffrey Garth at the end of this film.

The conflation of look and gaze that props up heterosexual masculinity is maintained, I would argue, by a simultaneous *separation* of gaze from spectacle. In other words, in order to maintain its ability to "pass" as the bearer of the gaze, the *look,* particularly the masculinist look which operates under the aegis of heterosexuality, must have something to look at, and, of course, the something at which it is most fond of looking is the lack inscribed on the body of "Woman," a lack which must be ritualistically displayed and fetishistically disavowed in order to reconsolidate the fragmented bodily ego of male heterosexuality. Indeed, the Countess has to be returned to the status of "mere" spectacle at the end of the film precisely *because of* her power to look, to lay claim to the gaze. At one crucial moment in the film, a moment linked emphatically with an erotic lesbian encounter, the Countess's look undoes the separation of gaze and spectacle by looking back—at another woman.

The scene to which I'm referring occurs after a failed consultation between the Countess and Jeffrey Garth, during which he suggests that the Countess overcome her not as yet clearly defined compulsion through an act of will similar to that required (at least in Garth's psychiatric practice) of alcoholic patients. The obvious failure in this scene of the heterosexual encounter and of the psychoanalytic cure, or perhaps of the heterosexual encounter *as* psychoanalytic cure, leads the film to devise its own recuperative strategies.

Immediately after Garth leaves the Countess's flat, her mysterious male servant, Sandor, enters to ask if they are going out that evening. The Countess, once again succumbing to her appetites, replies, "We're going to the studio. Tonight I paint, and I will need a model." The scene dissolves to Sandor in his hat and overcoat waiting furtively in the fog of a London night. A young and vulnerable woman walks by him and stops to gaze over the side of a bridge as if contemplating her suicide. Sandor interrupts her, telling her that his mistress is a painter who needs a model for the evening; in exchange, she will provide Lili (that is her name) with food and shelter. Lili agrees to return with him to the Countess's studio in Chelsea. Once there, she warms herself by the fire, eats some sandwiches, and engages in a conversation with the Countess, whose eager visual appraisal of Lili leads her to comment: "You have beautiful hands, but they're so white and bloodless." ("They're cold, ma'am," Lili responds.) She tells Lili that she is doing a study of "a young girl's head and shoulders" and asks Lili to remove her blouse. The camera follows Lili as she begins to undress behind a screen, and an odd montage sequence suggests that the Countess, too, is able to watch her from across the room. After stripping down to her slip, she steps out from behind the screen and announces, "I'm ready now." The Countess walks toward Lili as she lowers the straps of her slip, offering her a glass of sherry to warm herself. Lili accepts and steps closer to the fire at the Countess's request. She turns to reveal her naked and luminously beautiful back and shoulders. Looking back at the Countess, she asks, perplexed, "Why are you looking at me that way? Won't I do?" The Countess answers, "Yes, you'll do very well indeed." The Countess continues her approach, drawing Lili's attention to her ring, "Do you like jewels Lili? This is very old and very beautiful. I'll show it to you."

Intensified by the film's debt to the language of psychoanalysis in which "jewels" signify quite provocatively, this sexualized encounter has been carefully constructed by the camera. At this point, however, the uneasy two-shots that have framed Lili and the Countess together throughout most of this conversation give way abruptly to a frantic series of shot/reverse shots—from the Countess to Lili and back again—as if the camera were desperately attempting to maintain a proper separation between the two women at the very moment of erotic contact. As the questions and answers continue, we see the light refracted off the Countess's ring play across Lili's eyes. Mesmerized, she hesitates, but then murmurs, "I don't think I'll pose tonight. I'll think I'll go if you don't mind." The Countess continues to approach her and Lili cries, "Please don't come any closer!" Of course, the Countess comes quite close, confounding the divisive conventions of the reverse shot by literally walking beyond the frame and virtually overwhelming the screen as she moves toward the spectacle of Lili entranced by the hypnotic compulsion of the Countess's look and the play of light from her ring. The camera, as if unable to bear the approach of the overwhelming image of the Countess, leaps to a mask on the wall above Lili as she screams and the screen fades to black.

This extended scene provides us with the most sustained account of the Countess's vampiric compulsions. Functioning explicitly as a machine of projection, as the point from which light emanates, the Countess, in effect, "photo-graphs" Lili, producing her as a subject, and object, of lesbian desire. If, in imagining the Countess as the point from which light emanates, the film suggests that she in some way has disrupted the proper anonymity of the gaze, in this scene it suggests as well the "horrifying" consequences of that disruption. Here especially, Countess Zaleska exhibits a vision that ravishes—a vision capable of dissolving bodily and cinematic boundaries in violent and ecstatic ways, a vision, in other words, capable of dissolving the boundaries that maintain the illusory separation of spectacle and gaze. But the Countess's libidinal look (for how else can we understand her breathless pursuit of Lili?) is not the only erotic display in this scene. Lili's luminosity, the way she seems to exhibit a light of her own (as did the more famous film heroines in the 1930s and 1940s), produces her as a ravishingly seductive spectacle with its own power to enthrall.

Oddly enough, Lacan's famous story of the sardine can offers us a way to understand the uncanny effects of this luminosity. In this anecdote, Lacan explains that in his youth he had worked on a small fishing craft. One day, he writes, a friend, Petit-Jean, "pointed out to me something floating on the surface of the waves. It was a small can, a sardine can. It floated there in the sun. . . . It glittered in the sun. And Petit-Jean said to me—*You see that can? do you see it? well, it doesn't see you!*" Lacan remembers being singularly unamused, even distressed, by this little jest, and concludes that, though only an object, a bit of refuse, "in a sense, it was looking at me, all the same. It was looking at me at the level of the point of light, the point at which everything that looks at me is situated" (95). Suddenly animated and situated at the point of the gaze, the sardine can, in Lacan's anecdote, achieves an eerie vitality. Silverman, in her discussion of the Lacanian diagrams that schematize this story, dilates on the astonishingly provocative lesson embedded in it:

> Lacan makes clear that what is at issue in [this diagram] is the conflation of gaze and spectacle, a conflation which is made on the basis of what might be called the spectacle's "lit up" quality. Through the luminousness which imparts specularity to the object, it in effect looks back at the viewer, much like the sardine can in Lacan's anecdote. (151)

Though the end of the film attempts to return the Countess's gaze to the realm of spectacle in order to maintain a distance between look and gaze, in the scene described above the film has instead displayed the capacity of the spectacle, through an eroticized exchange, to be animated and animating, to function, in other words, "as" the gaze. As Silverman notes, "although our look can never function as the gaze for ourselves, it can have that metaphoric function for others, even at the moment that we emerge as spectacle. Exhibitionism unsettles because it threatens to expose the duplicity inherent in every subject, and every object" (151–52). The ravishing luminosity ascribed to Lili threatens to have much the same effect. Evoking the immaterial but enthralling images projected onto a movie screen, Lili's body, too, renders a hypnotic effect on the Countess as she is compelled ever closer. With the exception of the hypnotic play of light across Lili's face, the camera work in this scene is reproduced virtually unaltered from the Lugosi classic. But the encounter between Lili and Countess Zaleska does not reproduce the gendered looks that construct woman as spectacle and man as bearer of the gaze, but emblematizes instead the *coincidence* of gaze and spectacle, their impossible convergence. The film figures this convergence not only as vampiric in its representational force as the collapse of difference itself, but as the seductively hypnotic expression of lesbian desire. [8]

The return of the look in its capacity as prop or prosthetic to the gaze will be returned to Jeffrey at the end of the film. However, this return will be a return with a difference, since the look has been radically dislocated by its rerouting through an exchange between women. This exchange, which incorporates gaze and spectacle, is exactly what the film wants most to display, but can't bear to see, and produces unsettling effects for the scopic regime that would maintain sexual and *homo*sexual difference as determinative of subject status. Steadfastly refusing to look at this moment of coincidence between two women, the film repeats the gesture it performed earlier in the narrative, when it seemed unable to bear looking at the spectacle of the Countess in her erotic potential. This time, however, the camera effects a kind of upward displacement as it turns its gaze onto what must register, in the ideological framework of Hollywood in 1936, as a racially marked, and primitively other, African mask.[9] At once suggesting that the gaze embodied by the Countess is nothing more than a masquerade, this visual moment at the same time marks the unbearable spectacle that the film must mask, the point at which the symbolic can be read differently, a point of excess that unmasks heterosexuality itself as a kind of masquerade, as the purveyor of a look dissembling as the authority of the gaze.

Though it attempts to recuperate its authority by imagining Lili as the victim of the "forced hypnosis" practiced by the Countess, as opposed to the properly seductive strategies of the cinema, the film must enact a visual sleight of hand in order to accomplish its designs. The vertical jump the camera makes to the mask at the moment of Lili's "ravishment" suggests that the capacity to produce fixity and rigidity, a power that has previously been attributed to the Countess's gaze, has been assumed instead by the *camera* as it structurally interrupts this moment of coincidence between women. In other words, at the precise moment that the possibility of a lesbian encounter threatens to reveal the uncanny mobility of the gaze, its ability to inhere even in the spectacle, the apparatus of the camera assumes yet another posture—a flagrantly erect one—in order to seize the authority of the gaze.

III.

Though the cinematic apparatus momentarily recuperates the authority of the heterosexual gaze by figuring itself as rigidly erect, the duration of this moment, especially in a representational system which depends on the rapid movement of images, can be only temporary. After acknowledging the potentially disruptive encounter between Lili and the Countess, an encounter that baffles strict definitions of gaze and spectacle, the film must enact and sustain a more comprehensive strategy of recuperation; it must attribute the authority of the gaze to Jeffrey Garth as the placeholder for the cinema itself by imagining a technology of the gaze that renders it independent from the unpredictable desires of the body.

As I have suggested, heterosexual masculinity can only maintain its authoritative status by engaging in a kind of masquerade in which it erases the evidence of its own libidinal investments and by requiring a properly "feminine" spectacle of lack in order to maintain its own fictional coherency. On the other hand, as we have seen, the lesbian look, a libidinal and erotic one, undoes the strict separation of gaze and spectacle upon which the masquerade of heterosexual authority depends. But erotic investments, as we know, are typically enacted at a cost, and the film must separate itself from the vulnerability provoked by desire. While the film imagines the Countess able to exercise her hypnotic powers only as a function of appetite, it will attempt to identify Garth not with a body permeated by desire, but rather *as* the body of authority itself, as the machine of the cinema, an apparatus capable of inducing a hypnotic effect in the bodies it gazes upon with absolutely no cost to itself. The film will identify Garth as the appropriate proxy for a newly reinvented and properly *dis*embodied gaze.

In order to achieve this, of course, the film must first disentangle the apparatus of the cinema from the effects of lesbian eroticism with which it has been closely identified. But of course, this has been the project of the film from the beginning, to distinguish a properly symbolic and authoritative realm from an imaginary and inauthentic one, to distinguish the masculinist heterosexual gaze from the imaginary lesbian look, to distinguish the lawful living from the lawless undead who threaten to collapse the logic, or, more precisely, the illogic, on which the world of the living rests. In opposing the technology of the Countess's body, a technology whose seductive effects can undo the separation of gaze and spectacle upon which heterosexual hegemonies depend, with the technology of the machine, a machine that possesses the power to hypnotize and entrance, but that is immune to the vicissitudes of the body, the film effectively restructures and reaffirms the authority of the masculinist heterosexual gaze. It is as if the film, because of its failure to seize the apparatus of cinematic projection from the Countess earlier in the narrative, has reinvented the gaze, not in the image of the ravishing body of the lesbian, nor even in the image of the Lacanian *objet petit a*—the perpetually deferred object of desire, but, rather, in its own image, as an apparatus capable not only of producing visions, but of producing vision itself as the guarantor of the "truth" of sexual difference.

The film achieves this reappropriation of the gaze by fairly brutal means. After her encounter with the Countess, Lili is taken by ambulance to a hospital. Garth, who has been asked to aid in her diagnosis, decides that her affliction is a case of "forced hypnosis" which can only be countered by a relatively new therapeutic technique he has recently developed. In the ensuing scene, Garth, in effect, hypnotizes Lili again, but through the agency of a peculiar apparatus, a machine made up of spinning mirrors through which a beam of light is projected. The machine that Garth operates in order to put Lili in a hypnotic trance, of course, is an image of the projector, of the apparatus of cinema itself.

Though Lili protests and attempts to look away, Garth urges her to "look at it again for as long as you can" so that he can ascertain what he calls the "pictures behind her eyes" in order to piece together an image of the original trauma. Lili objects to Garth's treatment, crying out, "I don't want to pose." The film assumes that this expression of Lili's distress merely repeats, in therapeutic fashion, the trauma of her experience with the Countess. But in performing this repetition, the film, unwittingly perhaps, suggests that she is in fact protesting the violence of Garth's hypnotic suggestions. At this point we need to ask whether Garth is attempting to *read* the images behind Lili's eyes, or whether he is attempting to produce and manipulate them more directly. The projection of a series of fantasmatic images, after all, is exactly what the cinema effects, and the image of the hypnosis machine in the hands of a psychiatrist who has become more and more police-like as the film progresses suggests that the cinematic apparatus has been returned to its function as a disciplinary technology, one that regulates the very fantasies that saturate our erotic lives. The diagnosis of forced hypnosis clearly belongs to Garth and the apparatus of the cinema as he keeps pulling Lili's eyes brutally into the light of the hypnosis machine until she quietly dies.

Significantly, what kills Lili, in one respect at least, is not simply the cinematic apparatus, but Garth's manipulation of its mirrorlike capacity to bestow the illusion of identity.[10] In a scene introducing the relationship of heterosexuality to the logic of the mirror, Garth's ability to manipulate his own image proficiently is called into question. As he dresses for his first appointment with Countess Zaleska, Garth fails in that most marginal of masculine activities: facing a mirror and tying his bow tie. While Garth's failure to manage his own image in the mirror seriously undermines his ability to secure a coherent (even if imaginary)

identity, the *success* of that endeavor would signify a degree of fascination for the image, in this case Garth's own, that must be interpreted by
masculinist culture as essentially narcissistic, a representation that will
almost assuredly be mobilized homophobically. The scene can only conclude when his assistant Janet turns him away from the mirror, and
facing him, ties the tie herself. This odd dependence of Garth on the
ability of Janet to reflect his proper image back to himself, to act as the
mirror that secures and sustains heterosexual coherency, to tie him up in
a bow, is connected explicitly to Janet's carefully nuanced beauty. When,
in an anxious (but futile) bid for release from Janet, Garth asks his not-
so-attractive (at least by Hollywood standards) housekeeper to help him
with his tie, her flustered embarrassment as she struggles helplessly
with this task is not seen as girlishly charming, but as grotesquely
inappropriate. The film succeeds in establishing Janet as the proper
image of male fascination, it seems, because she is conventionally attractive; she has the slender body so admired in the Hollywood films of the
1930s and, unlike the mysteriously compelling gaze of the Countess,
or the vulnerable luminosity of Lili, Janet's face reassures rather than
provokes. [11]

While Janet turns Jeffrey away from the mirror and away from a
homophobically inflected narcissism, Jeffrey, of course, turns Lili back
toward the mirror. The compelling fascinations which come to be attributed to the entrancing effects of lesbian desire must be attributed instead
to a *female* narcissism which can always be recuperated, as writers from
Milton to Freud have demonstrated, as the hallmark of heterosexual
female desire. Indeed, while our culture insistently produces a spectacle
of male narcissism in order to read it phobically as homosexuality, the
spectacle of lesbian desire, as this film tirelessly demonstrates, must be
strategically collapsed into an instance of the "natural" narcissism of
women. Garth must intercept the eroticizing look between women with
the machine of the cinema in order to produce a female spectacle that
enthralls only insofar as it secures male heterosexual coherency.

But if the hypnosis machine that Garth uses to reappropriate the gaze
is, after all, merely an apparatus of illusion, a trick with light and
mirrors, what does this reveal about the apparatus of cinema? [12] The
regulatory function of the cinema depends on the production of images,
but its success is always mitigated by the vexing ephemerality of the
image. In spite of his successful manipulation of the hypnosis machine,

by the end of the film the Countess's "older, more ancient magic," her ability to enthrall and enrapture, still threatens Garth. Though he surrenders of his own volition in order to save Janet and the sense of coherency that she alone can provide for heterosexual culture, the film's relentless attempts to produce an image of the cinema apart from and in opposition to the Countess as a figure of fascination seem anxiously tenuous. In the final moments of the film, an arrow pierces the Countess's heart just as the image of Garth begins to blur out of focus, releasing him from her hypnotic powers. Janet awakens in his arms as the Countess dies alone, her face framed by the camera. Janet's reawakening, her reanimation as an appropriate object of male fascination, exists as a counterpoint to the Countess's now inanimate gaze. Although Garth remains fixed upon the spectacle of Janet in the final frames of the film, the *camera* compulsively returns to the Countess's staring face, which still exacts a compelling attraction. At the very moment that the Countess's death releases Garth from the entrancing power of the image, the image, in its potential as a disruptive lesbian eroticism, returns to haunt the cinematic apparatus. By attending to the figure of the lesbian which is constructed at the limit of the visible, we can begin to articulate a theory of the subject in which the body of the lesbian plays a crucial role, a cinematic body that both produces identities and threatens to undo them.

NOTES

This chapter is part of a longer project that considers the film *Dracula's Daughter* in relation to the representational practices of two exemplary nineteenth-century poems, Coleridge's "Christabel" and Tennyson's "The Lady of Shalott." I would like to thank the organizers of Inside/Out, the Third National Graduate Student Conference on Queer Studies, at the University of Minnesota at Minneapolis, where I presented a version of this essay. I would also like to thank Lee Edelman, Carol Houlihan Flynn, Sarah Jordan, Valerie Rohy, and Charles Trocano whose valuable criticism and advice have been exceeded only by their steady friendship and support.

1. *Dracula's Daughter*, 1936, directed by Lambert Hillyer. Starring Otto Kruger, Gloria Holden, and Marguerite Churchill. Distributed by MCA/Universal Home Video, Inc., 1992. For an account of the bizarre production history of this film see David J. Skal, *The Monster Show: A Cultural History of Horror* (New York: Norton, 1993) and *Hollywood Gothic: The Tangled Web of*

Dracula from Novel to Stage to Screen (New York: Norton, 1990), also by Skal.

2. For recent discussions of the relationship between lesbians and vampires, see Sue-Ellen Case, "Tracking the Vampire," *Differences* 3:2 (Summer 1991): 1–20 and Andrea Weiss, *Vampires and Violets: Lesbians and Film* (New York: Penguin Books, 1992).

3. See Terry Castle, *The Apparitional Lesbian: Female Homosexuality and Modern Culture* (New York: Columbia University Press, 1993), and Valerie Traub, "The (In)Significance of Lesbian Desire in Early Modern England," in *Queering the Renaissance*, ed. Jonathan Goldberg (Durham: Duke University Press, 1994), 62–83.

4. See Vito Russo's *The Celluloid Closet* (New York: Harper & Row, 1987) for an account of Hollywood's persistent fascination with the figure of the lesbian. For accounts of the place of lesbianism and lesbian desire in film theory see Teresa de Lauretis, "Film and the Visible," in *How Do I Look: Queer Film and Video*, ed. Bad Object-Choices (Seattle: Bay Press, 1991); *Queer Looks: Perspectives on Lesbian and Gay Film and Video*, ed. Martha Gever, John Greyson, and Pratibha Parmar (New York: Routledge, 1993); Judith Mayne, "Lesbian Looks: Dorothy Arzner and Female Authorship," in *How Do I Look*; Valerie Traub, "The Ambiguities of 'Lesbian' Viewing Pleasure: The (Dis)articulations of *Black Widow*," in *Body Guards: The Cultural Politics of Gender Ambiguity*, ed. Julia Epstein and Kristina Straub (New York: Routledge, 1991); and Patricia White, "Female Spectator, Lesbian Specter: *The Haunting*," in *Inside/Out: Lesbian Theories, Gay Theories*, ed. Diana Fuss (New York: Routledge, 1991).

5. The prolonged comic sequence that surrounds the issue of rats at Whitby jail seems to be a response to the Production Code's odd assortment of prohibited subject matter which extended to the genre of the horror film. The comments to one treatment of what would eventually become the script for *Dracula's Daughter* require the writers to "[p]lease eliminate the several rats referred to at the top of the page. The exhibition of rats on the screen at any time is generally considered to be bad theatre" (quoted in *The Monster Show*, 199). In striking contrast to the plague sequence in F. W. Murnau's *Nosferatu* (one of the earliest film adaptations of the Bram Stoker novel *Dracula*), in which hundreds of rats scurry through the streets, the rodents in *Dracula's Daughter* only ever appear as a slight disturbance of the soil as they burrow their way under the jail floor. This subterranean rendering works as an apt—though grotesque—figure for the film's treatment of lesbianism.

6. Jacques Lacan, *The Four Fundamental Concepts of Psychoanalysis*, ed. Jacques-Alain Miller, trans. Alan Sheridan (New York: Norton, 1978), 67–119. All further references will be made parenthetically in the text.

7. Kaja Silverman, *Male Subjectivity at the Margins* (New York: Routledge, 1992), 145. All further references will be made parenthetically in the text.

8. Lili's poignant vulnerability at this moment recalls that of any face mesmerized by the screen images which flicker over them in the anonymity of a

movie theater. At the same time that the film struggles with the mobility of a gaze which can seem to function at the level of object, it struggles as well with the implications of the passive pleasure induced by the screen image.

9. This odd moment in the film suggests a number of ways we might think about how race seems inevitably to be connected to the production of sexualities. Unable to prevent the collapse of gaze and spectacle, the film instead attempts to establish its ability to distinguish and determine identities by appealing to the putative transparency of race in order to establish yet another category of visual authority.

10. In *Dracula's Daughter* the logic of the mirror and its associations with masculinist assumptions about female narcissism are directly opposed to the logic of the painterly, which is emphatically connected to the Countess's desires for other women. For an important discussion of the relationship between the visual logics of painting and film insofar as they work to define particular representations of the gay male, see Lee Edelman, "Imag[in]ing the Homosexual: *Laura* and the Other Face of Gender," in *Homographesis: Essays in Gay Literary and Cultural Theory* (New York: Routledge, 1993).

11. The precarious nature of heterosexual dependence on the spectacle of fetishized female beauty becomes clear in Garth's exasperated, but slightly desperate, demand of Janet: "Will you tie this tie or won't you?" Janet replies, "You just hated to ask, didn't you?" Though she passes as the figure that ultimately redeems heterosexual hegemony, Janet's status as "society girl" turned "career girl," combined with her sharp wit, renders her highly troublesome in this film.

12. The problem with establishing the machine as the objective guarantor of truth has been incisively unfolded by Lacan. He writes:

> There is in optics a set of phenomena which can be said to be altogether real since we are also guided by experience in this matter, but in which, nonetheless, subjectivity is implicated at every moment. When you see a rainbow, you're seeing something completely subjective. You see it at a certain distance as if stitched on to the landscape. It isn't there. It is a subjective phenomenon. But nonetheless, thanks to a camera, you record it entirely objectively. So, what is it? We no longer have a clear idea, do we, which is the subjective, which is the objective. Or isn't it rather that we have acquired the habit of placing a too hastily drawn distinction between the objective and the subjective in our little thought-tank? Isn't the camera a subjective apparatus, entirely constructed with the help of an *x* and a *y* which take up residence in the domain which the subject inhabits, that is to say that of language? (*The Seminar of Jacques Lacan: Book I, Freud's Papers on Technique 1953–1954,* ed. Jacques-Alain Miller, trans. John Forrester [New York: Norton, 1991], 77)

Lacan's comments suggest that the stability of the camera as a device that can record an objective image is already undone by the subordination of perceptual logic to the logic of the signifier.

FOURTEEN

To Touch the Mother's C(o)untry: Siting Audre Lorde's Erotics

SHARON P. HOLLAND

[L]esbianism has served as a constantly shifting sign in our histories of feminism, and . . . to sharpen our sense of its momentary specificity in conflicting discourses is to accept new forms of political meaning. [1]

In women's groups, the political clones, the Dworkin-ites, see my studded belt and withdraw. I am obviously a sex pervert, and good, real true lesbians are not sex perverts. They are the high priestesses of feminism, con-juring up the "wimmin's" revolution. As I understand it, after the wimmin's revolution, sex will consist of wimmin holding hands, taking their shirts off and danc-ing in a circle. Then we will all fall asleep at exactly the same moment. If we didn't all fall asleep, something else might happen—something male-identified, objecti-fying, pornographic, noisy, and undignified. Something like an orgasm. [2]

[T]o lie with other women is a drive from the mother's blood. [3]

To speak, let alone to write, about a lesbian body is to give breath to both the erotic and the pornographic. The erotic, to echo Lorde, refers to women's power—a power located not just in an aroused body, but through a body made whole in connection with physical, spiritual and discursive selves. As a twist on the erotic, the pornographic reminds us that we are also entering the realm of the taboo—a moment where the unspeakable utters its own name, where sameness sleeps together. In returning to and examining Audre Lorde's work, I want to unravel the stated dichotomy between the two terms, I also want to focus on the erotic as not only a source of power, but also as a mechanism useful in dismantling the pornographic. If we agree that the pornographic "sells," to borrow Lorde's assessment, and the erotic "enlightens," then there is a powerful moment in this confrontation between terms wherein the erotic can and does enlighten what is known as the pornographic. For writers and critics like Monique Wittig and Elizabeth Meese, the erotic has a unique potentiality, as it is capable of moving the female and, in this case, lesbian body away from the object status implied by structural-ist/psychoanalytic discourse, creating this new body as the subject of its own text.[4] As its own subject, this body moves to the margins of an exchange of cultural production—that is, from a medium of the pornographic—into an empowered space where it writes itself. No longer a "subject of desire"[5] in patriarchal exchange, this lesbian body is somehow reconfigured and thus has the power to alter what we know as the pornographic.

In outlining the value of Lorde's work, I recall the perception of white lesbian feminist Anna Wilson who argues that Lorde's "textual practice also has the power to address not merely the problems of identity politics but also the issues of lesbian aesthetics."[6] What better place to locate lesbian aesthetics than in the implied margin between the pornographic and the erotic. Let me say at the outset that I am well aware of the debates, ambivalencies, and sheer paranoia that the term "pornography" excites in both puritan and academic North America. In the mid-1970s with the birth of Women Against Pornography (WAP) and the emergence of feminists deeply committed to the eradication of domestic violence and rape, debates raged about pornography indicting it as the "theory" which, in turn, launches rape as its "practice." At the close of the 1980s, feminists such as Deirdre English and Ellen Willis began critiquing the feminist position within the antipornography cam-paigns, recognizing the importance of political action against a misogy-nist culture, but also acknowledging that much of the antipornography debate had spiraled into and mirrored the conservative right, which preached a doctrine of protection of women under male patriarchy through campaigns to restrict women's access to abortion and health-care information. As well, lesbian feminists, including the creators of *On Our Backs,* rightfully began to fear antipornography propaganda as moving beyond theoretical discussions around the misuse of women's bodies in pornography to language which stigmatized certain sexual practices, in particular s/m sex.

Since the early 1980s, many academic feminists have moved away from narrow definitions of pornography into discussions of erotica and taste, boundaries and consent. Feminist critics such as Gloria Steinem and Robin Morgan have tried to create a distinction between pornography and erotica, but their definitions have been criticized as based on a network of prejudicial class distinctions—pornography is the cheap stuff of the working class and erotica is the sexy choice of the politically conscious and literate elite. If pornography can be, according to critic and lesbian activist Lisa Henderson, "any symbolic expression which seeks to arouse or which represents arousal,"[7] then those sentiments can be both negative and positive: It depends upon how the game is played and whose gaze is operative. For example, if I use Henderson's definition, I can experience a United Colors of Benetton advertisement of a black figure (wearing a Benetton product), with breasts exposed and nursing a white infant (Figure 14.1), as a form of pornography for the

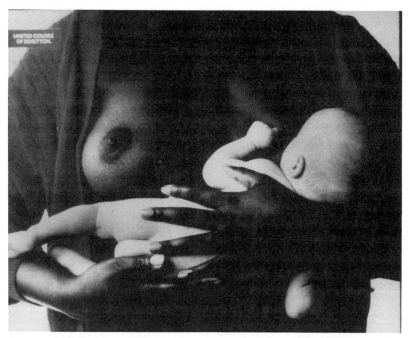

Controversial Benetton advertisement. Is this erotic? Courtesy of Benetton Services Corp.

mere fact that it seeks to arouse as well as depict arousal. But as a black woman I sense a negative connotation. While most women feel some sort of erotic sensation while nursing, I am assured by countless herstories that the bonding taking place in this Benetton advertisement is representative, instead, of bondage that is not based on consent, or in this case, conception. Perhaps *arousal* in the positive is erotic and in the negative (depending upon experience) is pornographic; for me, these two figures together *create* the pornographic by ceasing to appeal, by misrepresenting the erotic and by encasing an intimate exchange in the context of distorted and often abusive relationships between blacks and whites in American history. The figure nursing is clearly not the biological mother here, but the mammy. Moreover, the "woman" here is incomplete; what would have been a whole black woman is now just a black body. Decapitated, "she" is figuratively dead to us. However, if pornography is something that does arouse, to keep Henderson's definition, and "to arouse" is to awaken, as if from sleep, then both the negative and positive effects of the pornographic might yield sweet fruit, in the form of productive discussion and debate. After all, the owners of United Colors of Benetton contend that "these images have never been intended to express a particular point of view, but rather to encourage discussion about such important subjects as racism, AIDS, war and the environment. It is our hope that through dialogue greater understanding and positive change will occur." [8] But, my question is over whose (dead) body will this discussion take place? Blackness, in particular female blackness, always seems imminently expendable. Adding to this critique of pornography and erotica, Susanne Kappeler offers that erotica

> creates a positive problem for both anti-pornography activists and pro-erotica feminists. . . . The real consequences of failing to separate negative from positive sexual images would be the obligation to recognize that there is no fundamental difference between erotica and pornography, art and 'bad taste mass culture,' vaginas represented by men and vaginas represented by women—[there is] no way of attributing the scum exclusively to the bathwater. [9]

Kappeler concludes her discussion with an analysis that rests on the representation of women's bodies—on fine distinctions between "good" and "bad" and false notions of intent and injury. She gives little or no attention to the dynamics of representation in pornographic and erotic depiction, especially in terms of racialized subjectivities. For example, Kappeler's own introduction to her book *The Pornography of Represen-*

tation, involves the use of the torture death of a black Namibian worker named Thomas Kasire by a white farmer named van Rooyen as a segue into her theory of the pornographic. This lynching is considered especially horrific because van Rooyen's friends photographed the incident. Kappeler later states that these pictures "may also remind us, or some of us, of pornography, a woman in the place of the black man, the white men in their respective positions . . . behind the camera." [10] Kappeler proposes that the photograph of the slain Thomas Kasire is not pornography already, but is made so by substitution. However, I would have a hard time substituting a white woman (and I do believe that the woman alluded to by Kappeler is white) for a black man in these images because of the dynamics implied by these exchanged subject positions. If we substitute a white woman for the black man in this picture, we have a case of voyeurism, not a snuff film. Kappeler's proposal is as pornographic as Benetton's depiction of the (dead) black woman with the living white baby. For Kappeler, pornography only counts if we can substitute white for black, women in exchange for men, all of which sounds like the economic language of slavery to me. In the section quoted above, Kappeler seems to contend that changing the gender of the producers of both "good" and "bad" images of women blurs and shifts categories of representation and of subject and object, but the effect of "race" in this discussion of the erotic and the pornographic is devastatingly left without primacy.

Kappeler's theories of representation deal with pornography through veiled subject positions; the body is clearly a void entity to be exchanged and bartered. Still fixated on the figure, feminist critics have forgotten about the daily experience of the pornographic—a quintessentially American ideology steeped in the doctrine of separation and alienation, a form of divide and conquer practiced on black bodies and minds for centuries. Lorde stands as one of the few scholars of the erotic who focuses instead on the synergy of the erotic and the pornographic, which she locates not in the act of gazing, but in quotidian action itself. It is this new location that I find most compelling and would like to place my analysis of Lorde's work at the crossroads of this new tension. As Henderson reminds us, "[f]ew consider the women (and men) for whom sexual imagery is one link in a social and cultural lifeline, a link emblematic of their refusal to accept established sexual hierarchies and their will to make their own place." [11]

In "Uses of the Erotic," a paper delivered in 1978 during the Fourth Berkshire Conference on the History of Women, Lorde posits that "pornography represents the suppression of true feeling . . . . emphasiz[ing] sensation without feeling." [12] As a matter of fact, the erotic here is "an internal sense of satisfaction to which . . . we know we can aspire" (54). Creating a sense of fluidity between the two, Lorde's notion of the erotic appears as being birthed by the pornographic. As women loving one another, we move from the base(ness) of the pornographic to the heights of the erotic (an experience that is mythic, sublime, and highly politicized). Lorde's work seeks to move discussions of the pornographic and the erotic from the narrow focus upon a pleasure located solely in bodies, to a space highly volatile and creative where women are empowered to view themselves as able to change the myths that circumscribe and constrict their living.

I would like to begin here by pairing Lorde's biomythography, *Zami,* and her essay, "Uses of the Erotic: The Erotic as Power." Published before *Zami,* "Uses of the Erotic" can be seen as a road map for the sensual discourse which informs her unique autobiography and serves to facilitate her move through a pornographic America; moreover, it can be surmised that "Uses of the Erotic" not only informs *Zami,* but also defines, to borrow from Barbara Herrnstein Smith's analysis, the "use" and "value" of the erotic material presented in her text. [13] Commenting on Lorde's interface between the erotic and the pornographic, feminist deconstructionist critic Elizabeth Meese argues that "[m]uch remains unspoken in Lorde's essay. Other than [a] characterization [of the pornographic] by negation, Lorde leaves pornography undefined. Is it that pornography 'goes without saying' because we are certain to know what it is? Because it is too dangerous (messy/confusing) for us to define it?" [14] Meese's treatment of Lorde is perfunctory at best and misses the subtlety of Lorde's intention; in "Uses of the Erotic," Lorde ventures not to define the pornographic but to explicate the territory of the erotic, so often mistaken as the pornographic or so often represented and/or experienced as such. I would also ask why, in a text primarily focused on the aesthetics of lesbian erotics, a "definition" of pornography is so aggressively sought by Meese, and in the context of Lorde's work, in particular? To search for definitions in Lorde's essay would be to deny the reader the pleasure of viewing power as it remains undefined, disseminated, and vulnerable to collective sharing—a sharing both dangerous and empowering—and a definition of "power" as agency within women's communities. In a 1983 interview with Claudia Tate, Lorde expands upon her theory of the erotic:

> The work I did on the erotic was very, very important. It opened up for me a whole area of connections in the absence of codified knowledge, or in the absence of some other clear choice. . . . We tend to think of the erotic as an easy, tantalizing sexual arousal. I speak of the erotic as the deepest life force, a force which moves us toward living in a fundamental way. [15]

Lorde contends that the "erotic is a resource within each of us that lies in a deeply female and *spiritual* plane, firmly rooted in the power of our unexpressed or unrecognized feeling" (53, emphasis mine). The usefulness of Lorde's critique might be perceived as suspect here because she challenges academic feminists to pay attention to the spiritual—that nebulous cloud of women's energy which pervades popular culture but which lacks inclusion in the majority of feminist academic critiques. What Lorde expresses here is a subliminal interest in pairing two discourses, the spiritual and the political. Moreover, in prophetic fashion she challenges the impending split between "feeling" and "discourse" that informs contemporary lesbian criticism—a discourse, according to Elizabeth Meese, where the erotic *is* language, where the word "lesbian" is synonymous with writing, and subsequently, where feelings flow, riveted by and trapped within elements of the master's linguistics. Meese writes into her text *(Sem)Erotics* an exploration of this happening:

> when my tongue slides over the osmotic, lively breathing surfaces of your skin like words in the more elusive *glissement*, gliding like waves, one just over the other, enveloping their letters, as, in their representational capacity, they produce signification which we take as meanings. Or as the pen makes its tracks across the body of the page, its friction and its struggle to mark the course faithfully, our passions inscribed energetically in the body of language in the mind: a love letter. [16]

My intent here is not to undermine the beauty of Meese's prose or the validity of her response to contemporary debates centered on the lesbian body; in fact, I find her critique somewhat arousing. What I am attempting to engage is the specific *location* of lesbian feminist ideology in a body that is literally a page with skin composed of words. We're still concentrating on and theorizing about not only figures, but de-racialized ones—figures that can write arousal, but fail to comprehend the unique power of the erotic by offering an interrogation of the powers, desirous or otherwise, that compel the subject to write herself, or the powers that make it illegal for her to do so. Lorde's theory and use of the erotic bypass this obsession with the language of the father by concentrating on the experiential properties of the erotic which create poetry, that is writing, in the first place.

Working with this intersection of language, subjectivity, and writing, Claudine Raynaud offers a cogent analysis of Lorde's relationship with these categories in an article entitled, " 'A Nutmeg Nestled Inside Its Covering of Mace': Audre Lorde's *Zami.*" Raynaud, like Lorde, narrows the gap among myth, spirit, and textual production by conceiving of a theory that includes all possible entities as crucial in the genesis of writing. Raynaud concludes that "[Lorde] does not justify her life through her text, her writing does not fill the gap of her being. It is instead an affirmation of being; it celebrates a myth, i.e., a truth, a power." [17] This informative power in Lorde's work is the erotic; in *Zami* the erotic does not rewrite a male language; it writes and rewrites the herstory of itself.

One of *Zami*'s first erotic images is of Lorde as a child in bed with her mother. Of this Saturday morning exchange she writes:

> The click of her wedding ring against the wooden headboard. She is awake. Her smile. Her glycerine-flannel smell. The warmth. She reclines upon her back and side, one arm extended, the other flung across her forehead. A hot-water bottle wrapped in body-temperature flannel. . . . Her large soft breasts beneath . . . her nightgown. Below, the rounded swell of her stomach, silent and inviting touch.
>
> I crawl against her, playing with the enflanneled, warm, rubber bag, pummeling it, tossing it, sliding it down the roundness of her stomach to the warm sheet between the bend of her elbow and the curve of her waist below her breasts, flopping sideward inside the printed cloth. Under the covers, the morning smells soft and sunny and full of promise (33).

What is important about this beginning scene is Lorde's heading: "How I Became a Poet." This childhood rememory [18] is fueled by the forces of the erotic. Lorde travels back to a "mother," but this journey is not necessarily for the purpose of "evacuating patriarchal discourse in order to re-write writing" as Meese observes in lesbian writing. [19] Here Lorde wants simply to write, to create, and to utilize a lifeforce that she considers distinctly female in the service of women poets—in the service of poetry itself. She undermines the ownership implied by patriarchal oppression by allowing the sound of her mother's wedding ring to announce the beginning of this scene of daughter seducing mother; the slight "click" of her mother's ring is overpowered by the "crawl[ing]," "pummeling," "tossing," "sliding," and "inviting" that take place during this narrative. At the end of this excerpt the smells emanating from her own mother's body become conflated with the smells of morning itself, "soft, sunny and full of promise."

Toward the end of *Zami*, Lorde will remember this piece of erotica as a symbol of her bonding with "Afrekete." Lorde writes, "we loved that night into a bright Sunday morning, dappled with green sunlight from the plants in Afrekete's high windows. . . . I woke to her house suffused with that light . . . and Afrekete, known, asleep against my side" (248). Here, what earlier lay "silent" and "inviting touch" beneath her mother's stomach is now "known"—from her mother's house to Afrekete's there is no disruption. Lorde has accepted the invitation to touch her mother's c(o)untry. She has imploded the taboo of incest and touched not only the place from which she was born—her mother's vagina—as well as her mother's place of origin. She has gained access to forbidden herstory and fruit. Lorde's use of the erotic allows her to employ it as a transcending mechanism; she recreates the erotic bond with her mother *and* with other female lovers in the text, transforming what is taboo, what is considered pornographic, into a continuum of erotic exchange. She also tacitly subverts the traditional relationship between African Americans and the written word as an act of scrawling on a blank page, an act of imitating white action, by omitting the pen altogether and allowing this connection between women to conceive a homeland out of an intimate encounter far from the New York bedroom in which the image takes shape and is assigned meaning. This imagining, this poetry, can be utilized as language for an encounter with her "first playmate" and finally for the relationship which brings *Zami*'s journey to a close.

Later in "Uses of the Erotic," Lorde evaluates the erotic as "a measure between the beginnings of our sense of self and the chaos of our strongest feelings" (54). It is out of the chaos of her experience with cancer[20] that *Zami* is born. Lorde experiences this "sense of self" and emotional "chaos" during a forty-eight-hour period after an illegal abortion. I would argue that this forty-eight-hour event has substantial connection with both her experience that Saturday morning in bed with her mother and memories of her first period. She remembers that the catheter, "lay coiled inside of me like a cruel benefactor, soon to rupture the delicate lining and wash away my worries in blood" (110). Creating an intricate scene of pain and discovery, Lorde manages to return to her mother's house figuratively—she awakens to her birthday, but throws up her celebratory breakfast. She is helped by the mothering hands of a female abortionist and a washroom attendant but is haunted by the laments of "a crazy old lady . . . whose children paid rent for her not to live with them" (105). It is a strange scene of substitute mothers and abandoned daughters. As the catheter works its subtle magic, Lorde writes:

> The rest of the night was an agony of padding back and forth along the length of the hallway from my bedroom to the bathroom, doubled over in pain, watching clots of blood fall out of my body into the toilet and wondering if I was alright, after all. I had never seen such huge red blobs come from me before. . . . I was afraid I might be bleeding to death. (111)

If the erotic is a "lifeforce" which moves us "toward the living," then this passage is another example of its ability to dismantle the pornographic; of its intrusion into the void of silence and secrecy which surrounds abortion—both in 1950 and 1990 North America. Moving between a "sense of self" and the "chaos" of her "strongest feelings," Lorde's vision of the erotic sustains the revelation of both living and dying in this passage. Ultimately, the personal is political here, as Lorde's action causes another kind of rebirth. The erotic is no longer just sensual, but essential as well and every experience is mediated by the tenuous link between the erotic as feeling and the pornographic as a pull toward the stagnating affects of rationale. The next afternoon, Miz Lewis, the washroom attendant sighs, " 'Chile, why don't you go back home to your mama, where you belong?' " (114). Miz Lewis's remark is ironic, as she speaks to both Lorde, the daughter, and Lorde, the mother, who takes both destinies into her own hands, who moves from her mother's house and decides neither to create nor procreate one of her own. Lorde constructs a space in the narrative where issues of motherhood, origins, and conception are problematized. She realizes that she inhabits a space of continuous action; a space fueled by the erotic through the sensations of physical pleasure and informative pain.

Informed by the power of the erotic, Lorde implies a transformation from the chaos of the abortion to the sensation of an earlier memory. Describing her encounter with her mother, she observes, "I frolic with the liquid-filled water bottle, patting and rubbing its firm giving softness. I shake it slowly, rocking it back and forth, lost in sudden tenderness, at the same time gently rubbing against my mother's quiet body. Warm milky smells of morning surround us" (33–34). Claudine Raynaud has positioned this scene as reminiscent of an intimacy which has connections to the birthing process. She writes, "[t]he little girl would play with the water bottle, its softness and the liquid within suggesting uterine life." [21] If we are to keep Raynaud's assessment, then the menacing image of the coiling red and liquid-filled catheter is transformed by a rememory of the lolling swish of a water bottle over her mother's "quiet body." The catheter's invasion is subverted by the energy of uterine representation here. Erotic information, therefore, transgresses the boundaries between objects and subjects, formulating a new space not so much where the object status of women is replaced by their own inscribed subject status, but where relationships between objects and subjects are literally catheterized, where a catharsis of emotion replaces skewed object-subject relations prescribed by the American pornographic which prohibits intimacy with the mother and restricts a woman's fundamental right to choose. Watching a part of her break away and swirl down a communal toilet bowl allows Lorde to entertain the representation of her own blood and her own actions. The clotted blood that flows from the aftermath of the abortion is much like the image of blood from her first menstruation; the latter being a source of power and information, the former being an absolution into life.

In another scenario of bloodletting, Lorde remembers pounding spice for souse and savoring her first menses:

> As I continued to pound the spice, a vital connection seemed to establish itself between the muscles of my fingers curved tightly around the smooth pestle in its insistent downward motion, and the molten core of my body whose source emanated from a new ripe fullness just beneath the pit of my stomach. That invisible thread, taut and sensitive as a clitoris exposed, stretched through my curled fingers up my round brown arm into the moist reality of my armpits . . . . within that basin was a tiding ocean of blood beginning to be made real and available to me for strength and information. (78)

This "information" provides her with an empowered sense of self, in what she defines in her interview with Claudia Tate as the "absence of codified knowledge." [22] Elizabeth Meese's "pen" alluded to earlier, is transformed by a pestle; an instrument symbolic of women's work is utilized in place of a phallic symbol. Claudine Raynaud also notes that "the grounding experience of her female identity is both consistent with African culture and an inversion of African patriarchal mythology."[23] Throughout *Zami,* Lorde is constantly bombarded by a system of knowledge and a social fabric intent upon affecting her erasure by disallowing her as present and whole. In "Uses of the Erotic" Lorde outlines this system:

> The principal horror of any system which defines the good in terms of profit rather than in terms of human need, or which defines human need to the exclusion of the psychic and emotional components of that need— the principal horror of such a system is that it robs our work of its erotic value, its erotic power and life appeal . . . reduc[ing] work to a travesty of necessities, a duty by which we earn bread or oblivion for ourselves and those we love. (55)

Here "work" becomes a gross misrepresentation of the action performed; for Lorde this system is implied as the pornographic. The equation of "good" with "profit" constructs an institutional standard which has the capacity to alter and represent any action or figure in its own image. This implication of the pornographic undermines Meese's earlier contention that Lorde's "Uses of the Erotic" neglects to "define" pornography. What we have here is the power of the pornographic as an institution to subvert the private—what occurs in *Zami* is a complete inversion of this cycle of oppression. In the space where *Zami* grows, the erotic consistently dissolves the institutional efficacy of the pornographic, and, I would add, the hegemony of pen to paper as a male act of inscription, and hence, definition.

When her mother returns from the store and realizes that Audre has not completed the work assigned to her, she obliterates the thread that runs between blood and bowl: "She brought the pestle down inside the bowl of mortar with dispatch. . . . I heard the thump of wood brought down heavily upon wood, and I felt the harsh impact throughout my body, as if something had broken inside of me" (80). For Lorde, her mother attends to work in its most pornographic sense—as necessity. Later, Lorde repairs this rupture with the following vision:

> Years afterward when I was grown, whenever I thought about the way I smelled that day, I would have a fantasy about my mother, her hands wiped dry from the washing, and her apron untied and laid neatly away,

looking down upon me lying on the couch, and then slowly, thoroughly, our touching and caressing each other's most secret places. (78)

Take the word "mother" here as both literal and figurative and we can arrive at a continuum of feeling where the sensation which creates this "fantasy" is preserved and where it can feed and sustain Lorde's work with the erotic. Instead of the "oblivion" earned by working under institutions of the pornographic, she returns this work to the private sphere—a place animated by a combination of present and past, pregnant with possibility and erotic action. She also reaches into the incest taboo and transgresses the territory of the unspoken by not only giving words, but poetry to a feeling between mother and child which grows into loving between women in adult life.

Zami reaffirms this sense of the erotic stated in Lorde's earlier poems where the erotic touches upon bodily landscapes and continents of knowledge. Published in 1968, "On a Night of the Full Moon" sites the power to be extracted from the erotic; the poem is written in two phases, representing both the waxing and waning of the moon itself. Blending voice and physical attraction Lorde envisions a place of loving between women that is as yet unformed—a "shape" only—sought "for reason."[24] As Lorde argues in many of her essays, connection across differences is key to breaking the destructive patterns of racism, sexism, and homophobia that force women to view their lives through a pornographic lens. The erotic moment in Lorde is designed not only to encompass the designs of the flesh, but also to rework levels of the creative process. For Lorde, body parts such as the "eye," "skin," and "finger" represent pathways to knowing—the body itself becomes a repository for both feeling and knowledge.[25] Thus, the notion of the eroticized being as purely a sexual subject seeking climax is altered by Lorde's insistence upon deconstructing the sexual moment so that it becomes intertwined with creative force—it is literally conceived as loving takes place. Read on different levels, "On a Night of the Full Moon" is a poem about planetary function, individual apex, creative genesis, and the efficacy of the erotic in its myriad of forms. Echoing these principles, Miriam DeCosta-Willis proclaims that eroticism is

the powerful life force within us from which spring desire and creativity and our deepest knowledge of the universe. The life force that flows like an inscrutable tie through all things, linking man to woman, man to man, woman to woman, bird to flower, and flesh to spirit. Our ancestors taught us this in their songs of love, their myths of creation, their celebrations of birth, and their rituals of initiation. Desire. Pleasure. Wholeness.[26]

Lorde's work with the erotic and the pornographic demonstrates that a search for accurate definitions of either is both dangerous and unproductive. Constant focus on representational politics is necessary in feminist studies, but appears to lack attention to individual and collective action and experience, and in this case, black female experience. Moreover, Lorde's essay on the erotic, while often quoted, has been denied a close reading because it does not position the pornographic as primary by defining its nature, its essence. It appears that black lesbian experience is reflective of some measure of the pornographic and the erotic; therefore, Lorde leaves space for choice and difference, laughter and critique. Reminding us of the comic intersection of the pornographic and erotic, she writes of an interchange with a close womanfriend in *Zami:* "once we exchanged the word 'fucker' for 'mother' in a whole day's conversation, and got put off the Number 5 bus by an irate driver" (88–89).

NOTES

1. Katie King, "Audre Lorde's Lacquered Layerings: The Lesbian Bar as a Site of Literary Production," in *New Lesbian Criticism: Literary and Cultural Readings,* ed. Sally Munt (New York: Columbia University Press, 1992), 52.

2. Pat Califia, "A Secret Side of Lesbian Sexuality," in *S and M: Studies in Sadomasochism,* ed. Thomas Weinberg and G. W. Levi Kamel (Buffalo: Prometheus, 1983).

3. Audre Lorde, *Zami: A New Spelling of My Name: A Biomythography* (Freedom, CA: The Crossing Press, 1982), 256. All subsequent references are to this edition and are included in the text.

4. I am referring here to both Monique Wittig's *The Lesbian Body* (Boston: Beacon, 1973) and Elizabeth A. Meese's *(Sem)Erotics: theorizing lesbian : writing* (New York: New York University Press, 1992).

5. Namascar Shaktini, "A Revolutionary Signifier: The Lesbian Body," in *Lesbian Texts and Contexts: Radical Revisions,* ed. Karla Jay and Joanne Glasgow (New York: New York University Press, 1990), 300.

6. Anna Wilson, "Audre Lorde and the African-American Tradition: When the Family Is Not Enough," in *New Lesbian Criticism,* 78.

7. Lisa Henderson, "Lesbian Pornography: Cultural Transgression and Sexual Demystification," in *New Lesbian Criticism,* 175.

8. Oliviero Toscani and Luciano Benetton, advertisement. *Rolling Stone* (12 November 1992).

9. Susanne Kappeler, *The Pornography of Representation* (Minneapolis: University of Minnesota Press, 1986), 39–40. Alan Soble has offered that "erotica is better defined as 'acceptable pornography' rather than in opposition to pornography," in *Pornography: Marxism, Feminism, and the Future of Sexuality* (New Haven: Yale University Press, 1986), 179.

10. Kappeler, 6.

11. Henderson, 187.

12. Audre Lorde, "Uses of the Erotic," in *Sister Outsider* (Freedom, CA: The Crossing Press, 1984), 54. All subsequent references are to this edition and are included in the text.

13. Barbara Herrnstein Smith, *Contingencies of Value: Alternative Perspectives for Critical Theory* (Cambridge: Harvard University Press, 1988). See her critique of "use" and "value," 30–53.

14. Meese, 105.

15. Claudia Tate, ed., *Black Women Writers at Work*, Audre Lorde, interview (New York: Continuum, 1983), 115.

16. Meese, 3.

17. Claudine Raynaud, "'A Nutmeg Nestled Inside Its Covering of Mace': Audre Lorde's *Zami*," in *Life/Lines: Theorizing Women's Autobiography*, ed. Bella Brodzki and Celeste Schenck (Ithaca: Cornell University Press, 1988), 234.

18. I am using the word "rememory" here as a process of speaking about what has traditionally been omitted in both prose narrative and autobiography. Toni Morrison has defined "rememory" in an essay entitled, "The Site of Memory," in *Inventing the Truth, The Art and Craft of Memoir*, ed. William Zinsser (Boston: Houghton Mifflin, 1987).

19. Meese, 13.

20. Claudia Tate, interview. Here, Lorde comments: "[w]riting *Zami* was a lifeline through the cancer experience" (115).

21. Raynaud, 227.

22. Tate, 115.

23. Raynaud, 238.

24. Audre Lorde, "On a Night of the Full Moon," in *Chosen Poems Old and New* (New York: Norton, 1982), 20–21.

25. Ibid.

26. Miriam DeCosta-Willis, Reginald Martin, and Roseann P. Bell, eds., *Erotique Noire/Black Erotica* (New York: Doubleday, 1992), xxix.

FIFTEEN

Abrotica: The Lesbian Erotic and the Erotic Abject in Anaïs Nin's *House of Incest*

JOHANNA BLAKLEY

Anaïs Nin's *House of Incest* promises nothing more than a furtive glimpse at Freud's *unheimlich*—the un-home-like, the unfamiliar, the uncanny. Posing as nosey neighbors or peeping toms, we expect a tale of domestic horror or exotic eroticism; what we get is something in between, both but neither. We are ushered into "an edifice without dimension," [1] a home composed of one vomited heart and the bones of a dead lover. Its walls encompass various symbols of self-division, infertility, and dismemberment: we see a forest of bamboo women with faces sliced in two, a collection of white plaster eggs which will not hatch, and several "fragments of bodies, bodies armless and headless" (HI, 56). Each of its isolated rooms imprisons a character suffering from a love both self-destructive and self-indulgent—a woman in love with her brother, a hypersensitive and hopelessly self-absorbed modern Christ, and the house's own solipsistic architect, imprisoned in her own pages, in love with a woman of her own making.

Strewn with tortured bodies and the interminable flow of various bodily juices, *House of Incest* seems compelled to turn us away, to repulse and frighten us. We are seduced, however, by its incantatory poetic prose which creates a tension between form and content that ultimately contributes to its provocative character—we are invited to indulge in the erotic charge of images calculated to frighten us. Nin exploits incest as a pornographic motif and as a nightmarish symbol of debilitating and unacceptable intimacy. In *Speaking the Unspeakable*, Peter Michelson describes Nin's expansive use of incest as a "symbolic image of the dialectic of 'inner space'—between self and other, passive and active, male and female."[2] In her attempt to record "an incomplete but highly significant dream,"[3] Nin invokes binarisms only to wrench them apart and articulate the space in between. The result is an erotic lament, both arousing and oppressive. Her depiction of lesbian desire, which she presents as a type of incestuous behavior, is fraught with this titillating ambiguity: she glorifies the love between women for its lack of "mockery," yet she mourns its sterility and self-absorption (HI, 24).

I detect a similar ambivalence in Julia Kristeva's treatment of "abjection" in *Powers of Horror*. Kristeva proposes abjection as the experience of disrupted "identity, system, order" which occurs when "borders, positions, rules" are made ambiguous (PH, 4).[4] Substances which traverse bodily boundaries such as faeces, urine, blood, and vomit challenge definitions of self/other, inside/outside. Far from being "abnormal," abjection "preserves what existed in the archaism of pre-objectal relationship, in the immemorial violence with which a body becomes separated from another body in order to be" (PH, 10). Abjection is an inevitable experience for anyone who has entered the symbolic order where the difference between subject and object is crucial to identity. Rather than writing off the abject as inherently painful, Kristeva points to its proximity to *jouissance:* both are marked by the heterogeneous "I," an experience of self as other, and quite often, "victims" of abjection are "submissive and willing" (PH, 9).

By reading *House of Incest* and *Powers of Horror* side by side, we can examine a few methods of lesbian erotic representation in psychoanalytic terms. Both Nin and Kristeva explicitly address the complicated relationship between two sets of oppositional terms. Both authors investigate the territory between *attraction* and *repulsion* and ultimately question conventional distinctions between *difference* and *similarity*. Despite the fact that both of these works assume a heterosexual norm against which homosexuality is defined, the work of Nin and Kristeva will prove to be helpful to critics and readers interested in lesbian representation. Since the meaning of heterosexuality and homosexuality is grounded in assumptions about similarity and difference, any work which dedicates itself to deconstructing that binarism will also destabilize the taboo against homosexuality and the privileged position that heterosexuality enjoys. Without ignoring those moments when Nin and Kristeva shrink from the "sterility" of lesbian desire, I would like to concentrate on the ways they register abject alternatives to heterosexual notions of the "erotic."

Nin considered *House of Incest* "a woman's *Season in Hell*," [5] clearly suggesting that gender is a defining factor in this work and prompting Sharon Spencer to describe Nin's writing as "music of the womb." [6] Despite Nin's attempts to establish the tenets of a *féminine écriture*, her diaries reflect her unwavering belief that writing is ultimately a masculine activity:

> I sat at the typewriter, saying to myself: Write, you weakling; write, you madwoman, write your misery out, write out your guts, spill out what is choking you, shout obscenely. . . . Oh, to be free, to be masculine and purely artist. To care only about the art. [7]

The narrator in *House* withholds her name, only identifying herself as a woman writer grappling with madness. She also longs to stop choking and start writing like a man. However, her coherence as a representative of Nin's essentialist notion of "Woman" threatens to fall apart when she falls in love with another woman. Her agonizing efforts to identify herself and her lover are undermined by her dependence upon an essentialist definition of "woman": she oscillates between her belief that she is indistinguishable from Sabina and her conviction that their desire for one another must be based upon their fundamental differences. When she first sees Sabina, she cannot decide whether it is dawn or dusk, whether she is dreaming or awake: the night has been "unglued" from its photographic frame revealing the curled edges and the artificiality of "reality." In this surreal setting, Sabina's face appears in the garden, reeking of exotic savagery: incense spirals from her skin, her gestures arouse "a beat chant like the beat of the heart of the desert," and her voice is "rusty" from curses and orgasmic cries. Her overwhelming sexuality is infused with the power of death: a "simoun wind" blows from her eyes leaving the garden "shrivelled," her voice breaks what it touches, and she marches with an "inhuman rhythm" wearing a steel necklace "wrung of groaning machinery" (HI, 18–21). The narrator is utterly dominated by her: Sabina's voice threatens her, her breath blinds her, and she places a "steel bracelet" on the narrator's wrist, making her "pulse beat as she willed, losing its human cadence, thumping like a savage in orgiastic frenzy" (HI, 23).

Throughout these descriptions, the narrator emphasizes and eroticizes the differences between them: Sabina is a "dancer" who makes impressions upon the world while the narrator is the "writer," floating above it all, a shadow recording Sabina's exploits and saving all the "fragile things" that Sabina had thrown aside in her victorious march through the world (HI, 27). Despite the fact that both of them are ultimately "women," and therefore subject to certain eternal gender rules, the two complement one another, in many ways playing out the binary structure of desire used to "heterosexualize" homosexual desire. In her critique of psychoanalysis, Irigaray coins the term "hommosexuality" to describe Freud's explanation of lesbian desire which is underwritten by the male principle:[8] in his "Psychogenesis of a Case of Homosexuality in a Woman," he establishes a causal connection between his patient's desire for women, her "feminist" inclinations, and her "pronounced envy of the penis."[9] Labels such as "butch/femme" and "top/bottom" obviously owe a debt to hypotheses such as Freud's, and they seem to describe, all too well, the power relations between Sabina and the narrator. While Sabina fetishizes her puppets, the narrator describes herself as a "marionette pulled by unskilled fingers, pulled apart, inharmoniously dislocated; one arm dead, the other rhapsodizing in mid-air" (HI, 29–30). Each woman is distinctly aligned with the two opposing positions of sadomasochism: Sabina wears the typical fetishistic clothes of the dominatrix (a web-like dress, a black cape, steel jewelry), and her "nacreous" skin, her "ancient stare" (HI, 18), and her "labyrinthian smile" (HI, 23) conjure an image of the vampiric sadist. The writer poses as a willing but frightened victim who describes her pain as the predecessor to a "divine departure" (HI, 37). Clearly, the exaggerated power differences between these two women is coterminous with their erotic interplay: Sabina's acts of force and will have orgasmic results in her worshipful and "passive" partner. By explaining their desire for one another in terms of power (strength/weakness) and agency (activity/passivity) instead of gender (man/woman), the narrator's essentialist vision of Woman remains virtually unscathed.

Despite these elaborations on their sexual complementarity, their innate difference from one another, there are numerous passages devoted to the writer's anxiety about merging with Sabina and losing her identity while fulfilling her desire. She describes her vision as a mirror: as she gazes at Sabina, she sees "one woman within another eternally, in a far-reaching procession, shattering my mind into fragments, into quarter tones which no orchestral baton can ever make whole again" (HI, 22).

The phallic baton cannot arrest this *mise en abyme* which only seems possible if Sabina's gaze is also a mirror, making the "object" for either woman herself: "from all men I was different, and myself, but I see in you that part of me which is you. I feel you in me" (HI, 26). Face to face with Sabina, she is not herself, not different, but in Kristeva's terms, anchored "interiorly in the Other" (PH, 54). This simultaneous motion toward identification and desire characterizes both abjection and narcissism. Kristeva acknowledges their proximity but argues that abjection is "a kind of narcissistic crisis" which is "a precondition of narcissism." The two are "coexistent" but the abject is "the 'object' of primal repression" while narcissism is "a regression to a position set back from the other." Although Kristeva is apprehensive about assigning temporal primacy, she does claim that abjection precedes narcissism though the two may overlap in two opposing circumstances: when the Other is too strict, and when the Other has lapsed. "In both instances, the abject appears in order to uphold 'I' within the Other" (PH, 12–15).

Nin's depiction of lesbian desire appears to be an instance of a strict *and* a lapsed Other. Sabina's domineering presence and her status as "original" opposed to the writer as "copy" (or copier) suggests that this narcissistic crisis, this abjection, is half-grounded in the overwhelming authority of the Other: Sabina's voice invades her, her breath blinds her vision, she controls the writer's heartbeat, and she draws blood from her (HI, 24). The narrator's only power seems to come from her passive role recording Sabina's exploits: despite her constant self-effacement, the first-person narration grants her an authority and presence which she suddenly relinquishes:

> THIS IS THE BOOK YOU WROTE
> AND YOU ARE THE WOMAN
> I AM (HI, 28)

The Other, who might have been subject to this book, subjected to this writer, is abruptly in charge of her own description turning the I/You designation into an abysmal gesture that only refers to itself.

There are several passages, however, where Sabina represents the *lapsed* other. Occasionally, the narrator reaffirms her position as author and apostrophizes to her lover: "Come away with me, Sabina, come to my island." Nin's erotic island is infused with luxuriant danger: there are pomegranates "spurting blood," wild cats fighting, and a coral reef with a "body covered with long seaweeds." In yet another role reversal, the narrator offers the intoxicating glory of bodily decomposition and primal aggression to Sabina, her speechless addressee. Just before she offers to take Sabina to her island, she claims that Sabina is "losing her polarity" because she is "spreading herself" and has become incapable of "fusion" (HI, 25). A series of apostrophes follow, ending with the speaker posing as messiah:

> Step out of your role and rest yourself on the core of your true desires. Cease for a moment your violent deviations. Relinquish the furious indomitable strain.
>   I will take them up. (HI, 27)

In her Christ-like mode, the narrator takes control of an Other who is "trembling and shaking and gasping and cursing" because her "core" is finally located elsewhere (HI, 27). The essence of the original "I" is now in the copier's hands.

I find these instances of the "lapsed Other" particularly compelling because of Nin's repeated use of apostrophe. Jonathan Culler proposes that apostrophe "makes its point by troping not on the meaning of a word but on the circuit or situation of communication itself." [10] While an apostrophe establishes an I/Thou relationship, it might do so in order to constitute the speaker as poetical persona, one who has the power to invoke people, things, and forces of nature. In fact, the "thou" of the apostrophe can "be read as an act of radical interiorization and solipsism"—a way of "parcel(ing) out the self to fill the world" or "internaliz(ing) what might have been thought external." [11] In both instances, Kristeva might say that the "I" is upheld within the Other, that is, apostrophe might signify the narcissistic crisis which is related to abjection.

Perhaps the point at which these two contradictory circumstances, the strict and lapsed Other, occur simultaneously is the point at which abjection becomes eroticized. The Other is strict or lapsed only in comparison to something else—presumably, "I." In *House of Incest,* the I is not only "upheld within the Other" but *held up* by the Other: the "I" is held at gunpoint (or at bay), no longer a legible point of reference because its own position is not only dependent upon the difference the Other has to offer but also, to use Jonathan Dollimore's phrase, "mysteriously inherent within" it. [12] The subject is not only abjected, repulsed by her own boundaries, but attracted to them, in part, because they no longer seem to be her own. Dollimore's description of the "paradoxical perverse" is abundantly applicable here: the taboo against same/same desire, the foundation of abjection, is simultaneously upheld and destroyed—it is central to the narrator's repulsion and key to her delight. The erotic charge of a rule against a certain kind of eroticism is constantly in play and yet always on the brink of being overturned.

Kristeva's description of the erotic abject is appropriately fraught with ambiguity and "paradoxical perversity." Although Kristeva describes abjection (from *abicere* = to cast away) as a "universal phenomenon" which, by definition, should be universally abhorred (PH, 68), she acknowledges that it can become the object of desire. She claims that language must first come "undone": sound image and sight image are divorced—the condensation that first made the sign possible is denied and the semiotic overwhelms the symbolic.

> The body's inside ... shows up in order to compensate for the collapse of the border between inside and outside. It is as if the skin, a fragile container ... gave way before the dejection of its contents. Urine, blood, sperm, excrement then show up in order to reassure a subject that is lacking its "own and clean self." (PH, 53)

In order to replace the Other with the abject, Kristeva argues that the subject must regress to intersubjective relations with the mother. Instead of maintaining a distance from the Other, those who eroticize the abject delve into the bowels of the mother and try to give birth to themselves. Kristeva describes this process in surprisingly condescending terms: she calls it a "harebrained staging of an abortion, of a self-giving birth ever miscarried, endlessly to be renewed" (PH, 54). Her willingness to ridicule those who regard the abject erotically seems to signal a certain anxiety about the precarious position of the eroticized abject in her theory of abjection. This erotic exception to the rules of attraction and repulsion poses a problem to the symbolic order that Kristeva attempts to describe faithfully. Since Kristeva is primarily interested in "the *benefits* that accrue to the speaking subject from a precise symbolic organization" (PH, 67), she makes no attempt to invalidate cultural taboos. Although her definition of abjection helps explain the source of many anxieties about incest, narcissism, and homosexuality, for example, she does not call any of those anxieties into question; in fact, she displays some of that uneasiness in her description of the "harebrained" subject of the erotic abject.

Kristeva's analysis of the erotic abject is particularly strange because of the attention she pays to the difference between a man's experience and a woman's. Agreeing with Lacan that "Woman" does not exist, [13] Kristeva always assumes a male subject. We are surprised, then, when she emphasizes the profound differences between the male and female who eroticize the abject: while the man is a "frontiersman" and a "metaphysician," a woman is most likely doing it for a man and is "frequently absent" from her own actions. However, she imagines an exception which resonates with psychoanalytic commonplaces about the "lesbian":

> Rarely does a woman tie her desire and her sexual life to that abjection, which, coming to her from the other, anchors her interiorly in the Other. When that happens, one notes that it is through the expedient of writing that she gets there, and on that account she still has quite a way to go within the Oedipal mosaic before identifying with the owner of the penis. (PH, 54)

When a woman eroticizes the abject without the symbolic authority of a man, she must *become* him rather than relinquish him. Of course, this sounds eerily similar to the "masculinity complex" that Freud ascribes to lesbians: instead of *desiring* the owner of the penis, a lesbian identifies with him. Consequently, a woman's desire for the abject is implicitly lesbian: Kristeva makes it clear that "she as well as he" performs the "harebrained" abortion on the mother's body. Her Other is still her mother, just like her male counterpart.

Kristeva's atypical attention to a woman's experience as subject might indicate that the logic of the erotic abject is somehow indebted to or dependent upon the logic of gender differentiation in a way which is not true for narcissism, incest, paranoia, and voyeurism, all of which she discusses in this chapter without asides about "women." Her assertion that women experience the erotic abject through *writing* brings us quite close to the representation of lesbian eroticism in Nin's novel. Both of them regard "writing" and "identification with the owner of the penis" as corresponding steps taken by the abject woman on her route toward satisfaction and destruction, toward *jouissance*. Kristeva's emphasis upon the Judeo-Christian roots of the symbolic order explains her assumption that the writer and the owner of the penis are related; indeed, both of them are the direct inheritors of the Father's power to create with words. In reductive terms, authors are male and women who identify with them, women who write, suffer from a "masculinity complex" which shatters the Oedipal mosaic, and marks the beginning of a journey into the erotic abject.

The prologue to *House of Incest* foreshadows one of the predominant concerns of this work—the abject relationship between writing and the gendered body: "The morning I got up to begin this book I coughed. Something was coming out of my throat: it was strangling me. I broke the thread which held it and yanked it out. I went back to bed and said: I have just spat out my heart" (HI, no page number). Nin scandalizes the clichéd analogy between writing a book and giving birth by equating the book (or child) to a pile of vomit. While she submits to the temptation to equate writing with bodily excretion, this prologue obviously defies traditional notions of the writing process: the text is not sublime, nor cohesive, nor inspired by a transcendental signifier. As Kristeva mentions in her comments on "contemporary writing," writers of the abject taint the supposed sublimity of writing yet authorize their own literary work by soundly thrashing the pillars of the status quo such as Religion, Morality, and Law (PH, 16). Nin's description of the writing process simultaneously suggests that this book, this vomited heart, is a mode of self-expression and self-mutilation, a kind of hollowing within. Both productive and destructive, the writing of the abject produces culture while relentlessly tearing it apart at the seams.

The prologue continues with a description of the "quena" which goes beyond establishing a connection between writing and the body by bringing into the foreground the gender of that body and the erotic resonance of writing:

> There is an instrument called the quena made of human bones. It owes its origin to the worship of an Indian for his mistress. When she died he made a flute out of her bones. The quena has a more penetrating, more haunting sound than the ordinary flute.
> Those who write know the process. I thought of it as I was spitting out my heart.
> Only I do not wait for my love to die. (HI, no page number)

Even more shocking than her previous analogy, Nin equates writing with dismembering a *live* lover. While she originally emphasized the way in which writing is an act of self-expression and self-mutilation, this morbid anecdote depicts the writer as masochist *and* murderer: the text requires body parts from the author and her object of desire. She can sing her lover's praises only by robbing her lover of life . . . and writing the robbing itself. There is a gender slippage, however, in the comparison between the writer and the carver. It is initially unclear whether the narrator equates herself with the Indian or his mistress: the quena "owes its origin to the worship of an Indian . . . for his mistress." The reader stumbles through the passage—who is worshipped here? The Indian? . . . No, of course, the dead woman. If the narrator abides by gender alignments, she must be the mutilated mistress, risen from the dead, playing a flute whittled from her own bones.

It becomes apparent, in passages such as these, that writing is figured as a repository for (or a route toward) the erotic abject. When the subject of writing is writing, "the body's inside . . . shows up in order to compensate for the collapse of the border between inside and outside"— Kristeva's description of the onset of the erotic abject (PH, 53). Metadiscursive moments provide opportunities to delve not only into self-reflexivity but through it to a level neither self-expressed nor self-mutilated, neither whole nor fragmented, but an alien moment which is intimately related to the whole. Certain "revelations" take place on this plane of the text that resonate with Dollimore's "paradoxical perversity": the book seems to write about itself, distanced from the rest of itself and yet still the self-same book. While Nin's opening comments address the abjection of the writing process, she goes on to describe her literary production as a lethal trap which ensnares its own author: "I walked into my own book, seeking peace. . . . As I move within my book I am cut by pointed glass and broken bottles in which there is still the odor of sperm and perfume" (HI, 62). When the sign collapses—when sound image is divorced from sight image—Kristeva detects an "attempt at direct semantization of the body" (PH 53) which signals the erotic abject. The intertextuality of the author's body and book is dependent upon a "confusion" between the materiality of the sign and the materiality of the body. While Kristeva describes this as characteristic of both men and women who are attracted to the abject, she claims that only women experience the erotic abject through writing. In this context, Kristeva's assumption about women's relationship to writing and Nin's anxiety about her own bodily relationship to her work are both built upon an acknowledgment that writing is a masculine activity. Nin makes this assumption quite tangible when the narrator equates the landscape of her book to a collection of broken bottles once filled with sperm.

Nin consulted psychoanalysts while she wrote *House of Incest*, in part because of her anxiety about being a woman and a writer. Her second analyst, Otto Rank, tried to convince her to stop writing in her diary because he believed it was unnatural for women to be artists.[14] Rank explained that her "lesbian tendencies" and her diary were both unhealthy products of her identification with her father.[15] Two years earlier, under the influence of her first analyst, Nin had already connected her writing with her lesbian desires: after breaking off her relationship with June Miller (the model for Sabina) and resuming her affair with Henry Miller, Nin realizes

> how far I have moved away from lesbianism, and how it is only the artist in me, the dominating energy, which expands to fecundate beautiful women on a plane which it is difficult to apprehend and which bears no relation whatsoever to ordinary sexual activity.[16]

Nin's literary lesbianism is, indeed, a manifestation of the materiality of language and the erotic abject: her redistribution of sensory stimuli and bodily sites across the terrain of writing results in a text that is not "about" sexuality but an enactment of it. Where she "fecundates" women and cuts her skin with broken sperm bottles, we do not merely see the record of sexual desire but a bodily relationship to language which blurs the boundary between representation and reality.

Nin's preoccupation with the links between writing and the body necessarily implicates the body of the reader. In yet another passage about writing, Nin's narrator constructs an exotic Byzantine past for Sabina and herself where Sabina was "an idol dancing with legs parted; and I wrote with pollen and honey. The soft secret yielding of woman I carved into men's brains with copper words" (HI, 22). Due to the abrupt juxtaposition of Sabina's parted legs and the narrator's "pollen and honey," it seems possible that "the soft secret yielding of woman" which the narrator writes on men's minds is not only the subject of her writing but the substance itself, that is, her "ink." In another passage, she equates her ink to the acid that flows out of her body which she offers to her readers in "enormous mouthfuls" (32). In both instances, she depicts writing as an act of violent bodily inscription. Here, her readership is decidedly male, making the inscription on their bodies, their penetration by Sabina's "honey," an inversion of heterosexual sex. By replacing the phallic pen with womb-juice ink, and regendering the penetrated paper as male, Nin reverses the gendered roles of writer and reader in her description of lesbian desire.

All of these intersections between writing and the gendered body overflow with sexual connotation. The idea that writing has something to do with sex is certainly not new: any reader or writer of erotica has already assumed that representations can produce physical effects in readers. Considering Kristeva's crucial connections between women, writing, and the erotic abject, we should think more carefully about the *erotic* as a site for the explosion of the boundary between representation and reality.

Dictionary definitions tend to oscillate between describing the erotic as an inherent sexual quality in something or a sexual response that something elicits. This confusion is evidently grounded in the interdependence of the erotic subject and object: separating one from the other is particularly difficult when we consider reading or writing erotica. One reason we cannot seem to forge an adequate definition of the erotic is due to the paradoxical quality of "desire": since its presence always signifies an absence (a lack of something), it is difficult to determine whether the erotic creates desire or satiates it. Due to these complications, *Webster's New Twentieth Century Dictionary* attempts to stabilize this definitional tension with a moral judgment. Instead of establishing the difference between subject and object or desire and fulfillment, Webster describes eroticism as a "persistent and abnormal excitation or passion." According to this definition, eroticism is intrinsically excessive and will remain perversely distant from the "normality" that defines it. Webster's attempt to identify "eroticism" as inherently abnormal is rooted in a recognition that the erotic lingers somewhere between subjects and objects, desires and fulfillments, absolutely abject. Kristeva would call it a "harebrained staging of an abortion," a miscarried abortion whose product is illegible. An aberration. Abrotic.

With this "definition" in mind, I would like to suggest that discussions and depictions of the erotic are always abjectly lodged between theory and praxis. Both critiquing and practicing the erotic are exercises in reading and writing which take into account the body's relationship to meaning. Both Kristeva and Nin provide examples of the contradictions involved in such practice and critique: they both indulge in the erotic charge of the forbidden and censure that pleasure. The "moral" of *House of Incest* is appropriately delivered by the modern, drug-addicted

Christ: "If only we could all escape from this house of incest, where we only love ourselves in the other, if only I could save you all from yourselves" (HI, 70). Although his audience (which includes the narrator, Sabina, and Jeanne, a woman in love with her brother) doubts the plausibility of breaking out, Nin concludes the novel with the narrator's vicarious escape from it. In the final scene, the armless woman, who represents another facet of the narrator, initially dances her fears to a music unheard, but miraculously regains her arms (in order to give and forgive like Christ) and ends "dancing toward daylight" to a music that everyone hears (HI, 72).[17] The implications of this resolute ending are more disturbing than the disruptions that riddle the entire book. The "dialectic of inner-space"[18] and the erotic scene of the abject is presented as a prison while the social symbolic, the place where everyone hears and dances to the same music, is a sort of paradise of normality, fertility, and selflessness.

In her recent biography of Anaïs Nin, Noel Riley Fitch pieces together Nin's complicated erotic history from several different sources, including Nin's letters, her fiction, and the variously edited versions of her diaries. Although Nin included three women on her "Liste d'Amoureux" in an unpublished diary, she publicly denied that she ever had a lesbian relationship. In 1946, enraged by rumors that she was a lesbian, Nin defended herself in her published diary by writing that her work only "implied woman's love to woman."[19] Fitch's biography demonstrates that the relationship between Nin's publicly acknowledged erotic life, her private memoirs, and her fictionalized escapades are so desperately entangled that we cannot hope to know where reality ends and fantasy takes over. Nin's anxious attempt to separate fiction from fact, to designate firm boundaries between her writing and her body, illustrates her own abject relationship to the erotic abject.

NOTES

1. Anaïs Nin, *House of Incest* (1936; reprint, Athens, OH: Swallow Press, 1989): no page number. Hereafter, quotations from *House of Incest* are cited in the text with the abbreviation HI.
2. Peter Michelson, *Speaking the Unspeakable: A Poetics of Obscenity* (Albany: SUNY Press, 1993), 216.
3. Anaïs Nin, "Realism and Reality," in *The White Blackbird and Other Writings* (Santa Barbara: Capra Press, 1985), 19.

4. Julia Kristeva, *Powers of Horror: An Essay on Abjection*, trans. Leon S. Roudiez (New York: Columbia University Press, 1982), 4. Hereafter, quotations from *Powers of Horror* are cited in the text with the abbreviation PH.

5. Anaïs Nin, *The Diary of Anaïs Nin, 1934–1939*, vol. 2, ed. Gunther Stuhlmann (New York: Harcourt Brace Jovanovich, 1967), 151.

6. Sharon Spenser, "The Music of the Womb: Anaïs Nin's 'Feminine' Writing," in *Breaking the Sequence: Women's Experimental Fiction*, ed. Ellen G. Friedman and Miriam Fuchs (Princeton: Princeton University Press, 1989), 161–76.

7. Anaïs Nin, *Incest: From "A Journal of Love." The Unexpurgated Diary of Anaïs Nin, 1932–1934* (San Diego: Harcourt Brace Jovanovich, 1992), 308.

8. Luce Irigaray, *Speculum of the Other Woman* (1974) reprint, trans. Gillian C. Gill (Ithaca: Cornell University Press, 1985), 101–3.

9. Sigmund Freud, "Psychogenesis of a Case of Homosexuality in a Woman" (1920), in *Sexuality and the Psychology of Love*, trans. Barbara Low and R. Gabler (New York: Collier Books, 1963), 156.

10. Jonathan Culler, *The Pursuit of Signs: Semiotics, Literature, Deconstruction* (Ithaca: Cornell University Press, 1981), 135.

11. Ibid., 146.

12. Jonathan Dollimore, *Sexual Dissidence: Augustine to Wilde, Freud to Foucault* (New York: Oxford University Press, 1991), 121.

13. Julia Kristeva, "Women's Time," in *The Kristeva Reader*, ed. Toril Moi, trans. Alice Jardine and Harry Blake (New York: Columbia University Press, 1986), 205.

14. Nin, *Incest: A Journal*, 301.

15. Ibid., 298.

16. Ibid., 2.

17. Otto Rank insisted on this conclusion. See Noel Riley Fitch, *Anaïs: The Erotic Life of Anaïs Nin* (Boston: Little, Brown, 1993), 181.

18. Michelson, 216.

19. Anaïs Nin, *The Diary of Anaïs Nin, 1944–1947*, vol. 4, ed. Gunther Stuhlmann (New York: Harcourt Brace Jovanovich, 1967), 175–76.

SIXTEEN

Encoding Bi-Location: Sylvia Townsend Warner and the Erotics of Dissimulation

JANE GARRITY

In 1959, when Virginia Woolf's reputation as a writer was flagging, British author Sylvia Townsend Warner delivered a lecture entitled "Women as Writers" that revived interest in Woolf by alluding to and creating intertextual dialogue with Woolf's then forgotten essay, *A Room of One's Own.*[1] Woolf's observation that women writers experience a "splitting off of consciousness"—an ability to be both within and outside of culture simultaneously—is playfully echoed by Warner, who similarly invokes an image of women's dual-positionality:

> Women as writers are obstinate and sly.... There is, for instance, bi-location. It is well known that a woman can be two places at once.... She can practice a mental bi-location also.... Her mind is so extensive that it can simultaneously follow a train of thought, remember what it was she had to tell the electrician, answer the telephone, keep an eye on the time, and not forget about the potatoes.[2]

While Warner's characterization of the woman writer as "sly" and occupying a "bi-location" can be read as a description of Woolf's equivocal strategy in *A Room*, I want to suggest that these remarks—privileging duplicity and couching subversion within the realm of domestic familiarity—also have particular resonance for Warner's own fictional tactics. Her eccentric prose, which in one critic's words is always "pull [ing] the carpet from under the reader's feet," both obscures and reveals Warner's interest in encoding a lesbian thematic.[3]

Today, of course, Woolf's canonical status has never been more certain, while Warner's literary placement within the tradition of women's twentieth-century writing—despite her past prominence—is tenuous, at best. An author of prodigious imaginative scope, Warner's work includes nine books of poetry, seven novels, ten volumes of short stories, a translation of Proust, a biography of T. H. White, and many essays and reviews. One might argue, as does Warner's biographer Claire Harman, that the author's name eludes recognition precisely because her oeuvre is so tremendously varied and, as a result, difficult to categorize. Jane Marcus similarly speculates that Warner's exile from the canon has to do with her work in multiple genres, but she also argues that Warner's neglect is largely due to the fact that she was both a lesbian and an active member of the British Communist party.[4] While Warner's political writings on the Spanish Civil War have recently begun to be reassessed, her contribution to the development of both modernism and lesbian literary history still remains undertheorized.[5]

Warner's obscurity may indeed be linked to her involvement with Marxism and her passion for women, but I would additionally argue that her marginalization—in particular her exclusion from studies of literary modernism—has at least as much to do with her narrative style itself, which consistently employs the props of traditional storytelling. Warner never "broke the sentence" in any discernibly Woolfian sense; she never attempted to rupture or reconfigure prevailing linguistic structures. Instead, her desire, as Marcus recognizes, was to deconstruct "fundamental belief systems" through her use of elegant and witty, if seemingly conventional, English prose.[6] Although several of Warner's most important texts appeared between 1925 and 1948, she is rarely categorized as a "modernist"—even in studies which attempt to identify a predominantly sapphic aesthetic—presumably because her poetry and fiction are seen as formally conservative. Because the dominant critical discourse on modernism has tended to fetishize formal experimentation, readers today who encounter Warner for the first time are likely to assume, as does her biographer Wendy Mulford, that the author was completely unaffected by "the currents of modernism . . . [of] the twenties and thirties."[7] And yet, how are we to reconcile Mulford's dismissal of modernist influence with the claims of an earlier critic who argues that Warner was, in fact, "at heart a modernist"?[8] In terms of narrative structure, Warner's fiction, far from conventional or conservative, frequently melds social realism, fantasy, allegory, and literary allusion—

always with an eye toward subversion. The cumulative effect of her individually accessible sentence is never that of transparency. To carve a place within the canon for Warner's previously marginalized texts will necessarily alter our notions of canonicity; it will involve a rethinking of not only how Warner's work might conform to the aesthetics of modernism, but how the aesthetic itself is altered by her inclusion—the inclusion of a lesbian writer. Despite the thematic recurrence of same-sex desire in Warner's fiction and poetry, virtually never is she discussed as an author of lesbian fiction.[9] What one finds repeatedly in introductions to her work are oblique or sanitized references to her lifelong "friendship" with the poet Valentine Ackland (her partner of almost forty years), or, as is the case with the 1987 Virago reprint of *Summer Will Show,* a complete dismissal of the implications and representation of lesbian desire in the text itself.

The critical reception of Warner's work exposes a crucial interpretive problem: what are the implications of lesbian invisibility, and how does such erasure function to ensure—or, conversely, disallow—certain textual readings? Much recent work in lesbian literary theory has focused upon the text's latent content—upon what is not explicitly named, but rather, potentially inferred—as a way of extracting a lesbian reading that is not, oftentimes, immediately apparent. The influence of poststructuralism upon lesbian theory, as Sally Munt has recognized, reflects this desire to "read between the lines" by strategically "inhabiting the text of dominant heterosexuality" and at the same time "undo[ing] it, undermin[ing] it, and construct[ing] our own destabilising readings."[10] By suggesting that a book may require a different set of interpretive conventions, we recognize that the inscription of what we might call a lesbian aesthetic often necessitates a particular deconstructive process. Elizabeth Meese's provocative claim that " '[l]esbian' is a word written in invisible ink," understands not only that the representation of lesbian desire has historically been subject to the imposition of cultural restraints, but also suggests that lesbianism—as narrative practice—can be defined, for certain writers, as a kind of conspiratorial inscription.[11] For if the word "lesbian" is at times, as Meese intimates, a kind of disappearing hieroglyphic, readable and yet necessarily disguised, then the question arises: upon what conditions does its visibility depend?

It is here that Warner's theorization of "bi-location" is particularly salient, for the use of doubleness as a textual strategy is not only relevant

to Warner's own authorial tactics in *Lolly Willowes,* but is applicable to
our experience of reading this deceptively straightforward text. Warner,
I want to demonstrate, repeatedly draws attention to her own duplici-
tous intentions by explicitly thematizing the role of the double in her
novel, both through the juxtaposition of unlikely pairings, and by making overt reference to the protagonist Lolly's divided self. In utilizing
Warner's term, "bi-location," I want to emphasize what I identify as the
novel's two trajectories: its overt portrayal of a single, middle-aged
woman's psychic evolution, and its more covert, allusive mapping of a
lesbian subtext through its depiction of this independent spinster's muta-
tion into witch. To borrow from Willa Cather's biographer, Sharon
O'Brien, who rhetorically asks—regarding Cather's encodement of lesbian passion through the use of a male persona—"[w]hen is a male
character not a male character?"—I would similarly inquire, concerning
Warner: "when is a witch not a witch?" [12] The answer is arguably when
the witch is a lesbian. But to arrive at such a reading requires what
O'Brien, among others, has observed: that the sign of lesbian presence is
frequently detectable only through deflection, through that which is
subtle, symbolic, indirect, or covert—in short, lodged in textual places
that expressly demand that we become adept at multilayered readings.

Lolly Willowes flouts literary conventions by combining narrative
realism with satiric fantasy to tell the story of its eponymous heroine, a
forty-seven-year-old woman who is magically transformed from traditional spinster to self-empowered witch. While critics have rightly both
identified Lolly's retreat from marriage as a rejection of British patriarchal social values, and seen her psychic transformation as a sign of her
refusal of conventional femininity, no one has attempted to read the
figure of the spinster, or the witch, as codes for lesbianism, or analyzed
the way that Warner covertly maps lesbian desire by displacing it in the
text. [13] Lolly's celibacy is repeatedly celebrated as a result of her self-
induced autonomy, but is never contemplated as a sign of an alternative
sexuality; her spinsterhood is consistently read as asexual, that is within
the context of a heterosexual norm, rather than as a challenge to the
boundaries of what constitutes the sexual. Such critical interpretations
embody certain heterosexual assumptions about female desire, at the
same time that they work to eclipse and foreclose variant readings of
Lolly's character. I want, instead, to shift the contextual focus by situating Warner's novel within a different narrative space—one that prob-

lematizes the author's relationship to representation—in order to highlight what I observe as the text's undisclosed, yet arguably central, homoerotic focus. One might say my objective here is, in Bonnie Zimmerman's words, a "perverse reading," that is, a strategic lesbian-feminist appropriation of the text.[14] By foregrounding Warner's slyness as well as her eye for strangeness and her devotion to irreverence, I want to demonstrate how Lolly Willowes can most accurately be described in terms of its artful refusal, in essence, to play it "straight" with readers. By situating Warner's novel within the diverse context of what Shari Benstock has defined as "Sapphic modernism," we can begin to postulate a relation between Warner's sexual orientation and her interest in literary masquerade. Benstock, in her attempt to specify a lesbian tradition of modernist writing, distinguishes between women whose work was formally traditional, yet whose subject matter was overtly Sapphic (for example, Radclyffe Hall's Well of Loneliness), and those women "who filtered the lesbian content of their writing through the screen of presumably heterosexual subject matter or behind experimental literary styles" (such as Virginia Woolf, Gertrude Stein, and Djuna Barnes).[15] Warner's novel oscillates between these two extremes to the extent that her language, while formally accessible and seemingly transparent, disguises an alternate, homoerotic narrative. In this respect, Warner's lesbian modernist aesthetic is much more aligned with Willa Cather and Nella Larsen—whose encoded narratives appear conservative by high modernist standards—than it is with writers whose interest in a lesbian thematic is inextricable from radical innovations in syntax and style. It is particularly important to realize that Lolly Willowes was published during a transitional period in England when, despite the reconfiguration of sex-roles, obscenity laws were "freely used to censor the portrayal of 'immoral' sexual themes"; lesbianism was invariably one of the most prominent casualties of the postwar public censure of "perverse" behavior and desire.[16]

By situating Warner alongside modernists such as Cather and Larsen, I want to demonstrate how she employs a similar strategy of concealment and disclosure, for Lolly Willowes implicitly invites us to read the narrative mindful of the author's literary interest in the doubling and subterfuge of "bi-location." The novel opens with the death of Lolly's father, Everard, and her subsequent expulsion from the Willowes family home, a country estate whose name, "Lady Place," literalizes its affinity with the feminine and represents for her a kind of idyllic state in which the pressure to conform to a heterosexual model is virtually absent. The novel relates in flashback the autonomy Lolly enjoys at Lady Place, where she exhibits no interest in any potential male suitors, and instead immerses herself in what the text indicates are subversive pursuits for a woman: brewing beer, growing medicinal herbs, and devouring books on philosophy, demonology, and botany. In particular, it is Lolly's voracious and unrestricted appetite for unfeminine books—"Locke on the Understanding or Glanvil on Witches"—that signals her nonconformity, and unsettles the "neighboring mammas [who] considered her ignorant" because of her unfamiliarity with the conduct books that "*their* daughters" were reading.[17] Warner suggests that it is precisely the absence of a maternal presence (Mrs. Willowes dies early in the novel) that most emphatically enables Lolly to disregard the dictates of female convention and pursue alternative interests. This is not, however, to suggest that gender distinctions are not enforced at Lady Place, for the novel details the various ways in which Lolly's childhood reflects the late nineteenth-century's preoccupation with femininity as a protected sanctum. The text repeatedly associates heterosexuality with entrapment and confinement, at the same time that it illustrates how Lolly manages to circumvent her early socialization. Everard's gift to his newborn daughter is a little string of evenly matched pearls which "exactly fitted the baby's neck," and annually would be extended "until it encircled the neck of a grown-up young woman at her first ball" (12–13), a noose image which presages the sense of strangulation Lolly later experiences as a single woman in London. The mock-chivalric childhood scene in which her two older brothers, Henry and James, tie her to a tree in order later to rescue their "captive princess" (15)—only to be endlessly distracted from her predicament—similarly prefigures Lolly's feelings of captivity, entrapment, and neglect when, at twenty-eight, she becomes an "inmate" (3) of a masculine protectorate.

As a single woman Lolly has no hopes of inheriting Lady Place once her father dies, and instead is immediately absorbed into her eldest brother Henry's household in London; this process of commodification—she felt "as if she were a piece of property" (7)—signals her initiation into the world of paternalism, and indelibly marks her as a redundant woman. Henry's family is a microcosm of the novel's larger portrait of patriarchal privilege within British society, in which the

Willowes' conservatism and entrenched, "old-fashioned ways" (7) are Lolly's greatest impediment to any kind of self-determination or autonomy. The text equates the family's domestic mirroring of Britain's imperialist enterprise—relatives hoard "accumulations of prosperity" (90), amassing exotic treasures from their trips to the West Indies, the Sudan, and India—with the colonization of the female body. Lolly's Aunt Emma returns from a trip to India preoccupied with her aging niece's single status—"Why isn't she married already?"—and insists to Everard that a vacation to the colonies, "a season in India" (27), would improve the young woman's marital prospects. This linkage between heterosexuality and imperialism recalls the late nineteenth-century British practice of government-sponsored emigration of single English women to the colonies, but it also underscores the novel's acknowledgment that "[t]he price of Empire" (90) is inevitably the suppression of female liberty. Henry's wife, Caroline, dutifully "blink[s] her wider views in obedience to his prejudices" and "minister[s] to his imperiousness" (55), while as a couple they embody the tyranny of heterosexual privilege; Warner parodies this by depicting them as an unassailable fortress, "Henry was like a wall, and Caroline's breasts were like towers" (82), for they function as self-appointed arbiters of Lolly's matrimonial prospects.

One thing the novel indicates is that Lolly's subjugation is partially due to her own lack of consciousness about the possibilities of self-emancipation—an unawareness that, as we shall see, is directly linked with her latent lesbianism. Although some of her contemporaries are already challenging social and sexual conventions in 1902, Lolly, nearly thirty, is not yet prepared to "take up something artistic or emancipated" (6) when her father dies. The generous inheritance Everard leaves her—"five hundred a year" (6), exactly the sum that Woolf stipulates is necessary in *A Room*—is not immediately used to forge an independent existence. And yet, Lolly's evolution eventually undermines the binary operations of gender in the text. Through her, Warner examines both women's internalization of societal expectations regarding normative models of female behavior and illustrates how the single woman's assault on the conventions of femininity is inextricably bound with the political upheavals of the British suffrage movement. While critics have maintained that *Lolly Willowes* "ignore[s] history," I want instead to demonstrate how this fanciful text—punctuated throughout with historical dates—is in fact deeply embedded in the politics and culture of early twentieth-century England, when feminism and lesbianism were not only highly visible, but frequently linked in order to discredit the suffragist cause.[18] Lolly's status as a spinster is perhaps the text's most blatant indicator that she is not all that she appears to be, for despite its virginal connotations, the spinster is not at all a fixed or stable category. We know through historical sources that several feminists in England were choosing, before the First World War, not to have any sexual relations with men as a form of protest against female oppression, publicly maintaining that society "could only be improved . . . [with] a large class of celibate women."[19] Although these women did not always identify as lesbian, either because this would have been seen as invalidating their cause, or because they did not identify themselves as lesbians as defined by the medical discourse of the sexologists, the spinster was by her very existence, in Sheila Jeffreys' words, "a living reproach to men."[20] Because single women defied sexual classification, they were pathologized as deviants; they "threatened the social organization of society, and undermined the concept of separate spheres that guaranteed patriarchal hegemony."[21] Havelock Ellis, in his study of female inversion, classifies as homosexual precisely those forms of behavior for which spinster-feminists were being criticized by the antifeminists; accusations of lesbianism could effectively stigmatize and subvert women's attempts at emancipation.[22]

As Sheila Jeffreys argues, it is important to realize that "[a]ny attack on the spinster is inevitably an attack on the lesbian."[23] By the time that Warner was writing *Lolly Willowes* in the twenties, the visibility of the spinster—and specifically the liminality of her status—was unmistakable; her appearance in the press and the novel ensured that the spinster, with all of her homosexual connotations, was a part of public discourse, subject to speculation. While the novel never explicitly engages these debates, the text contains several passing references to the controversy over women's sexual and social autonomy, and Warner's use of the spinster category in 1926, I would argue, is itself an implicit signal of Lolly's double valence. At one point the text suggestively introduces the legalistic phrase, "*femme couverte*," which refers to a married woman, and then ultimately subverts its association by demonstrating that it is actually the spinster, "*femme sole*" (6), who is "covered over." Warner uses the language of concealment to mark the body of the single woman, expressly conflating her with the concept of dissimulation, of veiling. It is lesbianism, the text intimates, that Lolly's spinsterhood disguises, and works to camouflage. From the novel's opening pages we are aware that Lolly is not like most women, a perception that is reinforced throughout the text by references to her oddness, her tendency, for example, to interrupt a staid dinner party by asking one of the guests, a man her family hopes will marry her, if he is a "were-wolf" (58). Warner frequently utilizes the word "odd," or suggestions of queerness, in conjunction with Lolly's character; we learn, for example, that her clothes "smelt so queerly" (18), that she relishes telling "odd jokes" (98), gathering "strange herbs" (67), "behaving . . . oddly" (220), and probing "the strange places of [her] mind" (79). Increasingly, Lolly's eye gravitates toward the deviant, the "odd thing" (129). Terry Castle has recently argued that a "subterranean 'lesbian' meaning may be present in *odd* and its derivatives," for while the terms "homosexual" and "lesbian" are relatively new, there have "always been other words . . . for pointing to the lover of women."[24] Warner's text plays upon these associations, repeatedly offering the reader codes and clues regarding Lolly's indeterminate status. Thus, by the end of the novel Lolly remarks that one of the great advantages of associating with witches is that "they do not mind if you are a little odd" (250), a revelation that, as we shall see, has everything to do with the unleashing of her own repressed, homoerotic longings.

At a young age Lolly evinces what Warner suggestively terms a "temperamental indifference to the need of getting married," an aversion, the narrative intimates, that is further exacerbated by her close companionship with her father (26). While Lolly's intimacy with him is never pathologized, this identification with her father is a sign of her disdain for girlish trappings, for anything that might domesticate or "subdu[e] [her] into young-ladyhood" (19). Warner subverts the expectation that "a young woman's normal inclination [is] towards young men" (26) by illustrating Lolly's contentment with her father, who, despite his own traditional notions regarding gender, does not impede his daughter's rejection of the conventions of femininity. Thus, "[a]s innocently as the unconcerned Laura might have done, *but did not,* he waited for the ideal wooer," although he too repeatedly expresses relief when "budding suitors [are] nipped in their bud" (28, emphasis added). This suggestion of castration is consistent with other imagery within the text that aligns heterosexuality not merely with impotence, but with death. Prospective husbands are referred to as "likely undertakers" (56), while Lolly visualizes one of her potential mates as a cannibal, hunched over "upon all-fours with a lamb"—presumably herself—"dangling from his mouth" (59). Henry's wife, Caroline, is the novel's clearest example of the deadening effects of marriage; she at one point describes the orderliness of her undergarments as "graveclothes . . . folded in the tomb" (52). Elsewhere, at an anesthetizing family gathering, Lolly observes her sister-in-law Sibyl as one who "exchanged her former look of a pretty ferret for this refined and waxen mask," a face preparing "for the last look of death" (91). Given the repeated evidence of heterosexual union as a kind of living death, it comes as no surprise that Lolly would reject her family's efforts to transform her into yet another "memorial urn" (91). Yet at the same time, the novel's suggestion that Lolly's resistance to marriage stems also from her *"temperamental indifference,"* a predisposition which "her upbringing had only furthered" (26, emphasis added), anticipates Warner's later amplification of Lolly's lesbian identification. For Lolly, "her father . . . [and] Lady Place" (29) represent alternatives to the pressures of heterosexual conformity, alternatives which pave the way for her eventual substitution of the homoerotic "graces of the countryside" for London (78).

One way the text schematizes gender distinctions is through the contrast between the country, which is feminized throughout, and the city, which is aligned with masculinity and mechanization, and is portrayed as "fundamentally unnatural."[25] However, despite this seemingly neat dichotomy, the novel also problematizes the notion of what constitutes "the natural" through its representation of Lolly, whose refusal of the conventions of heterosexuality repeatedly threatens her family's idea of normative behavior. The neighbors' greatest fear when Lolly is a child is that "she might grow up eccentric," a suspicion that is subsequently realized when she rejects all male suitors and, at forty-seven, leaves her brother Henry's home. Warner's characterization of Lolly as "eccentric" anticipates Teresa de Lauretis's theorization of the lesbian as an "eccentric subject," that is, situated in a space that is excessive to, rather than contained by, "the sociocultural institution of heterosexuality."[26] Lolly's disidentification propels her to demand her inherited income from Henry, who without her knowledge has mishandled the bulk of her capital by transferring it to the "Ethiopian Development Syndicate"

(105), again suggesting a linkage between the imperialist enterprise and the domestication of women. Lolly's rhetoric to Henry anticipates Woolf's pronunciation in *A Room:* "Nothing is impracticable for a single, middle-aged woman with an income of her own" (104), and after procuring her inheritance she establishes her own cottage in a village called Great Mop—a comic allusion to the folklore of the witch's broom (17). Feminist critics' observation that the broomstick functions as "an emblem of female potency" is evident in Warner's text, which, as we shall see, links Great Mop with Lolly's expanded eroticism.[27] The various descriptions of Lolly as "a little odd" (251) hinge on what within the text are identified as her subversive impulses: her bibliophilia, her obsession with "unseasonable" (80) flowers—an addiction the family terms "naughty . . . [and] reckless" (81), her furtive consumption of French desserts (79), and above all, her transgressive expeditions to the Chilterns, the land of witchcraft. The tension between what Lolly appears to be in public, under her family's guardianship, and who she is in private, when she slips undetected to wander the countryside alone, is exemplified by the unstable position her name occupies in the novel. Depending upon the context she is either Lolly or Laura, a nominative split which recapitulates the feelings of duplicity she experiences in London—"two persons, each different" (62)—and underscores Warner's interest in thematizing the friction between her character's conscious and unconscious selves.

The turning point for Lolly, the point at which "[s]he felt as though she had awoken . . . from . . . [a] slumber," only to find her familiars "unrecognizable" (90), occurs in 1921, the year that British Parliament failed to criminalize lesbianism—not for progressive reasons, but rather, because the legislature feared an increase in lesbianism if it were given publicity.[28] *Lolly Willowes* makes no overt reference to this parliamentary debate, but Warner's use of 1921 as the watershed year in Lolly's life, the point at which she experiences her pivotal erotic and, as a result, political awakening, suggests the author's interest in subverting the governmental attempt to ensure the British lesbian's invisibility. We know through accounts by historians such as Lillian Faderman and Martha Vicinus that by the early twentieth century "traditional notions of the asexuality of single women was discarded," and that particularly after World War I—with the spread of psychoanalysis and its popularization by the work of the sexologists—spinsters, like lesbians, were increasingly pathologized.[29] By staging Lolly's most charged, and, I would argue, homoerotic moment—her interval of "great longing" at the greengrocer's (85)—during such a repressive period in England, Warner provides a corrective to the state's insistence that silence would render the lesbian invisible. At the same time, Warner counters the notoriety of the single woman as a sexual freak by depicting Lolly's moment of illumination, during the dead of winter 1921, as an experience of verdant lushness, bodily pleasure, and renewal. As Lolly wanders into the overcrowded florist shop, which is also the greengrocer's, she harbors "no particular intention of extravagance" (83), but extravagance is precisely what happens once she is finds herself inside the store—not in terms of consumption, but rather, with respect to herself. That is, what Lolly experiences in the shop as she gazes with rapture at the abundance of flowers, vegetables, bottled fruits in syrup, home-made jams, baskets of eggs, trays of walnuts, chestnuts, and filberts—all heaped together in "countrified disorder" (84)—is her own unrestraint, her own digression from moderation, from what her family views as the proper bounds of behavior for a woman. Standing in the midst of the shop's overgrown, earthy display, Lolly slips into a kind of sensual oblivion in which she "forgot the whole of her London life," and instead imagines herself standing alone in an orchard, her feet implanted in the grass "as though she were a tree herself," her arms extended, "stretched up like branches" (84–85). Warner gives Lolly's inarticulate desire a somatic dimension in this scene, physicalizing her "great longing" by illustrating the way in which it "weigh[s] upon her like the load of ripened fruit upon a tree" (85). But because Lolly herself here *is* the tree, her limbs alive with ripeness and fruition, the description of her fingers eagerly "seeking the rounded ovals of the fruit," her hands "search[ing] among the leaves" (85), can only be read as a self-reflexive gesture, signaling her body's autoerotic reverie. Not surprisingly, Warner tells us that Lolly "looked like a woman roused out of a fond dream" (86) when she is startled into wakefulness by a man's voice, for arousal is precisely what has occurred to Lolly in the shop. The seemingly impulsive purchase she makes as she prepares to leave, a bunch of glorious chrysanthemums with huge "curled petals . . . [a] . . . deep garnet colour within and a tawny yellow without," is not at all arbitrary. Lolly's fixation with "their sleek flesh," and her "long[ing] for the moment when she might stroke her hand over those mop heads" (86), recapitulates her interest in erotic exploration, and also alludes to Great Mop as the site of this pursuit. Warner here substitutes curled, fleshy petals for the female body, but her veiled meaning is not obscured.

Significantly, this indulgence of "her sensations" has a liberatory effect, instilling in Lolly the conviction that escape from convention is possible, that she can leave London and create her own material reality out of "the country of her autumn imagination" (87)—in other words, out of pleasure. Warner's use of 1921 as the turning point for this conversion alludes to the assault on lesbian visibility, but the date has additional import because it marks the publication of a book that was highly influential for Warner's text, Margaret Murray's *The Witch Cult in Western Europe*. Murray is one of the first historians to counter the conventional wisdom, initially disseminated by the Catholic church, that witches are the perpetrators of Satanic evil; her book explores the late medieval period in Great Britain to demonstrate that the witch cult was a highly developed, pagan religion which Christianity was determined to eradicate. The author makes note of the fact that sexual rites played a role in the rituals of witchcraft, and her evidence suggests that partici- pants engaged in sexual activity with members of the same as well as the opposite sex. Murray's influence on *Lolly Willowes* is evident in War- ner's representation of the witch as an eroticized figure, but Warner decontextualizes the witch by transporting her to the twentieth century in order to politicize her as a feminist agent. Just one year after Lolly's electric moment in the greengrocer's, she is completely transformed: "She, Laura Willowes, in England, in the year 1922, had entered into a compact with the Devil" (172), a compact that has as its source a heretofore unacknowledged erotic basis. The reading of Lolly as "old- maidishly" (227) nondesiring is persuasive only superficially, to the extent that she has no lover, but it is misleading in light of her eroticized relation to nature, her passionate identification with Great Mop, and particularly the repeated references to her enigmatic, indefinable, longing.

Underlying all of these attractions is Lolly's relation to her own body which, despite popular critical opinion, is not devoid of eros. While critics have argued that Lolly's self-possession "resists the erotic," that her rapture is analogous to that of "St. Teresa as the bride of Christ," I want instead to demonstrate the ways that Lolly's "recurrent autumnal fever" (78)—in other words, her desire—destabilizes these suppositions.[30] As a young woman, Lolly distracts herself from Caroline's talk of marriage by picking a red geranium and staining her wrist "with the juice of its crushed petals" (3), a cosmetic gesture similar to her girlhood experience of "stain[ing] her pale cheeks" in order to gaze at her reflection (3). These details are not the signs of a woman unconcerned with physicality; indeed, we see ample evidence of Lolly's susceptibility to corporeal pleasure. But because Lolly's attention to the somatic is never linked with the objective of inciting male attention, critics have mistakenly read her body as a kind of blank slate, unmarked by desire. Warner contrasts the austerity and asceticism of Lolly's life in London, where bodily excess is realized through the consumption of "extra trivialities such as sardines and celery" (51) once a week, with the gratification of the senses that Lolly repeatedly cultivates, alone, on her secret sojourns to the country. She subverts her family's practice of English economy by allowing herself little indulgences of the body: hidden packets of roasted chestnuts "taken home for bedroom eating"; the experimental purchase of "expensive soaps"; and the sumptuous pleasure she takes in eating "*marrons glacés*" (79). In particular, Lolly's attraction to French culture underscores her deviation from British propriety, a fact exemplified by the prominence in her new cottage of a classical print of the French Empress Josephine, the consort of Napoleon, complete "with ruined temples, and volcanoes" (110); such an exhibit of wantonness would have been inconceivable in London.

Yet what I'm reading as Lolly's intermittent indulgence of the senses is juxtaposed with multiple references to an insatiable, *psychological* longing, a "groping after something that eluded her experience" (78). This slippery "something" is Lolly's lesbianism, for the text offers us several suggestive "clue[s] to her disquiet" (78), disclosures that invite us to interpret Lolly's spinsterhood as a site of contradiction, a space of instability which ultimately privileges the homoerotic. "What It was exactly, she would have found hard to say" (76), for Lolly lacks not only the social exposure that would facilitate self-recognition, but the language that would enable self-representation. Embedded within the text are many references to Lolly's nebulous desire, her "ghost-like feeling" that is described as both "familiar" and "underground" (64), conjuring an image of her split subjectivity. We see repeated examples of this doubleness in Lolly, instances where "while her body" sits passively with Henry and Caroline, "her mind walked by lonely seaboards, in

marshes and fens, or came at night to the edge of a wood" (77). Warner's portrayal of Lolly's psychic dissociation here invokes Teresa de
Lauretis's description of the unconscious as a point of resistance, "*a*
resistance to identification . . . with femininity."[31] It is significant that
Lolly "never imagined herself in these places by daylight" (77), for her
wanderings have to do with tapping into that subversive part of herself
that "lurked in waste places, that was hinted at by the sound of water
gurgling through deep channels" (78), in other words, her lesbian sub-
conscious. The language Warner uses to portray Lolly's state during
these episodes—"day-dreaming . . . almost a hallucination" (77)—suggests that lesbian resistance may not be directly accessible, but at the
same time the novel demonstrates that the source of Lolly's feminist
transformation into a witch is precisely these oppositional moments of
semiconsciousness. Warner's description of Lolly's sensations as ghostly
recalls Terry Castle's recent analysis of the literary lesbian as a spectral
figure, historically dematerialized by Western culture, "as if vaporized
by the forces of heterosexual propriety."[32]

Castle's term, "apparitional," provides us with a way of characteriz-
ing Lolly's lesbianism, of situating her submerged, unconscious longing—her groping for "something that was shadowy and menacing, and
yet in some way congenial" (78)—within a sexual context. This elusive
desire, her "scarcely knowing what it was that she knew" (172), is
explicitly linked with several references to Lolly's "secret"—a word we
might consider replete with homosexual connotation—which in turn is
tied to her transformation into a witch, itself a category that suggests
lawlessness and subversion. Warner's reference to Lolly's "aptness for
arousing . . . a kind of ungodly hallowedness" (78) foreshadows her
witchery at Great Mop, but it also underscores the author's interest
in identifying Lolly with the incongruous, with the destabilization of
conventional juxtapositions. The most marked example of this unlikely
coupling is, of course, Lolly herself, whose embodiment of the spinster/
witch dualism both camouflages and exposes "her own secret" (78). Yet
the revelation of this secret requires an intervention; it necessarily
"wait[s] to be interpreted" (139) by the reader. *Lolly Willowes* contains
various suggestive statements that invite us to read the text metacriti-
cally, for the language of detection—clues, secrets, interpretation—invariably has as much to do with our hermeneutic experience as readers
as it does with Lolly herself, who, like us, searches until "she had almost

pounced on the clue . . . to the secret country of her mind" (137). Claire Harman's observation that Warner's words often contain a double, or "second meaning," is evident in this novel, where the word "natural" is repeatedly used in conjunction with Lolly's metamorphosis to mark her lesbianism as normative.[33] Warner arguably stresses that "it seemed most natural" (251) for Lolly to become a witch in order to illustrate the lesbian body's "dignity of natural behaviour" (249), for this was a time in England when both lesbians and spinsters were routinely regarded as sexual deviants. Warner maintains that "the true Laura . . . was a witch by vocation" (178). Even in the old days of Lady Place the elusive "impulse had stirred in her" (178), a predilection that Warner explicitly sexualizes when she states that "unrealized, had Laura been carrying her talisman in her pocket" (178), a code for female genitalia. Illustrative of this point is an additional veiled reference to Lolly's sexual organs, in which the "warmth between her knees"—literally, a kitten on her lap—figuratively signals her unmatched bodily "contentment" (176) as a witch. What the text repeatedly indicates is that spinster-lesbians, like witches, are frequently "under cover" (149).

The text is ultimately based upon a series of substitutions, in Judith Butler's words, a "specific practice of dissimulation," that point toward Lolly's lesbianism.[34] Butler's recent discussion of Willa Cather, in which she argues that "lesbian sexuality within [her] text is produced as a perpetual challenge to legibility," provides us with a cogent way of understanding Warner's own strategy in Lolly Willowes, where the workings of lesbian desire are never discursively immediate.[35] Rather, Warner constitutes the lesbian through a process of displacement and exchange. Nature is a feminized presence throughout the text, described at one point as so "moist and swell[ing]" that Lolly languishes with "the contentment of the newly awakened" (186) in its lushness. Yet this is not a landscape, from her perspective, that is subject to male co-optation. At one point her nephew Titus, surveying the view at Great Mop, confesses that he "should like to stroke it," a remark that sends a "cold shiver" through Lolly because she "loved [the landscape] so jealously" (162). Lolly experiences Titus's love as a "horror" because "[i]t was different in kind from hers," but what precisely her "kind" of love is, is left undisclosed (162). The only clue Warner offers is that, since Titus's arrival, "[Lolly] had not been allowed to love in her own way" (163), a suggestive allusion to her homoerotic impulses. Titus is represented as a colonizer, a "usurping monarch" (160) who "loved the countryside as though it were a body" (162), a female body that, "[without] struggle" (163), he could appropriate at will. Rather than desiring to be "in possession" (163) of the countryside, Lolly, who had staked everything to come to Great Mop, pursues a more reciprocal relation with nature. So that, for example, when Titus's "dynastic will" (227) encroaches on her solitude, the anthropomorphic countryside "withdrew itself further from her," the woods "hushed their talk," and the hills "locked up their thoughts" (164) whenever he is in her company. Yet when Titus is away, the winds release "exciting voices" (109) for her pleasure and the hills fold "themselves round her like the fingers of a hand" (129); this image suggests a woman's conspiratorial embrace, for nature, with her "rising undulations" (108), is always coded feminine. By casting nature as a woman's body that is "congenial to [Lolly's] spirit" (109) only when Titus is elsewhere, Warner illustrates the degree to which lesbian eroticism is dependent upon the absence of masculine intervention. Warner explicitly states that Lolly had not chosen Great Mop in order "to concern herself with the hearts of men," and indeed we see that the revelation of "her own secret, if she had one" (129) hinges upon her circulation within what is clearly a feminized community—despite the seeming appearance of men. Lolly's friend, Mr. Saunters, a man who "darned [socks] much better than she" (133) and "mother[s] his chicks" (147) just like the fairytale "henwife" (149), is the text's clearest example of this feminization.

Although Lolly's secret remains elusive at this point, she longs to "yield herself" (136) to its logic and realizes that "Great Mop was the likeliest place to find it" (138); what follows in the text are various manifestations of the way in which she gives herself over to the inducements of the village. This giving over is twofold, with both a political and a sexual dimension. Even before Lolly pledges herself to Satan, her psychic evolution as a witch is apparent—"[s]he was changed, and knew it" (152)—a shift that is expressed in explicitly feminist terms. In recollecting her prior life in London, Lolly thinks about the oppressiveness of her family and concludes that there was "no question of forgiving them," allegedly because she does not have a "forgiving nature" (152). Upon further reflection, however, she draws a parallel between the imperial will of the family and that of society, seeing a relation between the tyranny of the domestic and the larger patriarchal sphere: "If she were to start forgiving she must needs forgive Society, the Law, the Church, the History of Europe, the Old Testament . . . the bank of England, Prostitution, the Architect of Apsley Terrace, and half a dozen other useful props of civilization" (152). Although obviously politicized here, Lolly's consciousness does not compel her to intervene and attempt to transform the social body, either through legislative or any other direct feminist action; rather, she resolves, simply, to "forget them" (152). Critics have interpreted this effacement as Lolly's flight from reality, as evidence of her political apathy; from this perspective, her retreat—into an ahistorical, fantasy world of oblivion—illustrates the novel's "disjunction between feminist theory and concretely lived elaborations of the theory."[36] This interpretation, in my view, has a heterosexual bias, for it neglects to consider the political aspect of Lolly's nonintervention, ignoring the degree to which her feminism is inflected by her unarticulated lesbianism. Warner's text imaginatively intervenes in the politics of Britain by rejecting the demonization of lesbianism and creating an alternative space—literally, an English community—of female desire and autonomy. We might call Lolly a prototypical separat-ist, to the extent that her decision to live in Great Mop has a political basis, for the language Warner uses to characterize the villagers' kinship is replete with homosexual connotations. Lolly, for example, wields the rhetoric of inclusion when making an appeal on the group's behalf: "If they were different from other people, why shouldn't they be?" (131). Renowned for its eccentricity, Great Mop "had a name for being differ-ent . . . [it was] an out-of-the-way place if ever there was one" (131). An equivalence between the witch's minority status and that of the lesbian is suggested when Lolly refers to the villagers' demeanor as "odd," the same word used in conjunction with her, and is conveyed through her identification with the community's difference: "She felt at one with them, an inhabitant like themselves" (131). Lolly's incorporation is acknowledged by nature, which homoerotically coos to her: "We will not let you go" (172). Later, at the witches' Sabbath Lolly observes that "[a] single mysterious impulse seemed to govern the group" (197), another oblique reference, I would suggest, to the villagers' shared sexu-ality.

From historical accounts we know that one of the crimes that witches were accused of, and persecuted for, was engaging in homosexual sex, although the extent to which this actually occurred remains speculative.

What is evident, however, is that the codification of witchcraft by Church authorities emphasized that the participants in ceremonial rites "indulge[d] in the most loathsome sensuality, having no regard to sex."[37] Although Warner is never explicit about sexual acts, her eroticized depiction of the witches' Sabbath is arguably based upon these associations. It is as a witch that Lolly experiences her most emphatically lesbian moment when she attends the Sabbath, a frenzied affair of ecstatic dancing during which time "a nameless excitement caught hold of her" (200). Lolly's most overtly eroticized interlude is dancing with "red-haired . . . half-naked" Emily (199), a witch whose physical proximity—they are described as whirling "fused together like two suns" (195)—she clearly finds arousing. A strand of Emily's hair brushes across Lolly's face as they "danc[e] with a fervour that annihilated every misgiving"—an indication that what transpires is taboo—and the contact electrifies her body, making her uncontrollably "tingle from head to foot" (195). The sensuality of the moment, for Lolly, is unparalleled: "She shut her eyes and dived into obliviousness—with Emily for a partner she could dance until the gunpowder ran out of the heels of her boots" (196). This is not, I would venture, the response of a woman preoccupied with chastity, or resistant to the lures of physical desire. But because the etiquette of a Sabbath requires constant circulation—"one rule only: to do nothing for long" (197)—Lolly is eventually left by Emily to be entertained by other dance partners, both male and female. While various people "please and excite" (201) her, nothing approximates the homoerotic pleasure she experiences with Emily. However, Emily is not the only woman whom Lolly finds compelling.

I read the figure of Satan as a feminized figure, a homosexual signifier, and want to suggest that Lolly's attraction to him is further evidence of her repressed lesbian identification. Several critics have correctly interpreted Satan as Lolly's alter-ego, seeing him as a kind of double for her mysterious underside, but no one has aligned this subterfuge with sexuality, or registered the way that Warner positions him as a lesbian mirror. When Lolly first encounters him at the Sabbath he is disguised as a woman, so that our first impression of the Devil is of a man in drag. Queer theorists have argued for a relation between the theatricality of drag and homosexuality, seeing the parodic and performative promotion of identity as a way of understanding the fictive foundation of sexuality.[38] If, in other words, the body straddles a variable gender boundary, then the seeming coherence between sex and gender is destabilized; drag is a vehicle that works to denaturalize heterosexuality. The most salient aspect of Satan is his dissimulation, his gender play. Lolly initially believes that she sees the face of a "Chinaman" when Satan appears, and only in full light realizes that he wears a lifeless mask that "was like the face of a very young girl," whose narrow eyes, slanting brows, and small, curved mouth she finds "entranc[ing]" (203). Warner depicts Satan's girlish disguise as Asian here in order to further underscore Lolly's attraction to what would clearly be regarded as "other" within the Willowes' British context. The author codes Satan's campy performance as gay in order to signal that Lolly's alter-ego is homosexual; the fact that Satan is—however provisionally—male is important, because it mediates Lolly's lesbian identification. Lesbianism is never figured mimetically in this novel, so Satan could not in fact *be* a woman; instead, his transvestism merely enables him to look like one. Nonetheless, his feminine concealment appears somewhat redundant, for beneath Satan's masquerade what surfaces are the traces of a female physique: his "lithe body" approaches Lolly "[m]incing like a girl," and through his "imitation face" she observes "the hollow of [a] girlish throat" (203). The cracks in Satan's drag, rather than revealing a masculine body, seem to ground a female identity. The spectacle of his bodily gestures is clearly an act—he purposely licks Lolly's cheek at one point, much to her annoyance—functioning as evidence of his duplicity. Warner writes that Satan comes to Lolly's side with "secretive and undulating movements" (203), echoing the language she utilizes earlier to describe the feminized landscape (as undulating) and Lolly's relation to Great Mop (where her secret resides). Lolly's observation that "a flicker of life" pulses through Satan's throat as though "a pearl necklace slid by under the skin" (203) invokes and subverts the earlier image of Lolly's pearl necklace as a sign of strangulation, for here Satan, miming the feminine, has seemingly ingested the offending object.

Warner feminizes Satan and pointedly alludes to Lolly's girlhood pearls in order to signal their affinity as doubles, for the most salient characteristic they share is their duplicity. Satan not only represents Lolly's own subversive alter-ego, the "dangerous" underside of the "typical genteel spinster" (242–43), but is himself a double as well, a split that recapitulates her Lolly/Laura dualism. He appears to her both in his guise as the representative of the "Powers of Darkness" (205), at the

Sabbath, and in his incarnation as the protective gamekeeper in gaiters and a corduroy coat, when she is in nature. Like Lolly herself, Satan is more than one thing; "inscrutable as ever" (205), his innocuous behavior repeatedly challenges her expectations concerning the demonic, much in the same way that Lolly's crypto-lesbianism destabilizes the reader's assumptions regarding her spinsterhood. Warner utilizes spectatorial imagery in conjunction with both Lolly and Satan in order to convey this notion of the "hidden" (179) self, for like duplicity, the problem of (in)visibility—of seeing and remaining unseen—speaks to the novel's interest in thematizing lesbian dissimulation. Each of them exhibits "an amusing sense of superiority" (219) through undetected observation, so that as Satan watches Lolly with "unseen eyes" (203) through the slits in his mask, elsewhere she herself "releas[es] her gaze" (221) on Titus while "remaining unseen" (219). For both, the visual pleasure here has less to do with voyeurism than it does with concealment, a motive for secrecy that extends beyond the specificity of the moment to encode homosexual discretion. Satan comments upon the remarkableness of "how invisible one is" (233) within the countryside of Great Mop, for this is the realm of the clandestine, a fact alluded to by Lolly's claim that she is Satan's witch "in blindness" (244)—that is to say, through a process of deliberate dissimulation. Like Lolly herself, whose lesbian identity hinges upon deception, Satan operates primarily through stealthiness and evasion.

Warner's representation of Satan as Lolly's double invokes Freud's notion of the uncanny as that which is both familiar and congenial, and at the same time so terrifying that it is concealed and kept out of sight. According to Freud, the "quality of uncanniness can only come from the circumstance of the 'double' . . . dating back to a very early mental stage." [39] In other words, the uncanny has to do with the repression of something familiar that "ought to have been kept concealed but which has nevertheless come to light." [40] This notion of the uncanny as that which has been estranged through a process of repression provides us with a way of understanding Lolly's relationship to Satan; "he had never been far off" (179), psychically speaking, because he is the trace of her lesbian identification. "How [Lolly] had come to Great Mop she could not say; whether it was of her own will, or whether . . . Satan had at last taken pity upon her bewilderment, leading her by the hand into the flower-shop" (179). This ambiguity regarding the status of Lolly's volition speaks to Warner's interest in problematizing her heroine's sexuality, for does she become a witch by her own desire or is it Satan's intention? The novel ultimately suggests that the two are interchangeable, a fact underscored by the book's rarely cited, full title: *Lolly Willowes or the Loving Huntsman*. Warner significantly utilizes Lolly, and not Laura, in her novel's title because her objective is concealment, to disguise her heroine's otherness. Satan is Lolly's double to the extent that he represents her repressed lesbianism, for from the outset it is he who has been her stimulus, guiding her away from her role as London spinster and, with the "sweet persuasions" (179) of a lover, easing her into her subversive calling as a witch. Lolly even refers to him in conventional romantic terms, seeing him as "a kind of black knight, wandering about and succouring decayed gentlewomen" (238). Because she yields to her desire, Satan considers her his "conquest" (245). Although Freud locates one example of the uncanny in magic and witchcraft, he never associates the prohibition against the familiar, the proximate, with homosexuality. The novel, however, enables us to read the doubling of Satan and Lolly in terms of precisely this equation. Sue-Ellen Case's assertion that "[t]he queer is the taboo-breaker, the monstrous, the uncanny," has particular resonance for Warner's juxtaposition of the demonic and the domestic, for the connective between Satan and Lolly is sexual sameness.[41]

If we read Satan as an uncanny figure for Lolly's lesbian unconscious—despite his strangeness, he "struck her as being familiar" (232)—then he can be said to make representable what the novel largely implies, but in effect leaves out. By casting Lolly as a witch who pledges herself to Satan, Warner invokes the associations of female sexuality as dangerous and susceptible to demonic control; as Lolly puts it, "women . . . know they are dynamite" (241). The reference to Satan as "the loving huntsman" (179) underscores his affiliation with the erotic forces of nature, for throughout Lolly's residence in Great Mop, "all the time, whether couched in the woods or hunting among the hills, he drew closer" (179). At one point Satan's words—"Remember, Miss Willowes, that I shall always be very glad to help you" (209)—are echoed by nature's feminine voice, which murmurs consolingly: "Remember, Miss Willowes. . . . Remember" (210). The text's focus on recollection— "[s]he remembered, and understood" (210)—has to do with Satan's role as the harbor of Lolly's vestigial memory, her repressed lesbian identification. The intimate conversation between the pair at the end of the novel recalls Warner's theorization of bi-location, for the language can be read as a coded dialogue, between doubles, that itself has a double meaning. Satan's promise to Lolly: "You will always find me in the wood" (209), positions him in the space of the homoerotic, an alignment that is later reiterated when he repeats to her: "Once a wood, always a wood" (234). This sentence, which appears again twice within the same paragraph, is meaningful only if understood in terms of lesbian displacement, for what the text posits is an equivalence between the invariability of the wood and Lolly's sexuality. It is this context in which Lolly contemplates her own "natural leaning towards the Devil," ironically contrasting her deviancy with the behavior of "respectable people like Henry and Caroline" (234). She identifies herself here with the prohibitive, with the persistently marginalized, "the other people, the people of Satan" (234). The text identifies patriarchy as the most oppressive force that lesbian eroticism has to contend with; only Satan represents the possibility of liberatory escape: "Custom, public opinion, law, church, and state—all would have shaken their massive heads against her plea, and sent her back to bondage" (223). Satan asserts: "Well, you're a witch now," and Lolly concurs: "Yes . . . I really am, aren't I?" (236). That this conversation is constituted on the basis of substitution is made explicit when Lolly reflects upon Satan's language, and "thought [that] a *deeper meaning* lay beneath his words" (237, emphasis added). Here, as elsewhere, the subtext is not revealed, but the substitutability of lesbianism is implicit. Lolly's promise—"I shall never wish to escape you" (237)—is about preserving her own sexuality, for the denial of her alter-ego would mean the annihilation of her erotic self.

Only by reading the novel slant, then, can we fully appreciate the extent to which Warner thematizes Lolly's homosexuality both by multiple examples of her oddness, and by constructing sentences that subvert the expected order throughout her text. By this I mean the various places in which Warner posits the conceptual inversion of heterosexual paradigms through literal reversal. Thus, for example, as a young woman Lolly describes her "'coming out'"—the point at which she is to appear as a débutante—as an occasion that actually signals her "going-in" (19). Or elsewhere, toward the end of the text when Lolly and Satan are engaged in dialogue, Warner inverts the biblical narrative by having Lolly—who earlier is referred to as "Eve" because of her "unladylike curiosity"—offer Satan the desired apple, which in this case leads not to expulsion, but merely friendship (134). Yet even this designation of Lolly as "Eve" is itself further inverted, when Warner writes that Lolly "was like God," who, "after casting out the rebel angels . . . use[d] Adam as an intermediate step" (143). Here, the conventional hierarchy of the creation story—the myth of heterosexual origin—is repeatedly scrambled, until it is Lolly, as a feminized God, who utilizes Adam's body as a means to the creation of Eve. The text frequently transposes the expected sequence, and upsets any presumption of certainty, particularly where heterosexuality is figured. At one point, Lolly's sister-in-law Caroline condescendingly refers to her as the "unused virgin," while maintaining that her own role as a wife and mother is "emotionally plumper" (60)—even though she herself is depicted as an asexual "Mother Superior" (51). The text continually upsets this dichotomy by associating heterosexuality not with the generative, but with images of death and confinement, while Lolly—the "barren spinster"—is associated with fruit and vegetation, images of ripeness and renewal. At her father's funeral, held in a botanical garden, Lolly dismisses the pastor's banalities about the inevitability of death and revises conventional logic by rejecting Christian dogma, yet at the same time asserting, "[i]n the midst of death, we are in life" (40). It is through the accumulation of such moments of reversal that Warner's novel alludes to Lolly's inversion without precisely naming what it is.

Warner's novel radicalizes the model that "English witches . . . define[d] by inversion the acceptable social role for women" by depicting the witch herself as a figure for the invert.[42] Lolly's final, feminist speech to Satan fuels the superstitious terror regarding witches, that they perverted women's natural roles of wife and mother, by aligning herself with the destabilization of gender norms. What is compelling about Lolly's passionate oration is her vision of feminism as a covert practice; her colloquy with Satan, both intimate and flirtatious, emphasizes their role as homosexual doubles. Satan responds to Lolly's initial request— "if I am really a witch, treat me as such . . . [t]ell me about yourself"— by requiring that she expose herself: "Tell me first what *you* think" (238). Warner stages this pedagogical dynamic, not in order to depict Satan as withholding, but to facilitate Lolly's self-disclosure: "I [Satan] encourage you to talk, not that I may know all your thoughts, but that you may" (244). Satan's perceptions about himself never deviate from Lolly's own, because as her alter-ego, "he did not know much more . . . than she did herself" (249). What Satan enables is a kind of transference, through which her dark side is able to speak: "When I think of witches, I seem to see all over England, all over Europe, women living and growing old . . . unregarded . . . wives and sisters of respectable men . . . listening to men talking together in the way that men talk and women listen" (239). Lolly's feminist manifesto encompasses all women whose lives are sacrificed by patriarchy, but the context suggests that her words specifically address the "subjection" (239) of the lesbian body. Warner's signifier for this body is a stick of dynamite, waiting for the moment of ignition: "for so many, what can there be but witchcraft? That strikes them real. Even if other people still find them quite safe and usual . . . they know in their hearts how dangerous, how incalculable, how extraordinary they are" (241). What Warner conveys here is that, beneath the spinster's appearance of conformity and dormancy, there lurks the dangerous, if latent, possibility of a lesbian explosion: "Even if they never do anything with their witchcraft, they know it's there—ready!" (241). We can read Satan's closing injunction to Lolly—"[d]on't try to put me in your pocket" (245)—as counsel against her proclivity for hiding her sexuality, but the novel provides no avenue for such unmediated expression. Because Lolly's lesbianism is constituted precisely through displacement and dissimulation, the text ends, notably, with a cover-up. Warner leaves us with a sexualized image of Lolly, reflecting upon her "odd" yet "most natural" vocation, imagining herself about to "penetrate into a wood and burrow herself a bed" where, undisturbed, she will repose "couched in the Devil's coverts" (251).

NOTES

I want to thank Elizabeth Abel and Laura Green for their invaluable assistance on an earlier version of this essay. I am also indebted to Terry Castle, whose graduate seminar on lesbian literature at Berkeley helped to inspire this reading.

1. Jane Marcus makes this observation in her introduction to Sylvia Townsend Warner in *The Gender of Modernism*, ed. Bonnie Kime Scott (Bloomington: Indiana University Press, 1990), 535.

2. Virginia Woolf, *A Room of One's Own* (New York: Harcourt Brace Jovanovich, 1929), 101; *The Gender of Modernism*, 535.

3. See Claire Harman's introduction to *Sylvia Townsend Warner: Collected Poems* (New York: The Viking Press, 1982), xv.

4. See Jane Marcus's introduction to Warner in *The Gender of Modernism*, 534, and her essay, "Alibis and Legends: The Ethics of Elsewhereness, Gender and Estrangement," in *Women's Writing in Exile*, ed. Mary Lynn Broe and Angela Ingram (Chapel Hill: University of North Carolina Press, 1989), 69–94.

5. Barbara Brothers, "Through the 'Pantry Window': Sylvia Townsend Warner and the Spanish Civil War," in *Rewriting the Good Fight: Critical Essays on the Literature of the Spanish Civil War*, ed. Frieda S. Brown, et al. (East Lansing: Michigan State University Press, 1989), 161–73; "Writing Against the Grain: Sylvia Townsend Warner and the Spanish Civil War," in *Women's Writing in Exile*, 350–68.

6. Marcus, "Alibis and Legends," 285.

7. Wendy Mulford, *This Narrow Place: Sylvia Townsend Warner and Valentine Ackland: Life, Letters and Politics, 1930–1951* (London: Pandora Books, 1988), 46.

8. Glen Cavaliero, "The Short Stories," *Poetry National Review* 23 (1981): 45.

9. The notable exception is Terry Castle's ground-breaking analysis, "Sylvia Townsend Warner and the Counterplot of Lesbian Fiction," in *The Apparitional Lesbian: Female Homosexuality and Modern Culture* (New York: Columbia University Press, 1993), 74. The other notable article that deals explicitly with the theme of homosexuality in Warner's work is Gillian Spraggs, "Exiled to Home: The Poetry of Sylvia Townsend Warner and Valentine Ackland," in *Lesbian and Gay Writing: An Anthology of Critical Essays*, ed. Mark Lilly (Philadelphia: Temple University Press, 1990), 109–250.

10. Sally Munt, "Introduction," to *New Lesbian Criticism: Literary and Cultural Readings* (New York: Columbia University Press, 1992), xxiii.

11. Elizabeth A. Meese, *(Sem)Erotics: Theorizing Lesbian: Writing* (New York: New York University Press, 1992), 18.

12. Sharon O'Brien, "'The Thing Not Named': Willa Cather as a Lesbian Writer," in *The Lesbian Issues: Essays from Signs*, ed. Estelle B. Freedman, et al. (Chicago: University of Chicago Press, 1985), 87.

13. For an analysis of Warner's novel as a celebration of celibacy see: Barbara Brothers, "Flying the Nets at Forty: Lolly Willowes as Female Bildungsroman," *Old Maids to Radical Spinsters: Unmarried Women in the Twentieth-Century Novel*, ed. Laura L. Doan (Urbana: University of Illinois Press, 1991), 195–212; Robert Caserio, "Celibate Sisters-in-Revolution: Towards Reading Sylvia Townsend Warner," in *Engendering Men: The Question of Male Feminist Criticism*, ed. Joseph A. Boone and Michael Cadden (New York: Routledge, 1990), 254–74; Jane Marcus, "A Wilderness of One's Own: Feminist Fantasy Novels of the Twenties: Rebecca West and Sylvia Townsend Warner," *Women*

Writers and the City, ed. Susan Merrill Squier (Knoxville: University of Tennessee Press, 1984), 134–60.

14. Bonnie Zimmerman, "Perverse Reading: The Lesbian Appropriation of Literature," in *Sexual Practice, Textual Theory: Lesbian Cultural Criticism,* ed. Susan J. Wolfe and Julia Penelope (Oxford: Blackwell, 1993), 139.

15. Shari Benstock, "Expatriate Sapphic Modernism: Entering Literary History," in *Lesbian Texts and Contexts: Radical Revisions,* ed. Karla Jay and Joanne Glasgow (New York: New York University Press, 1990), 185.

16. Cate Haste, *Rules of Desire: Sex in Britain, World War I to the Present* (London: Chatto and Windus, 1992), 29.

17. Sylvia Townsend Warner, *Lolly Willowes or the Loving Huntsman* (Chicago: Academy Chicago Limited, 1978), 24–25. Further citations from this edition are incorporated in the text.

18. J. Lawrence Mitchell, "The Secret Country of her Mind: Aspects of the Novels of Sylvia Townsend Warner," *Poetry National Review* 8: 3 (1981): 55.

19. Sheila Jeffreys, *The Spinster and Her Enemies: Feminism and Sexuality, 1880–1930* (London: Pandora Press, 1985), 88.

20. Ibid., 92.

21. Susan Kingsley Kent, *Sex and Suffrage in Britain, 1860–1914* (Princeton: Princeton University Press, 1987), 204.

22. Jeffreys, 106.

23. Jeffreys, 100. In addition to Jeffreys, Lillian Faderman, in *Surpassing the Love of Men* (New York: Morrow, 1981), and also her more recent volume, *Odd Girls and Twilight Lovers* (New York: Columbia University Press, 1991), discusses the relation between lesbianism and the spinster figure. Other notable critics who observe a similar linkage include: Lyndie Brimstone, "Towards a New Cartography: Radclyffe Hall, Virginia Woolf and the Workings of Common Land," in *What Lesbians Do in Books* (London: Women's Press, 1991); Carroll Smith-Rosenberg, "The New Women as Androgyne: Social Disorder and Gender Crisis, 1870–1936," in her *Disorderly Conduct: Visions of Gender in Victorian America* (New York: Oxford University Press, 1985); Elaine Showalter, "Odd Women," in her *Sexual Anarchy: Gender and Culture at the Fin De Siècle* (New York: Viking, 1990); Martha Vicinus, *Independent Women: Work and Community for Single Women, 1850–1920* (Chicago: University of Chicago Press, 1985).

24. Terry Castle, 9–10. Judith Butler also discusses the derivation of the word "queer" in *Bodies That Matter: On the Discursive Limits of "Sex"* (New York: Routledge, 1992), 176.

25. Brothers, "Flying the Nets at Forty," 197.

26. Teresa de Lauretis, "Eccentric Subjects: Feminist Theory and Historical Consciousness," *Feminist Studies* 16: 1 (Spring 1990): 144, 127.

27. Leslie Wilson, "Broom, Broom," *London Review of Books* (2 December 1993): 26.

28. For a discussion of the British attempt to criminalize lesbian activity see: Haste, 85; Jeffreys, 106; Jane Lewis, *Women in England, 1870–1950: Sexual*

Divisions and Social Change (Bloomington: Indiana University Press, 1984), 128.

29. Martha Vicinus, *Independent Women: Work and Community for the Single Woman, 1850–1920* (Chicago: University of Chicago Press, 1985), 206; Lillian Faderman, *Odd Girls and Twilight Lovers* (New York: Columbia University Press, 1991), 93.

30. Caserio, 273. Marcus, "A Wilderness of One's Own," 148.

31. De Lauretis, 126.

32. Castle, 7.

33. Claire Harman, *Sylvia Townsend Warner: A Biography* (London: Chatto and Windus, 1989), 219.

34. Butler, *Bodies,* 145.

35. Ibid.

36. Caserio, 264.

37. Carolyn Matalene, "Women as Witches," *International Journal of Women's Studies* 1: 6 (November/December 1978): 574. For other accounts of the relation between witchcraft and homosexuality, see Randy P. Conner, *Blossom of Bone: Reclaiming the Connection between Homeroticism and the Sacred* (San Francisco: Harper Collins); Arthur Evans, *Witchcraft and the Gay Counterculture* (Boston: Fag Rag Books, 1978); Anne Llewellyn Barstow, *Witchcraze: A New History of the European Witch Hunts* (San Francisco: Pandora, Harper Collins, 1994).

38. See, for example: Judith Butler, "Imitation and Gender Insubordination," in *Inside/Out: Lesbian Theories, Gay Theories,* ed. Diana Fuss (New York: Routledge, 1991), 18–25; and also in the same volume, Carole-Anne Tyler, "Boys Will Be Girls: The Politics of Gay Drag."

39. Sigmund Freud, "The 'Uncanny'" (1919), *Collected Papers,* vol. 4, ed. Ernest Jones (New York: Basic Books, 1959), 389.

40. Ibid., 394

41. Sue-Ellen Case, "Tracking the Vampire," *differences* 3: 2 (Summer 1991): 3.

42. Matalene, 585.

For Further Reading

Nonfiction

Abelove, Henry, Michèle Aina Barale, and David Halperin, eds. *The Lesbian and Gay Studies Reader.* New York: Routledge, 1993.

Almaguer, Tomas. "Chicano Men: A Cartography of Homosexual Identity and Behavior." *differences* 3:2 (Summer 1991): 75–100.

Alonso, Ana Maria, and Maria Teresa Koreck. "Silences: 'Hispanics,' AIDS, and Sexual Practices." *differences* 1:1 (Winter 1989): 101–24.

Apfelbaum, Bernard, Martin Williams, and Susan Greene, "Couple Sex Therapy Assignments." In *Expanding the Boundaries of Sex Therapy,* edited by Bernard Apfelbaum, 79–88. Berkeley: Berkeley Sex Therapy Group, 1979.

Assiter, Alison. *Pornography, Feminism and the Individual.* London: Pluto Press, 1989.

Bad Object-Choices, ed. *How Do I Look? Queer Film and Video.* Seattle: Bay Press, 1991.

Bell, Adam, and Martin Weinberg. *Homosexualities: A Study of Diversity Among Men and Women.* New York: Simon & Schuster, 1978.

Berger, Ronald J., Patricia Searles, and Charles E. Cottle. *Feminism and Pornography.* New York: Praeger, 1991.

Bernheimer, Charles. "Penile Reference in Phallic Theory." *differences* 4:1 (1992): 116–32.

Bersani, Leo. "Is the Rectum a Grave?" In *AIDS: Cultural Analysis, Cultural Activism,* edited by Douglas Crimp, 197–222. Cambridge: MIT Press, 1987.

Borges, Jorge Luis. *A Universal History of Infamy.* Harmondsworth: Penguin, 1975.

Bright, Susie. *Susie Bright's Sexual Reality: A Virtual Sex World Reader.* Pittsburgh: Cleis Press, 1992.

———. *Susie Sexpert's Lesbian Sex World.* Pittsburgh: Cleis Press, 1992.

———. "Undressing Camille." *Out/Look* (Spring 1992): 9–14.

Brodski, Bella, and Celeste Schenck, eds. *Life/lines: Theorizing Women's Autobiography.* Ithaca: Cornell University Press, 1988.

269

Broe, Mary Lynn, and Angela Ingram, eds. *Women's Writing in Exile.* Chapel Hill: University of North Carolina Press, 1989.

Burch, Beverly. "Another Perspective on Merger in Lesbian Relationships." In *Handbook of Feminist Therapy,* edited by L. B. Rosewater and L. E. A. Walker, 100–109. New York: Springer, 1985.

———. *On Intimate Terms: The Psychology of Difference in Lesbian Relationships.* Urbana: University of Illinois Press, 1993.

Butler, Judith. *Bodies That Matter: On the Discursive Limits of "Sex."* New York: Routledge, 1993.

———. *Gender Trouble: Feminism and the Subversion of Identity.* New York: Routledge, 1990.

Butler, Judith, and Joan Scott, eds. *Feminists Theorize the Political.* New York: Routledge, 1992.

Califia, Pat. *The Lesbian S/M Safety Manual.* Boston: Alyson, 1988.

———. *Sapphistry: The Book of Lesbian Sexuality.* 3rd. ed. Tallahassee, FL: Naiad, 1988.

———. *Sensuous Magic.* New York: Kasak Books, 1993.

Card, Claudia. "Intimacy and Responsibility: What Lesbians Do." In *At the Boundaries of Law: Feminism and Legal Theory,* edited by Martha Albertson Fineman and Nancy Sweet Thomadsen, 77–94. New York: Routledge, 1991.

Case, Sue-Ellen. "Toward a Butch-Femme Aesthetic." *Discourse* 11:1 (Fall 1988/Winter 1989): 55–73.

———. "Tracking the Vampire." *differences* 3: 2 (Summer 1991): 1–20.

Castle, Terry. *The Apparitional Lesbian: Female Homosexuality and Modern Culture.* New York: Columbia University Press, 1993.

Cohen, Ed. "Legislating the Norm: From Sodomy to Gross Indecency." *South Atlantic Quarterly* 88:1–2 (1989): 181–221.

Cover, Robert. "Violence and the Word." *Yale Law Journal* 95 (1986):1601.

Creet, Julia. "Daughter of the Movement: The Psychodynamics of Lesbian S/M Fantasy." *differences* 3:2 (Summer 1991): 135–59.

Crimp, Douglas, ed. *AIDS: Cultural Analysis, Cultural Activism.* Cambridge: MIT Press, 1987.

Crompton, Louis. "The Myth of Lesbian Impunity: Capital Laws from 1270–1791." *Journal of Homosexuality* 6:1–2 (Fall 1980/Winter 1981): 11–25.

Cruikshank, Margaret, ed. *Lesbian Studies: Present and Future.* New York: The Feminist Press, 1982.

Culler, Jonathan. *The Pursuit of Signs: Semiotics, Literature, Deconstruction.* Ithaca: Cornell University Press, 1981.

Davis, Angela. *Women, Race and Class.* New York: Random House, 1981.

de Lauretis, Teresa. *Alice Doesn't: Feminism, Semiotics, Cinema.* Bloomington: Indiana University Press, 1984.

———. "Eccentric Subjects: Feminist Theory and Historical Consciousness." *Feminist Studies* 16:1 (Spring 1990): 115–50.

———. *Technologies of Gender: Essays on Theory, Film, and Fiction.* Bloomington: Indiana University Press, 1987.

Dolan, Jill. "The Dynamics of Desire: Sexuality and Gender in Pornography and Performance." *Theatre Journal* 39:2 (May 1987): 156–74.

Dollimore, Jonathan. *Sexual Dissidence: Augustine to Wilde, Freud to Foucault.* New York: Oxford University Press, 1991.

Duberman, Martin Bauml, Martha Vicinus, and George Chauncey, Jr., eds. *Hidden from History: Reclaiming the Gay and Lesbian Past.* New York: Meridian Press, 1989.

Dworkin, Andrea. *Pornography: Men Possessing Women.* New York: Perigee, 1981.

Ebert, Teresa L. "The Difference of Postmodern Feminism." *College English* 53 (1991): 886–904.

———. "The Politics of the Outrageous." *Women's Review of Books* (October 1991), 12–13.

Echols, Alice. *Daring to Be Bad: Radical Feminism in America, 1967–1975.* Minneapolis: University of Minnesota Press, 1989.

Edelman, Lee. *Homographesis: Essays in Gay Literary and Cultural Theory.* New York: Routledge, 1993.

Ellis, Havelock. *Studies in the Psychology of Sex.* Vol. 1, part 4, *Sexual Inversion.* New York: Random House, 1942.

Engelhardt, H. Tristram, Foreword to *Homosexuality in Perspective* by William Masters and Virginia Johnson. Boston: Little, Brown, 1979.

Faderman, Lillian. *Odd Girls and Twilight Lovers: A History of Lesbian Life in Twentieth-Century America.* New York: Columbia University Press, 1991.

———. *Surpassing the Love of Men: Romantic Friendship and Love Between Women from the Renaissance to the Present.* New York: William Morrow, 1981.

Findlay, Heather. "Freud's 'Fetishism' and the Lesbian Dildo Debates." *Feminist Studies* 18:3 (Fall 1992): 563–80.

Foucault, Michel. *Discipline and Punish.* New York: Random House, 1979.

———. *The History of Sexuality.* New York: Vintage, 1980.

Freedman, Estelle et al., eds. *The Lesbian Issue: Essays from Signs.* Chicago: University of Chicago Press, 1985.

Freud, Sigmund. *Dora: An Analysis of a Case of Hysteria.* New York: Macmillan, 1963.

———. "Femininity." In *New Introductory Lectures on Psychoanalysis,* edited by James Strachey, 99–119. New York: Norton, 1965.

———. "Fetishism." In *Sexuality and the Psychology of Love,* edited by Philip Rieff, 214–19. New York: Collier, 1963.

———. "The Psychogenesis of a Case of Homosexuality in a Woman." In *Sexuality and the Psychology of Love,* translated by Barbara Low and R. Gabler, 133–59. New York: Collier Books, 1963.

———. "The 'Uncanny.'" In *Collected Papers*, vol. 4, edited by Ernest Jones, 368–407. New York: Basic Books, 1959.

Frye, Marilyn. *Willful Virgin: Essays in Feminism*. Freedom, CA: Crossing Press, 1992.

Fuss, Diana, ed. *Inside/Out: Lesbian Theories, Gay Theories*. New York: Routledge, 1991.

Gabriel, Susan, and Isaiah Smithson, eds. *Gender in the Classroom: Power and Pedagogy*. Urbana: University of Illinois Press, 1990.

Gagnier, Regenia. "Feminist Autobiography in the 1980's." *Feminist Studies* 17:1 (Spring 1991): 135–48.

Gallop, Jane. *Thinking Through the Body*. New York: Columbia University Press, 1988.

Gever, Martha, John Greyson, and Pratibha Parmar, eds. *Queer Looks: Perspectives on Lesbian and Gay Film and Video*. New York: Routledge, 1993.

Goldstein, Nancy. "Discipline and Publish: Henry Fielding's Policing of 'Lesbian' Sexuality in *The Female Husband*." Unpublished manuscript, Boston, MA.

Gordon, Michael. "Marital Education Literature, 1830–1940." In *Studies in the Sociology of Sex*, edited by James M. Henslin, 37–42. New York: Appleton-Century-Crofts, 1971.

Gore, Jennifer. *The Struggle for Pedagogies: Critical and Feminist Discourses as Regimes of Truth*. New York: Routledge, 1993.

Grosz, Elizabeth. "Lesbian Fetishism?" *differences* 3:2 (1991): 39–54.

Guillory, John. *Cultural Capital*. Chicago: University of Chicago Press, 1993.

Gupta, Sunil. "Black, *Brown* and White." In *Coming On Strong: Gay Politics and Culture*, edited by Simon Shepherd and Mick Wallis, 163–79. London: Unwin Hyman, 1989.

Hall, Marny. "Ex-Therapy to Sex Therapy: Notes from the Margins." In *Gays, Lesbians and Their Therapists*, edited by Charles Silverstein, 84–97. New York: Norton, 1991.

Halperin, David M. *One Hundred Years of Homosexuality*. New York: Routledge, 1990.

Haste, Cate. *Rules of Desire: Sex in Britain, World War I to the Present*. London: Chatto and Windus, 1992.

Hoagland, Sarah. *Lesbian Ethics: Toward New Value*. Palo Alto, CA: Institute of Lesbian Studies, 1990.

Irigaray, Luce. *Speculum of the Other Woman*, translated by Gillian C. Gill. Ithaca: Cornell University Press, 1985.

Jay, Karla, and Joanne Glasgow, eds. *Lesbian Texts and Contexts: Radical Revisions*. New York: New York University Press, 1990.

Jay, Karla, and Allen Young. *The Gay Report: Lesbians and Gay Men Speak Out About Sexual Experiences and Lifestyles*. New York: Simon & Schuster, 1979.

———, eds. *Lavender Culture*. 1978; rpt. New York: New York University Press, 1994.

Jeffreys, Sheila. *The Lesbian Heresy: A Feminist Perspective on the Lesbian Sexual Revolution*. North Melbourne: Spinifex Press, 1993.

——. *The Spinster and Her Enemies: Feminism and Sexuality 1880–1930*. London: Pandora, 1985.

Kappeler, Susanne. *The Pornography of Representation*. Minneapolis: University of Minnesota Press, 1986.

Katz, Jonathan Ned, comp. *Gay American History: Lesbians and Gay Men in the U.S.A.* New York: Thomas Crowell, 1976.

——. *Gay/Lesbian Almanac*. New York: Harper Colophon, 1983.

Kennedy, Elizabeth Lapovsky, and Madeline D. Davis. *Boots of Leather, Slippers of Gold: The History of a Lesbian Community*. New York: Routledge, 1993.

Kent, Susan Kingsley. *Sex and Suffrage in Britain 1860–1914*. Princeton: Princeton University Press, 1987.

Krestan, Joann, and C. S. Bepko. "The Problem of Fusion in Lesbian Relationships." *Family Process* 19 (1980): 277–89.

Kristeva, Julia. *The Kristeva Reader*, edited by Toril Moi, translated by Alice Jardine and Harry Blake. New York: Columbia University Press, 1986.

——. *Powers of Horror: An Essay on Abjection*, translated by Leon S. Roudiez. New York: Columbia University Press, 1982.

Kuhn, Annette. *The Power of the Image: Essays on Representation and Sexuality*. London: Routledge, 1985.

Lacan, Jacques. *The Four Fundamental Concepts of Psychoanalysis*, edited by Jacques-Alain Miller, translated by Alan Sheridan. New York: Norton, 1978.

——. "The Meaning of the Phallus." In *Feminine Sexuality: Jacques Lacan and the Ecole Freudienne*, edited by Juliet Mitchell and Jacqueline Rose, translated by Jacqueline Rose, 74–85. New York: Norton, 1985.

——. *The Seminar of Jacques Lacan: Book I, Freud's Papers on Technique 1953–1954*, edited by Jacques-Alain Miller, translated by John Forrester. New York: Norton, 1991.

Laclau, Ernesto, and Chantal Mouffe. *Hegemony and Socialist Strategy*. London: Verso, 1985.

Laplanche, Jean, and Jean-Bertrand Pontalis. "Fantasy and the Origins of Sexuality." *Formations of Fantasy*, edited by Victor Burgin, James Donald, and Cora Kaplan, 5–34. New York: Methuen, 1986.

Lather, Patti. *Getting Smart: Feminist Research and Pedagogy With/In the Postmodern*. New York: Routledge, 1991.

Lewis, Jane. *Women in England 1870–1950: Sexual Divisions and Social Change*. Bloomington: Indiana University Press, 1984.

Lily, Mark, ed. *Lesbian and Gay Writing: An Anthology of Critical Essays*. Philadelphia: Temple University Press, 1990.

Ling, Amy. *Between Worlds*. New York: Pergamon Press, 1990.

Lister, Anne. *I Know My Own Heart: The Diaries of Anne Lister, 1791–1840*, edited by Helena Whitbread. New York: New York University Press, 1992.

——. *No Priest but Love: The Journals of Anne Lister, 1824–1826*, edited by Helena Whitbread. New York: New York University Press, 1993.

Lorde, Audre. *Sister Outsider: Essays and Speeches.* Freedom, CA: Crossing Press, 1984.

———. *Zami: A New Spelling of My Name: A Biomythography.* Freedom, CA: Crossing Press, 1982.

Loulan, JoAnn. *The Lesbian Erotic Dance: Butch, Femme, Androgyny, and Other Rhythms.* San Francisco: Spinsters Book Company, 1990.

———. *Lesbian Passion: Loving Ourselves and Each Other.* San Francisco: Spinsters Ink, 1987.

MacCannell, Juliet Flower. "Resistance to Sexual Theory." In *Texts for Change: Theory/Pedagogy/Politics,* edited by Donald Morton and Mas'ud Zavarzadeh. Urbana: University of Illinois Press, 1991.

MacKinnon, Catharine A. *Feminism Unmodified: Discourses on Life and Law.* Cambridge: Harvard University Press, 1987.

Masters, William, and Virginia Johnson. *Human Sexual Response.* Boston: Little, Brown, 1966.

Marcus, Greil. *Lipstick Traces.* Cambridge: Harvard University Press, 1989.

Matalene, Carolyn. "Women as Witches." *International Journal of Women's Studies* 1:6 (November/December 1978): 573–87.

McConnell, Joyce. "A Feminist's Perspective on Liberal Reform of Legal Education." *Harvard Women's Law Journal* 14 (1991): 77–80.

Meese, Elizabeth. *(Sem)Erotics: Theorizing Lesbian : Writing.* New York: New York University Press, 1992.

Michelson, Peter. *Speaking the Unspeakable: A Poetics of Obscenity.* Albany: SUNY Press, 1993.

Morton, Donald, and Mas'ud Zavarzadeh, eds. *Texts for Change: Theory/Pedagogy/Politics.* Urbana: University of Illinois Press, 1991.

Munt, Sally, ed. *New Lesbian Criticism: Literary and Cultural Readings.* New York: Columbia University Press, 1992.

Newfield, Christopher. "Democracy and Male Homoeroticism." *Yale Journal of Criticism* 6:2 (1993): 29–62.

Newton, Esther. *Cherry Grove, Fire Island.* Boston: Beacon Press, 1993.

Padgug, Robert A. "Sexual Matters: On Conceptualizing Sexuality in History." *Radical History Review* 20 (1979): 16–18.

Paglia, Camille. "Feminists Lead Women Astray on the Threat of Rape." *Philadelphia Inquirer* (15 February 1991), 23A.

———. *Sex, Art, and American Culture.* New York: Vintage Books, 1992.

———. *Sexual Personae: Art and Decadence from Nefertiti to Emily Dickinson.* New Haven: Yale University Press, 1990.

Parmar, Pratibha. "Gender, Race and Class: Asian Women in Resistance." In *The Empire Strikes Back: Race and Racism in 1970s Britain,* edited by Centre for Contemporary Cultural Studies, 212–35. London: Hutchinson, 1982.

Pearsall, Ronald. *The Worm in the Bud: The World of Victorian Sexuality.* Harmondsworth: Penguin, 1969.

Post, Robert. "Tradition, the Self, and Substantive Due Process." *California Law Review* 77 (1989): 559–60.

Reich, June. "Genderfuck: The Law of the Dildo." *Discourse* 15:1 (Fall 1992): 112–27.

Reti, Irene. *Unleashing Feminism: Critiquing Lesbian Sadomasochism in the Gay Nineties.* Santa Cruz: HerBooks, 1993.

Robson, Ruthann. "Embodiments: The Possibilities of Lesbian Legal Theory in Bodies Problematized by Feminisms and Postmodernisms." *Journal of Law and Sexuality* 2 (1992): 37–80.

———. "Incendiary Categories: Lesbians/Violence/Law." *Texas Journal of Women and the Law* 2 (1993): 1, 28.

———. *Lesbian (Out)Law: Survival Under the Rule of Law.* Ithaca: Firebrand Books, 1992.

———. "The Specter of a Lesbian Supreme Court Justice: Problems of Identity in Lesbian Legal Theorizing." *St. Thomas Law Review* 5 (1993): 433–58.

Roof, Judith. *A Lure of Knowledge: Lesbian Sexuality and Theory.* New York: Columbia University Press, 1991.

Rothblum, Esther D., and Kathleen A. Brehony, eds. *Boston Marriages: Romantic But Asexual Relationships among Contemporary Lesbians.* Amherst: University of Massachusetts Press, 1993.

Rubin, Gayle. "The Traffic in Women: Notes on the 'Political Economy' of Sex." In *Toward an Anthropology of Women,* edited by Rayna Reiter, 157–210. New York: Monthly Review Press, 1975.

Russell, Diana. *Against Pornography: The Evidence of Harm.* Berkeley: Russell Publications, 1993.

Said, Edward. *Orientalism.* New York: Peregrine Books, 1985.

Samois, ed. *Coming to Power: Writing and Graphics on Lesbian S/M.* 3rd ed. Boston: Alyson, 1987.

Schor, Naomi. "Female Fetishism: The Case of George Sand." In *The Female Body in Western Culture: Contemporary Perspectives,* edited by Susan Rubin Suleiman, 363–72. Cambridge: Harvard University Press, 1986.

Scott, Bonnie Kime, ed. *The Gender of Modernism.* Bloomington: Indiana University Press, 1990.

Scott, James. *Domination and the Arts of Resistance.* New Haven: Yale University Press, 1990.

Sedgwick, Eve Kosofsky. *Between Men: English Literature and Male Homosocial Desire.* New York: Columbia University Press, 1985.

———. "Queer Performativity: Henry James's *The Art of the Novel.*" *GLQ* 1:1 (1993): 1–16.

———. *Tendencies.* Durham: Duke University Press, 1993.

Showalter, Elaine. *Sexual Anarchy: Gender and Culture at the Fin de Siècle.* New York: Penguin Books, 1990.

Silverman, Kaja. "The Lacanian Phallus." *differences* 4:1 (1992): 84–115.

———. *Male Subjectivity at the Margins.* New York: Routledge, 1992.

Skal, David J. *Hollywood Gothic: The Tangled Web of Dracula from Novel to Stage to Screen.* New York: Norton, 1990.

———. *The Monster Show: A Cultural History of Horror.* New York: Norton, 1993.

Smith, Anna Marie. "Resisting the Erasure of Lesbianism: A Challenge for Queer Activism." In *Modern Homosexualities: Fragments of Lesbian and Gay Experience,* edited by Ken Plummer, 200–216. London: Routledge, 1992.

Smith, Barbara Herrnstein. *Contingencies of Value: Alternative Perspectives for Critical Theory.* Cambridge: Harvard University Press, 1988.

Snitow, Ann, Christine Stansell, and Sharon Thompson, eds. *Powers of Desire: The Politics of Sexuality.* New York: Monthly Review Press, 1983.

Soble, Alan. *Pornography: Marxism, Feminism, and the Future of Sexuality.* New Haven: Yale University Press, 1986.

Squier, Susan, ed. *Women Writers and the City.* Knoxville: University of Tennessee Press, 1984.

Stein, Arlene. "Sisters and Queers: The Decentering of Lesbian Feminism." *Socialist Review* 22:1 (January/March 1992): 33–55.

Suyin, Han. *Between Worlds.* New York: Pergamon Press, 1990.

Tate, Claudia. *Black Women Writers at Work.* New York: Continuum, 1983.

Thompson, Mark, ed. *Leatherfolk: Radical Sex, People, Politics, and Practice.* Boston: Alyson, 1991.

Traub, Valerie. "The (In)Significance of Lesbian Desire in Early Modern England." In *Queering the Renaissance,* edited by Jonathan Goldberg, 62–83. Durham: Duke University Press, 1994.

Valverde, Mariana. *Sex, Power, and Pleasure.* Toronto: Women's Press, 1985.

Vance, Carol S., ed. *Pleasure and Danger: Exploring Female Sexuality.* New York: Routledge, 1973.

Vicinus, Martha. *Independent Women: Work and Community for Single Women, 1850–1920.* Chicago: University of Chicago Press, 1985.

Wagner, Peter. "The Discourse on Sex—or Sex as Discourse: Eighteenth-Century Medical and Paramedical Erotica." In *Sexual Underworlds of the Enlightenment,* edited by G. S. Rousseau and Roy Porter, 46–68. Chapel Hill: University of North Carolina Press, 1988.

Walker, Alice. *In Search of Our Mother's Gardens: Womanist Prose.* New York: Harcourt Brace Jovanovich, 1983.

Warner, Michael, ed. *Fear of a Queer Planet.* Minneapolis: University of Minnesota Press, 1993.

Weeks, Jeffrey. *Coming Out: Homosexual Politics in Britain from the Nineteenth Century to the Present.* London: Quartet Books, 1977.

West, Celeste. *A Lesbian Love Advisor.* San Francisco: Cleis Press, 1989.

Williams, Linda. *Hard Core: Power, Pleasure, and the "Frenzy of the Visible."* Berkeley: University of California Press, 1989.

Wilson, Leslie. "Broom, broom." *London Review of Books* (2 December 1993), 26.

Wolfe, Susan J., and Julia Penelope, eds. *Sexual Practice, Textual Theory: Lesbian Cultural Criticism.* Oxford: Blackwell, 1993.
Woolf, Virginia. *A Room of One's Own.* New York: Harcourt, 1929.

Fiction

Note: Some of the anthologies in this section also contain nonfiction essays.

Allain, Carol, and Rosemund Elwin, eds. *Getting Wet: Tales of Lesbian Seductions.* Toronto: Women's Press, 1992.
Antonious, Laura, ed. *Leather Women.* New York: Rosebud, 1993.
Arrowsmith, Pat. *Somewhere Like This.* London: Gay Men's Press, 1990.
Barbach, Lonnie, ed. *Erotic Interludes.* New York: HarperPerennial, 1987.
———. *Pleasures: Women Write Erotica.* New York: Perennial, 1985.
Barber, Karen, ed. *Afterglow: More Stories of Lesbian Desire.* Boston: Alyson, 1993.
———. *Bushfire: Stories of Lesbian Desire.* Boston: Alyson, 1993.
Barrington, Judith, ed. *An Intimate Winderness: Lesbian Writers on Sexuality.* Portland, OR: Eighth Mountain Press, 1991.
Borgstrom, Wendy. *Rapture and the Second Coming.* Boston: Alyson, 1990.
———. *Short Rides.* Boston: Alyson, 1992.
Bright, Susie, ed. *Herotica: A Collection of Women's Erotic Fiction.* San Francisco: Down There Press, 1988.
Bright, Susie, and Joani Blank. *Herotica 2.* New York: Plume, 1992.
Brossard, Nicole. *Sous la Langue/Under Tongue.* Montreal: Gynergy, 1987.
Califia, Pat. *Doc and Fluff: The Distopian Tale of a Girl and Her Biker.* Boston: Alyson, 1990.
———. *Macho Sluts.* Boston: Alyson, 1988.
———. *Melting Point: Short Stories.* Boston: Alyson, 1993.
Chester, Laura, ed. *Deep Down: The New Sensual Writing by Women.* Boston: Faber and Faber, 1988.
Chrystos. *In Her I Am.* Vancouver: Press Gang Publishers, 1993.
Corinne, Tee. *Dreams of the Woman Who Loved Sex.* Austin: Banned Books, 1987.
———. *Lovers: Love and Sex Stories.* Austin: Banned Books, 1989.
———. *The Sparkling Lavender Dust of Lust.* Austin: Banned Books, 1991.
———, ed. *The Body of Love.* Austin: Banned Books, 1993.
———. *Intricate Passions.* Austin: Banned Books, 1989.
———. *The Poetry of Sex: Lesbians Write the Erotic.* Austin: Banned Books, 1992.
———. *Riding Desire: An Anthology of Erotic Writing.* Austin: Banned Books, 1991.
Cotrell, Georgia. *Shoulders.* Ithaca: Firebrand, 1987.

Dane, Roslyn. *The Assistance of Vice.* Austin: Banned Books, 1989.
DeCosta-Willis, Miriam, Reginald Martin, and Roseann Bell, eds. *Erotique noire/Black Erotica.* New York: Doubleday, 1992.
Edda, Stud. "Packin' It." *On Our Backs* (March/April 1991): 15ff.
Feinberg, Leslie. *Stone Butch Blues.* Ithaca: Firebrand, 1993.
Fleming, Lee, ed. *By Word of Mouth: Lesbians Write the Erotic.* Montreal: Gynergy, 1990.
Folisade, Lee. *Quicksand!* Oakland: Black Angels Press, 1994.
———, ed. *By Word of Mouth: Lesbians Write the Erotic.* Palo Alto, CA: Black Angels Press, 1993.
Forrest, Katherine, and Barbara Grier, eds. *The Erotic Naiad.* Tallahassee, FL: Naiad, 1992.
Griffin, Aarona. *Passage and Other Stories.* New York: Masquerade Books, 1992.
Hardy, Jan, ed. *Wanting Women: An Anthology of Erotic Lesbian Poetry.* Pittsburgh: Sidewalk Revolution Press, 1990.
Herrera, Barbara. *Seasons of Erotic Love.* San Diego: Paradigm, 1992.
Israel, Katherine. "Midnight Blue." *Frighten the Horses* 11 (Winter 1993): 32–35.
Kotz, Cappy. *The First Stroke.* Seattle: Lace Publications, 1988.
Lorde, Audre. *Chosen Poems Old and New.* New York: Norton, 1982.
Nestle, Joan. *A Restricted Country.* Ithaca: Firebrand Press, 1987.
———, ed. *The Persistent Desire: A Femme-Butch Reader.* Boston: Alyson, 1992.
Nin, Anaïs. *House of Incest.* 1936. Rpt. Athens, OH: Swallow Press, 1989.
Reynolds, Margaret, ed. *Erotica.* New York: Fawcett Columbine, 1990.
Sands, Regine. *Alarming Fiction: Erotic Fiction.* Boston: Alyson, 1991.
Senos, Anna Conchita. "The Shower." *On Our Backs* (July/August 1991): 30ff.
Sheba Collective and Sheba Feminist Publishers, eds. *Excitement: Sexual Stories for the '90s.* Pittsburgh: Cleis Press, 1992.
———. *More Serious Pleasure.* Pittsburgh: Cleis Press, 1990.
———. *Serious Pleasure: Lesbian Erotic Stories and Poetry.* Pittsburgh: Cleis Press, 1989.
Sommers, Robbi. *Behind Closed Doors.* Tallahassee, FL: Naiad, 1993.
———. *Kiss and Tell.* Tallahassee, FL: Naiad:, 1991.
———. *Players.* Tallahassee, FL: Naiad, 1990.
———. *Pleasures.* Tallahassee, FL: Naiad, 1989.
———. *Uncertain Companions.* Tallahassee, FL: Naiad, 1992.
Thornton, Louise, Jane Sturtevant, and Amber Coverdale Sumrall, eds. *Touching Fire: Erotic Writings by Women.* New York: Carroll & Graf, 1989.
Tsui, Kitty. *The Words of a Woman Who Breathes Fire.* San Francisco: Spinsters Ink, 1983.
Verel, Shirley. *The Bee's Kiss.* Tallahassee, FL: Naiad, 1989.
Warner, Sylvia Townsend. *Collected Poems.* New York: Viking Press, 1982.

————. *Lolly Willowes or the Loving Huntsman*. Chicago: Academy Chicago Limited, 1978.

Weathers, Carolyn. *Crazy*. Los Angeles: Clothespin Fever Press, 1989.

————. *Shitkickers and Other Texas Stories*. Los Angeles: Clothespin Fever Press, 1989.

Welsh, Lindsay, *Private Lessons*. New York: Rosebud, 1993.

Wittig, Monique. *The Lesbian Body*. Boston: Beacon, 1973.

Woodrow, Terry, ed. *Lesbian Bedtime Stories*. Little River, CA: Tough Dove Books, 1989.

————. *Lesbian Bedtime Stories 2*. Willits, CA: Tough Dove Books, 1990.

Zahava, Irene, ed. *Lesbian Love Stories*. Freedom, CA: Crossing Press, 1989.

————. *Lesbian Love Stories, Volume 2*. Freedom, CA: Crossing Press, 1991.

Film

The following books provide information on lesbian films.

Hadleigh, Boze. *The Lavender Screen: The Gay and Lesbian Films: Their Stars, Makers, Characters and Critics*. New York: Citadel, 1993.

Russo, Vito. *The Celluloid Closet*. New York: Harper & Row, 1987.

Weiss, Andrea. *Vampires and Violets: Lesbians and Film*. New York: Penguin, 1992.

Contributors

DONNA ALLEGRA's recent publications include *All the Ways Home: Short Stories About Children and the Lesbian and Gay Communities,* and she has also contributed pieces to *Sportsdykes,* edited by Susan Fox Rogers, *Sister/Stranger,* edited by Jan Hardy, *Woman in the Window,* edited by Pamela Pratt, and *Lesbian Culture,* edited by Julia Penelope and Susan J. Wolfe. She is currently at work on a novel.

JOHANNA BLAKLEY has a master's degree in English from the University of Oregon and is completing a Ph.D. in English at the University of California, Santa Barbara. Her dissertation, "In-Between Means and Ends," addresses poststructuralist theories of "the between" and the works of Gertrude Stein, Mina Loy, Djuna Barnes, and Anaïs Nin.

BONNIE BURNS is a doctoral candidate in the Department of English at Tufts University where she is completing her dissertation on representation and the spectacle of lesbianism in nineteenth- and twentieth-century British and American culture.

S. ELAINE CRAGHEAD is currently completing her dissertation, entitled "Female Homosociality and Homoeroticism in Twentieth-Century American Texts: An Analysis of Subversion," at the University of Rhode Island.

ANN CVETKOVICH is Associate Professor of English at the University of Texas at Austin. She is the author of *Mixed Feelings: Feminism, Mass Culture, and Victorian Sensationalism,* and articles about film, video, and popular culture. She is working on a book about intersections between lesbian cultures and mass culture.

JANE GARRITY is Assistant Professor of English at the University of Colorado, at Boulder. Her essay, "Nocturnal Transgressions in *The House of Sleep*: Anna Kavan's Maternal Registers," has appeared in *Modern Fiction Studies*. She is currently at work on a book tentatively entitled, *Telling It Slant: British Women Modernists and the Experimental Novel*.

MARNY HALL, Ph.D., has lived, worked, and played in the San Francisco Bay Area for twenty-five years. She is currently writing a book about lesbian sex, tentatively entitled *What Sappho Never Knew*. She has contributed articles to several anthologies and is the author of *The Lavender Couch: A Consumer's Guide to Psychotherapy for Lesbians and Gay Men*.

SHARON P. HOLLAND is an Assistant Professor of English at Stanford University. She is currently at work on a manuscript entitled "Qualifying Margins: The Discourse of Death in Native and African American Fiction." Her areas of specialty include Contemporary African American and Afro-Native Studies with an emphasis on twentieth-century literature by women. Presently she devotes much of her time to the political writings and poetry of Audre Lorde, June Jordan, Adrienne Rich, and Alice Walker. Educated at Princeton (A.B.) and the University of Michigan (Ph.D.), Sharon is originally from Washington, D.C.

SANDY HUSS is an Associate Professor who teaches fiction writing in the M.F.A. program at the University of Alabama. Her first book is *Labor for Love: Stories*.

KARLA JAY is Professor of English and Women's Studies at Pace University. She has co-edited many anthologies, including *Lesbian Texts and Contexts: Radical Revisions* (with Joanne Glasgow) and *Lavender Culture* and *Out of the Closets: Voices of Gay Liberation* (both with Allen Young).

COLLEEN LAMOS is Assistant Professor of English at Rice University. She is the author of essays published in *The Lesbian Postmodern*, edited by Laura Doan, and in *Joyce in Context*, edited by Vincent Cheng and Timothy Martin. Her articles and reviews have appeared in *Signs*, the *James Joyce Quarterly, Contemporary Literature, Pretext, NWSA Journal*, and the *Lesbian and Gay Studies Newsletter*. An earlier version of "Taking on the Phallus" was runner-up for the 1992 Crompton-Noll Award of the MLA Lesbian and Gay Caucus. She is currently completing a book manuscript, *Going Astray: Gender and Sexual Errancy in Modernist Literature*.

ANNA LIVIA was born in Dublin, grew up in Africa, spent eighteen years in London, and now lives in the Bay Area where she is finishing a Ph.D. in French linguistics. She is the author of two collections of short stories and four novels including *Minimax* and *Relatively Norma*. Her translation of writings by Natalie Clifford Barney, *A Perilous Advantage*, was published in 1992. She is currently working on a translation of *The Angel and the Perverts* by Lucie Delarue-Mardrus to be published in 1995.

ELIZABETH MEESE is Professor of English and Adjunct Professor of Women's Studies at the University of Alabama. She is the author of *Crossing the Double-Cross: The Practice of Feminist Criticism* (1986), *(Ex)Tensions: Re-Figuring Feminist Criticism* (1990), and *(Sem)Erotics: Theorizing Lesbian : Writing* (1992). She co-edited, with Alice Parker, *The Difference Within: Feminism and Critical Theory* (1989) and *Feminist Critical Negotiations* (1992).

KARIN QUIMBY is a doctoral student at the University of Southern California studying contemporary American film and literature and lesbian literature.

RUTHANN ROBSON is Professor of Law at City University of New York School of Law. Her recent work includes *Lesbian (Out)Law: Survival Under the Rule of Law*, numerous articles addressing the possibilities of lesbian legal theory, as well as two books of lesbian fiction.

ANNA MARIE SMITH is Assistant Professor of Political Theory in the Department of Government at Cornell University. She is the author of *New Right Discourse on Race and Sexuality: Britain, 1968–1990*. She is currently working on her second book, *The Politics of Post-Marxism*, which will be published in 1995.

JENNIFER TRAVIS is a Ph.D. candidate in the Department of English at Brandeis University. She is currently completing her dissertation, "Emotional Distress: Configurations of Law and Literature," which analyzes "pain" as a representational domain emerging alongside (and, in some sense, compensating for) a new form of economic subjecthood in the United States in the late nineteenth and early twentieth centuries.

KITTY TSUI appeared on the cover of *On Our Backs* in two issues, Summer 1988 and October/November 1990, and in the gay pride issue of the *Village Voice*, 30 June 1992, vol. XXXVII, no. 26, the first time the *Voice* featured a female nude on the cover. In addition, she has modeled for The Shanti Project and DIFFA/Chicago (Design Industries Foundation for AIDS). She has also appeared in books and in numerous calendars, most recently in the 1991 Women of the Games, athletes at Gay Games III, and the 1994 Breast Plates calendar. A competitive bodybuilder, she won the bronze medal at Gay Games II in San Francisco in 1986 and the gold medal in same-sex pairs at Gay Games III in Vancouver in 1990.